With Picks, Shovels, and Hope

The CCC and Its Legacy on the Colorado Plateau

Dr. Wayne K. Hinton with Elizabeth A. Green

Foreword by Robert W. Audretsch

2008

MOUNTAIN PRESS PUBLISHING COMPANY

MISSOULA, MONTANA

Cover photos courtesy National Park Service; Utah Historical Society;
Cline Library Special Collections and Archives, Northern Arizona University
Cover design by Christopher Eaton

Library of Congress Cataloging-in-Publication Data
  Hinton, Wayne K., 1940-
    With picks, shovels & hope : the CCC and its legacy on the Colorado
    Plateau / Wayne K. Hinton with Elizabeth A. Green.
      p. cm.
    Includes bibliographical references and index.
    ISBN-13: 978-0-87842-546-4 (pbk. : alk. paper)
    ISBN-10: 0-87842-546-2 (pbk. : alk. paper)
    1. Civilian Conservation Corps (U.S.)—Colorado—History. 2.
    Conservation of natural resources—Colorado—History. 3. Forest
    conservation—Colorado—History. I. Green, Elizabeth A., 1944–
    II. Title. III. Title: With picks, shovels, and hope.
    S932.C6.H56 2008
    333.76'15097881—dc22
                                                    2008019275

PRINTED IN HONG KONG BY MANTEC PRODUCTION COMPANY

Published in cooperation with
Peaks, Plateaus & Canyons Association
Mountain Press Publishing Company
P.O. Box 2399 • Missoula, MT 59806
406-728-1900

This book is dedicated to the thousands of young men who, at a critical moment in the history of the United States, seized the opportunity offered by a concerned nation to join the Civilian Conservation Corps. They performed works of wonder to conserve natural resources and build a marvelous infrastructure of roads, trails, bridges, buildings, campgrounds, and services on public lands that would serve visitors to the Colorado Plateau for decades to come. While supporting their families they also developed skills, self assurance, discipline, and the courage that restored hope to a generation.

"I PROPOSE TO CREATE A CIVILIAN CONSERVATION CORPS TO BE
USED IN SIMPLE WORK. . . . MORE IMPORTANT, HOWEVER, THAN
THE MATERIAL GAINS WILL BE THE MORAL AND SPIRITUAL VALUE
OF SUCH WORK."

—FRANKLIN DELANO ROOSEVELT, MARCH 9, 1933

Contents

Foreword

History has always fascinated me. As an undergraduate my first in-depth studies focused on the anti-slavery movement and the chaotic time leading to the Civil War. After coming to the Grand Canyon in 1988, I studied the Ancestral Puebloan people, seeking to understand how they lived in the harsh environment of the American Southwest. Later my interests turned to the question of hikers' survival (and death) below the rim of the Grand Canyon.

All of these studies shared a common compelling theme—survival. How did our nation survive? How did human beings survive?

In January 2002 I was touched deeply by the words of a stranger. He spoke of how, at age seventeen, he had lost all hope in the future. "I still hear the sobbing of my siblings as they cried themselves to sleep because of the hunger in their bellies," he said. That stranger was Roy Lemons whose presentation at the Grand Canyon History Symposium told his personal story about how the Civilian Conservation Corps (CCC) saved him and his family from hunger during the Great Depression. Why did Roy touch the many people in that room so dramatically? Because we could feel his emotion, his authenticity, his truth.

As a teenager in 1936, Roy witnessed the predicament of his family. He saw the sullen, unemployed men standing in groups, their heads down, hands in their pockets, muttering despondently about the lack of work and their families' hunger. He heard these men talk of neighbors losing their farms and town folk their businesses. He knew that many small-town banks had failed. He could see evidence of severe drought in the Dust Bowl near his home in west Texas. He could not find even the most menial job to help alleviate his family's despair. Then a friend told him about the Civilian Conservation Corps. When Roy walked into the courthouse in town to enroll in the CCC, he took a giant step toward survival.

Roy Lemons went from a boy in despair to a man with hope. He credits his survival, and the survival of the country, to a program that was pulled together in just a matter of weeks. It was a program that, on paper, should not have worked. It envisioned government agencies working together that had never cooperated before—a mix that many officials believed would doom it to failure. But the Civilian Conservation Corps did work, and it served Roy Lemons well. He became a hard working, productive citizen and went on to be a husband, a father, a grandfather, a hopeful man.

All CCC projects—whether fighting fires, enhancing rangelands, or building trails, structures, or stone walls—are interwoven with personal stories like Roy's. Frequently they are stories of courage, bravery, triumph and, of course, survival, and you will find such stories in the lines of this book.

Words and images combine to tell us about CCC projects specific to the Colorado Plateau, but they also tell a deeper story about the boys themselves. Many had traveled far from home, perhaps for the first time, only to find themselves in an alien environment. Upon arriving at his camp in northern Michigan, one big-city boy from Detroit exclaimed, "The land is barren; what the hell am I doing here?" The dramatic landscape of the Colorado Plateau must have evoked equally strong reactions. When I look at the beautiful dioramas at Mesa Verde National Park's museum I see one CCC boy who helped create them. That boy, Meredith Guillet, later became a successful park ranger and eventually returned to Mesa Verde as its superintendent.

When I look at the photos of Grand Canyon National Park's River Trail, I can't forget the story of a Texas boy, Louis Purvis, who learned at an early age to work hard and hone skills taught by a great supervisor. "The skills I learned in the CCC were . . . to be resourceful. I learned to respect people," said Louis. When I walk along the rim at the Grand Canyon and look down at the trans-canyon telephone line I think about another Texas boy, Roy Lemons, who sent money home to feed his brothers and sisters and met his bride at the Grand Canyon. And what about that CCC boy at Grand Canyon who was helping build the boundary fence? He looks not a day over fifteen! Did the recruiters in his little Utah town unofficially waive the eighteen-year minimum-age requirement knowing that his family was desperate for food? Nevada CCC enrollee Ralph Hash said, "Things were so bad that for a year and a half my parents, my brother, and my three sisters lived on my [monthly] $25."

The CCC is a story both personal and global. More than three million boys and their families survived the Great Depression with the help of the Civilian Conservation Corps. The United States survived as a nation because of the many New Deal programs like the CCC that built confidence in our democratic system of government at a time when many people believed that a dictatorship was the only way to deal with issues as all-encompassing as those of the Great Depression.

This is the story of a program that was both altruistic and practical. It was Franklin Delano Roosevelt's "scheme on a gargantuan scale," said J. J. McEntee, CCC director in 1942. It was the "reclamation of wasting natural resources and reclamation of young American manhood."

It is the story of a program that was at the same time unique and ubiquitous—unique in that it has not been surpassed as the nation's largest peacetime mobilization ever; ubiquitous in that it touched more lives and more places than any other non-wartime program until the building of the interstate highway system several decades later. The CCC program impacted every small town in the West by creating jobs for poor, unskilled boys, employing local experienced men as supervisors, and providing needed income to local businesses that supplied their camps.

America emerged from the Great Depression a strong country with the help of the CCC. "In the end," says author Jonathan Alter, "FDR's seemingly impractical brainstorm not only protected the country from unrest and eased suffering, it symbolized the spirit of rebirth and regeneration." A generation of young men survived with the help of the CCC. "I sincerely believe that the Cs has done more to rehabilitate and restore confidence in American youth than any other organization ever existing," said Idaho enrollee Donald Tanasoca. Another enrollee said simply, "It saved my life."

Robert W. Audretsch
Historian
Park Ranger, Grand Canyon National Park

Acknowledgments

Many people were of assistance in researching this book. Rob Richards and the staff at the Denver Federal Records Center were of particular help, as were Leslie Courtright and Vickie Parkinson at Zion National Park and Michael Plyler and Lyman Hafen at Zion Natural History Association; Vickie Webster at Arches National Park and Sam Wainer and Cindy Hardgrave at Canyonlands Natural History Association; Anne Worthington and Keith Durfey at Capitol Reef National Park and Shirley Torgerson at Capitol Reef Natural History Association; Ann Elder at Dinosaur National Monument; Richard Millett at Intermountain Natural History Association; Paul Roelandt and Steve Robinson at Cedar Breaks National Monument; Jan Stock and Dan Ng at Bryce Canyon National Park and Gayle Pollock and Paula Henrie at Bryce Canyon Natural History Association; Liz Bauer and Erica Campos Thompson at Mesa Verde National Park; Lisa Claussen, Bruce Nobel, and Bobbie June Fisher at Colorado National Monument and Renee Creeden at Colorado National Monument Association; Wendy Bustard at Chaco Culture National Historical Park; Terry Nichols, Grady Griffin, and Cyresa Montanari at Aztec Ruins National Monument; Colleen Hyde, Michael Anderson, Pam Cox, Bob Audretsch, and Michael Quinn at Grand Canyon National Park and Pam Frazier and Brad Wallis at Grand Canyon Association; Scott Williams at Petrified Forest National Park; Scott Travis at Canyon de Chelly National Monument; Gwenn Gallenstein at Walnut Canyon and Wupatki National Monuments; Jane Jackson at the National Park

Service/USDA Forest Service Interpretive Partnership Program; Chris Anderson at Western National Parks Association; Bill Cantine and Andrea Bornemier at Pipe Spring National Monument; and Greg Cox and Tessy Shirakawa at Mesa Verde National Park.

Janet Seegmiller at the Southern Utah University Special Collections Library and Janice Richards in the interlibrary loan department of the university library were helpful, as were Barbara Valvo at Northern Arizona University's Cline Library Special Collections and Archives, Britt Kendall at the Washington City Museum in Washington County, Utah, Khaleel Saba at the Western Archaeological Center, and Todd Ellison and Nik Kendziorski at Fort Lewis College's Center of Southwest Studies.

Special thanks are due to Doug Leen of Ranger Doug Enterprises and Jerome Eberharter of White Cloud Coffee for their generous research grant.

WAYNE K. HINTON

Preface

Virtually every visitor to national parks and monuments, national forests, and other public lands on the Colorado Plateau benefits from a program instituted in 1933 to put young men to work. They became stewards of the land and builders of the facilities we enjoy to this day. Many of the roads we travel, the paths we walk, the visitor centers we explore, the campgrounds we stay in, and so much more, are the results of the most successful New Deal work program, the Civilian Conservation Corps.

Many histories and articles have told fragments of the CCC story, but none has concentrated on CCC endeavors on the Colorado Plateau, with particular emphasis on the difference the "Cs" made to federal lands. Who better to tell that story now than the cooperating associations that enhance visitor experiences through exhibits, educational programs, publications, and book stores? The Peaks, Plateaus & Canyons Association is a consortium of nonprofit educational organizations that cumulatively serve thirty-nine National Park Service sites, thirteen USDA Forest Service units, thirteen Bureau of Land Management units, and numerous other public land management agencies and municipalities on the plateau.

This book looks at the impact of the Great Depression, which gave rise to the CCC and other New Deal programs, as it affected the states that make up the Four Corners region of the American Southwest: Arizona, Utah, Colorado, and New Mexico. The distinctive landscape of the region's Colorado Plateau offered unparalleled opportunities for unemployed men to make a difference while having what for many of them proved to be a life-altering experience. Drawing on public land agency and college archives, previously published works, countless oral histories, and the Internet, this book explores who these young men were, what life was like in their camps, the remarkable contributions they made to the region, and the lasting impact of the CCC on the Colorado Plateau.

It is a collaborative effort involving many contributors. Armed with a grant from the Peaks, Plateaus & Canyons Association, Dr. Wayne K. Hinton, professor of history at Southern Utah University, conducted background research and wrote the preliminary manuscript. Peaks, Plateaus & Canyons Association members combed the archives of numerous national parks and monuments to bring life to the story. Lyman Hafen contributed a compelling word portrait of the Colorado Plateau. Jane Jackson, a volunteer interpretive ranger in the National Park Service/USDA Forest Service Interpretive Partnership Program in Flagstaff, Arizona, wrote not only about Arizona's Schultz Pass CCC camp, but also provided other research material from the area; Jane even spends her summers living on the site of the former Mount Elden CCC camp. Dr. Duane A. Smith, professor of history at Fort Lewis College, lent his expertise and his interview records on CCC at Mesa Verde National Park. Elizabeth A. Green conducted additional research, and knitted all the information together into the book you now hold.

A few words of explanation are in order. Officials and enrollees are identified by their full names unless CCC records contain only a last name. To avoid an alphabet stew of federal relief programs, references to New Deal programs have been simplified. In the early years, the Emergency Conservation Work (ECW) program put young men to work through public lands agencies.

Partway through the program's existence, in 1937, it was re-named the Civilian Conservation Corps. However, over time the program has come to be called the CCC throughout its nine-and-one-half-year existence and will therefore be referred to as the CCC in this book. Similarly, a separate Indian Division is described herein as the CCC-ID, even though it actually was the ECWID in its early years. The Soil Conservation Service (U.S. Department of Agriculture) did not come into existence until 1934 when it supplanted the Soil Erosion Service (U.S. Department of Interior). Unless otherwise noted, discussion in this book refers to the Soil Conservation Service (SCS).

Much of the personal information in this text is derived from oral histories or Web site histories, most of them collected around the fiftieth anniversary of the program. The tales of these young men's lives in the CCC have been left intact as the men expressed them, in colorful, sometimes grammatically flawed, language. While their years in the 3Cs were, according to many of them, the most meaningful in their lives, it must be acknowledged that oral history is fundamentally subjective history. It is likely the CCC was not run identically throughout the country, but the degree of those variations may, at times, be ascribed to faulty memories as well as regional differences. Stories vary, for example, on how much the men kept from their monthly wages, in part because of different pay levels for leaders and assistant leaders, but also, perhaps, because the numbers weren't as clear, decades later, for some of the men. While information has been corroborated to the degree possible, there may be factual errors in their personal stories. They do nothing, however, to detract from the magnitude of the individuals' experiences or the profound contributions of the CCC to this nation's public lands.

SEE AMERICA

UNITED STATES TRAVEL BUREAU

MADE BY WORKS PROGRESS ADMINISTRATION · FEDERAL ART PROJECT NYC

Chapter One

THE GREAT DEPRESSION AND THE CCC

The 1920s were a boom time for the United States. Americans were feeling prosperous, so confident of their future that they eagerly borrowed money to buy houses, cars, and consumer goods. They invested in companies they were certain would grow and richly reward them.

Building their future on borrowed money proved to be disastrous. On October 29, 1929, the stock market crashed. Many investors were wiped out, and the dominoes started to tumble.

Initially, the country rebounded, at least somewhat. Government and business spending actually increased in the first part of 1930, and wages held steady. It wasn't enough, however, to counteract people's sudden, profound loss of confidence in the economy. They grew cautious and consumer spending declined. At the same time, a severe drought devastated summer crops in agricultural states, which lost a sixth of their tillable soil. With spending on the decline, prices dropped, nowhere more dramatically than in farming areas.

THOUSANDS OF FAMILIES LOST THEIR HOMES DURING THE GREAT DEPRESSION. —COURTESY FRANKLIN D. ROOSEVELT PRESIDENTIAL LIBRARY AND MUSEUM

FRANKLIN D. ROOSEVELT'S FEDERAL ART PROJECT PUT ARTISTS AND PHOTOGRAPHERS TO WORK CREATING DESIGNS TO PROMOTE EDUCATION, HEALTH, SAFETY, AND TRAVEL. —COURTESY DOUG LEEN, RANGER DOUG ENTERPRISES

More than 700 banks failed in 1930 alone, as people found it harder and harder to make payments on the loans they had taken out during the good times. Lower consumer demand led to lower production and more people lost their jobs. In 1932, 32,000 businesses failed. The downward spiral seemed irreversible as it spread around the world. By 1933, more than a quarter of employable Americans were jobless. Those who still had jobs were earning less than half what they had earned before the Depression. No one was impacted more than the nation's youth, hundreds of thousands of whom approached adulthood without ever having a job, or at best only occasional day jobs.

Meanwhile, public lands were suffering as well. Insect infestations and disease had taken a dramatic toll on forests, as had drought and fire. Overharvesting of timber was an even bigger factor, prompting state and federal officials to search for long-term solutions. Conservation-minded leaders had seen what was coming. As governor of New York in 1928–29, Franklin D. Roosevelt created a reforestation program on state and county lands, expanding it in subsequent years to include acquisition of private lands for reforestation. By 1931, the New York legislature established a program to hire unemployed men to plant trees, fight fires, control insects, build roads and trails, improve forest ponds and lakes, and develop recreational facilities—a model FDR would employ on a far greater scale two years later.

Professional foresters shared Roosevelt's concerns even before the Great Depression. By the 1930s, the nation's once abundant timberland was reduced to a thousandth of what it had been. Deforestation had become so serious that in 1932 the Society of American Foresters proposed a program that would employ men in national and state forests and national parks to protect the denuded land through erosion control, road and trail construction, and firefighting.

When he accepted the Democratic nomination for president, FDR asserted that "converting many millions of acres of marginal and unused land into timber land through reforestation" would help resolve unemployment and problems in agriculture. Only days after his inauguration as president, he acted on that belief, offering measures to "relieve stress, to build men, to accomplish constructive results in our vast Federal, State, and private forest properties."

FDR REASSURED AMERICANS WITH FREQUENT RADIO "CHATS."
—Courtesy Franklin D. Roosevelt Presidential Library and Museum

The idea could not come too soon for the USDA Forest Service, whose 1934 budget was cut by 50 percent. The National Park Service was in similar condition, with master plans on the books for improvements to park and monument facilities, but no funding for the labor force or materials needed to carry them out.

Starting in 1933, several federal programs were created that included a provision for conservation work. The National Industrial Recovery Act established the Public Works Administration (PWA) in June 1933 to employ skilled workers hired by private contractors to do construction. That November, as the nation entered one of its coldest winters in fifty years, the Civil Works Administration (CWA) was created. With a goal of employing four million workers to build and repair roads, develop parks, dig sewers, and prevent erosion, the short-lived CWA was labor-intensive and spent most of its funds on wages. It was terminated in July 1934, largely because of its cost. In 1935 the Works Progress Administration (WPA, with the "P" later changed to "Projects") was created

3

to provide employment to all able-bodied, unemployed men over twenty-three years of age, and paid more than relief checks but less than prevailing wages. The workers, three-fourths of them unskilled or semiskilled, built highways, public buildings, parks, and irrigation ditches, worked on flood and erosion control, and planted trees, as well as completing many projects that did not specifically involve construction.

However, the program with the greatest impact on public lands—including the Colorado Plateau—was the Civilian Conservation Corps. The CCC was the first of the national public works programs approved by Congress on March 31, 1933, although that was not the official name until 1937. Roosevelt proposed enrolling 250,000 young men, and within three months the Labor Department had exceeded that goal, selecting 275,000 civilian enrollees to serve for six months. The enabling legislation spelled out who could participate—single men between eighteen and twenty-five—and the work they would do.

> . . . *provide for employing citizens of the United States who are unemployed, in the construction, maintenance and carrying on of works of a public nature in connection with the forestation of lands belonging to the United States or to the several States which are suitable for timber production, the prevention of forest fires, floods and soil erosion, plant pest and disease control, the construction, maintenance or repair of paths, trails and fire lanes in the national parks and national forests, and such other work on the public domain, national and State, and Government reservations incidental to or necessary in connection with any projects of the character enumerated, as the President may determine to be desirable. . . .*

A third CCC goal, added in 1934 and enlarged in 1937, was to provide educational opportunities to enrollees. CCCers were to be housed in semi-military camps and paid a subsistence wage of $30 a month, of which $25 was sent home to their parents. Hard-workers could advance to junior leadership positions and increase their pay. At a time when young men were dropping out of school and hopping freight trains in search of work, the prospect of a place to sleep and three meals a day was attractive. Having some pocket money as well, and being able to help their families back home made the CCC a godsend. Army privates called to work in CCC camps were envious of their civilian charges, since their pay equaled only $21 per month.

"While I was a child, I'd chop cotton for maybe a dollar a day, maybe six bits a day; cut wood, haul it into town for a dollar a rick. In the early spring, I would go into town with a team and plow gardens for people to make a dollar," recalled Jess "Buck" Forester, an Oklahoman who was assigned to Grand Canyon National Park in 1937. "It was quite a thing in my life realizing that I was going to be able to go to work, help my parents, and then return to school."

Jake Barranca also went to the Grand Canyon after he enrolled in the CCC in Albuquerque, New Mexico. His father had died when he was a toddler, and the family's finances were desperate. Barranca earned 25¢ a day herding cattle "sunrise to sunset" and helping out on farms. "Then I had to buy my own meal out of that."

The nation was divided into corps areas, with overall administration handled by the army. In the West, Colorado, New Mexico, and Arizona were part of the Eighth Corps area, headquartered in Houston, Texas. Utah was in the Ninth

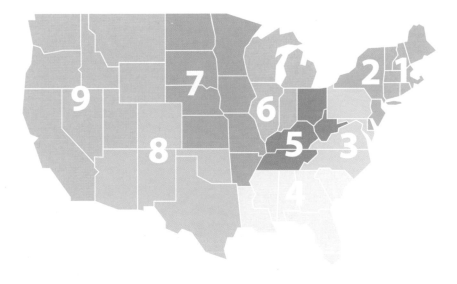

CCC WORKERS WERE ASSIGNED TO CORPS AREAS.
—MAP BY AMANDA SUMMERS

5

Corps area, with headquarters in San Francisco, California. The Ninth Corps area received one-third of all the CCC camps authorized in 1933. That region alone processed more men per day in May and June 1933 than the combined army and navy did per day recruiting soldiers and sailors for World War I.

Each state received enlistment instructions and a quota based on its population. For every ten young, unskilled enrollees, they would be able to sign up one slightly older, experienced worker—24,375 nationwide. These local experienced men, or LEMs, would be hired to help set up the camps and guide the junior enrollees in their work. They had to be over twenty-five, registered with the welfare office, and have work experience that would be of use in the various CCC projects. The Forest Service, National Park Service, and other "technical agencies" chose LEMs based on agency needs and the applicants' abilities in such matters as handling horses and equipment. Living close to a CCC camp became a distinct advantage for such men, who could be married or single. Existing state welfare agencies made the actual selections under guidelines set by the Department of Labor.

The CCC brought together young men from diverse regions, life experiences, and cultures. A Division of Grazing camp near Blanding, Utah, was populated with boys from New York, New Jersey, and Delaware initially. Many of the fifty Italian boys and twenty-two Puerto Ricans spoke in their native tongues. Later, thirty-five local boys from Moab, Monticello, and Blanding were assigned to the camp.

At the inception of the CCC, Executive Order 6129 authorized enrollment of 25,000 World War I veterans, with the Veterans Administration responsible for certifying eligibility and making the selections. Each state was entitled to one veteran for every ten junior enrollees.

Native Americans also were identified as a target enrollment group, with their selection and work projects handled by the Bureau of Indian Affairs in the Interior Department. Organization and administration of the CCC-Indian Division was much more flexible than the parent CCC and had great impact in the Southwest where so many Native Americans resided on reservations. Up to 10,000 Native Americans could be enrolled, without restrictions based on age or marital status, primarily to work on tribal lands or areas adjacent to reservations. Additionally, using Indian CCC workers did not count against the state's quota for junior enrollees.

As early as 1934, an agreement between the forest service and the Bureau of Indian Affairs provided for cooperative firefighting. Soon, similar arrangements were reached between the bureau and the park service, setting a precedent for further cooperation. When cuts came to the CCC-Indian Division, cooperative agreements became even more popular. Oral histories from Colorado-based CCCers, in particular, sometimes refer to "Indian" enrollees in their companies, suggesting that not all Native American CCCers participated in CCC-ID programs.

"When we arrived at the camp [near Grand Junction, Colorado], the guys who were there were mostly from little farm towns in Oklahoma. These fellows were unable to speak without cussing and I soon found that my speech habits had changed accordingly," recalled Morris Grodsky, decades after he left his Denver, Colorado, home to work in two Bureau of Reclamation camps in western Colorado in 1940. "Later on we acquired a contingent of Native Americans from a nearby reservation. These guys hardly spoke at all."

The 1933 legislation authorizing the Civilian Conservation Corps contained an amendment stipulating that "no discrimination shall be made on account of race, color, or creed." Nonetheless, despite pressure from African Americans to integrate and provide racial justice, the CCC's dealings with them were difficult and less than totally successful. Black unemployment was twice the national average in 1933, yet black enrollment was consistently limited. The failure was due, in part, to a conservative director from the segregated state of Georgia and also to the role of the recalcitrant, tradition-bound, segregated army. Prevalent attitudes toward African Americans also spawned crude racist remarks in some camp newspapers, entertainment that ridiculed blacks, and disproportionate disciplinary actions against them.

Black enrollment in 1933 was only half the quota set for African Americans. Local and state enrollment processes, unfortunately, allowed for discrimination based on local customs. In Colorado, with a total population of 1,035,791, including 41,431 blacks, most of the state's few black enrollees were sent to a segregated camp in New Mexico.

Up until 1934, Corps commanders could decide on policy relative to camp make-up, which allowed commanders in the Eighth and Ninth corps areas to maintain some mixed companies. Other areas had total segregation, and some had very few African American enrollees. In September 1934 CCC director Robert Fechner issued an order that black enrollees be placed in black-only camps. The War Department followed up with an April 1935 order segregating camps, making separation of blacks the general rule. When numbers of blacks in a state were insufficient to form an all-black company, the corps could continue mixed companies, but the African Americans generally received the least desirable assignments.

Despite involving the departments of War, Agriculture, Interior, and Labor—a seeming administrative monstrosity—the CCC functioned smoothly, largely because their individual roles were well defined. Labor selected the recruits. Army was responsible for establishing and running the camps with military discipline, while Agriculture and Interior—the "technical service" agencies—took over during working hours, determining and supervising projects.

President Roosevelt insisted that the army participate in this civilian unemployment relief effort, a diversion from its primary function of national defense. Even as war preparations stepped up in 1939, the army retained its association with the program. It was an arrangement that would prove especially beneficial when the United States entered World War II.

The army supplied clothing, food, and equipment; constructed the camps, and saw to the general welfare of enrollees by providing sanitation and medical care. Regular officers were placed in charge of the camps at first, but later unemployed Army Reserve officers were called to active duty for service in the CCC camps. Each camp was under the command of an officer, most of them army captains, although there were lieutenants occasionally. Each company also had a junior officer, sometimes referred to as the adjutant, welfare officer, or mess officer. These camps shared military doctors while some camps used civilian doctors contracted to the CCC. Military personnel attached to camps usually rotated often.

Enrollee morale was dependent largely on the attitudes and abilities of the army officer, the technical staff, and, later, the educational advisor. Since the military personnel rotated much more often than the technical service personnel, the civilian superintendents and foremen were able to gain loyalty among the men. The army made assignments without consulting the technical agency, insisting that it could move its CCC camp commanders as it saw fit. Sometimes moving, or failing to move, army officers caused concerns to the technical service leaders, and most decidedly the enrollees and LEMs. When a commander earned the men's respect, they were sorry to see him leave. Many commanders learned to gain the admiration and cooperation of the company members while others were less effective.

"The park service people, their supervisors, that was the ones that taught you everything," recalled Lynn Atwood, a young Texan whose family had moved to New Mexico, then Arizona, because of his father's health. Atwood left his Prescott, Arizona, home to work in the Grand Canyon. "They kept an eye on you, [saw] that you stayed healthy, saw that you stayed safe, and above all, learned what you were supposed to be doing and do it well."

In contrast, Atwood had little interaction with the army personnel who ran the camp. "They had business of their own," he explained. "They couldn't be bothered with you. They'd see that you were fed, housed, and clothed, and as long as you behaved yourself, you got along real well."

Quotas for enrollment in the CCC were based on the population of each state. However, with the preponderance of the population in the East, and the vast public lands in the West, many enrollees had to be sent far from their homes. In a three-month period, special trains carried 55,000 men an average of 2,200 miles to camps in the West.

William Ivy Byrd, who grew up in Alabama, had never been more than fifty miles from home when he joined the CCC in 1940 after graduating from high school. "I tell people I did not grow up in the country—you had to go through the country to reach our location," he recalled. Until he enrolled in the CCC and went to Eureka and Green River, Utah, he had never ridden on a train.

CCC enrollees were assigned to companies, which in turn were sent to camps. In the nine and one-half years of the program, company and camp

designations changed, sometimes seasonally and other times with new assignments. The results can be confusing when trying to determine where camps were
and who was assigned to them.

Camp designations identified the state in which they were located and
the technical service agency that ran the work program there. For example, "F"
indicated a forest service camp and "NP" a National Park Service camp. Later
when the Grazing Service, the Bureau of Reclamation, and Soil Conservation
Service were allotted camps, they were designated respectively "GS," "BR," and

CAMP NP-5, CEDAR BREAKS
NATIONAL MONUMENT, UTAH
—COURTESY UTAH STATE
HISTORICAL SOCIETY

"SCS." The National Park Service also coordinated CCC work in state parks, whose camps were designated "SP."

"We landed in Thompson, Utah, which was an isolated place," recalled Frank "Bo" Montella, who was seventeen when he left his Brooklyn, New York, home to join the CCC in Utah. "We thought it was out of this world."

From the beginning, the CCC was a temporary program. Men enrolled for a six-month period, with the option of re-enlisting for a second term. Later, as enrollment declined, men were allowed to serve more than two terms. Others were able to advance into leadership positions and spend years with the CCC. Congress had to re-authorize the program every two years.

The spirit of cooperation among agencies and the popular program's success led to an increase in enrollees and camps in 1935 legislation. By 1936, the CCC had doubled in size, from nearly 300,000 to almost 600,000 men. Again in 1937 and 1939, Congress extended the life of the CCC, but by 1937 it was becoming more difficult to fill quotas and keep the camps at authorized strength. As potential CCC boys found employment in the private sector, the age range was expanded to include men between seventeen and twenty-eight, and eliminated the requirement that they be on relief. Soon, younger recruits made up more than 30 percent of the enrollees. With their homesickness, desertion increased significantly, as did dishonorable discharges. Some of the slack in construction work on public lands, however, was taken up by the WPA.

Increasing threats of war stimulated the economy and provided private sector job opportunities for CCC veterans as well as prospective enrollees. Enrollment declined from 600,000 in 1936, to 200,000 in late 1940, and 150,000 in June 1941. An expanding military also drained off many camp officers and enrollees, and when the United States entered World War II in December 1941, the CCC shrank to fewer than 600 camps with fewer than 100,000 men. By June 1942, increased industrial employment and competition from the military and the National Youth Administration (a special program to hire young people on a part-time basis to help keep them in school and to teach skills), brought the demise of the CCC. When Congress voted to end the program, it was already quietly expiring of natural causes, but not of failure or public disfavor.

Sometimes referred to as "Roosevelt's Tree Army," CCCers planted more than four billion trees, greater than had been planted in the entire prior history of the United States. The CCC had lasted nine and one-half years, through nineteen six-month enrollment periods, longer than any other New Deal work relief program. In that time, nearly 3.5 million CCCers improved public lands, learned valuable skills, and contributed to their families' finances. It was, undoubtedly, one of the most popular and successful of FDR's programs.

"That's how it was in the Cs. A period I'll always remember with gratitude," Morris Grodsky reflected. "I learned how to chew tobacco and hated it. I worked at physical labor harder than I would ever do again in my life. I would never again be as lean and fit as I was during that brief interlude with 'Roosevelt's Tree Army.'"

Chapter Two

For many of the CCC boys, the abrupt transition from their boyhood homes to the Colorado Plateau of the American Southwest must have been akin to landing on a new planet. All of a sudden, a young man who had known nothing but the rolling grass prairies of the Midwest, or the densely treed glens of the South, or the urban jungles of the Northeast, found himself smack in the middle of the deep canyons, the towering peaks, and the vast slickrock mesas of the Colorado Plateau.

Hobart Feltner, who came from Kentucky, considered Utah "the damnedest country" he had ever seen in his life. He was accustomed to the lush forests and grassy meadows of his boyhood home and had no use for all the desert's "briar stuff." For a time, Feltner found the sparsely vegetated, dusty landscape of the Colorado Plateau "hard to look at." But as is the case for many people, it didn't take long for it grow on him. And he never left.

Yet for Joseph Arnold the fruit orchards that lined the Colorado River near Grand Junction, Colorado, were "unbelievably fertile to my New England eyes." He must have felt grateful to be employed as a CCCer when worsening dust bowl conditions drove "desperately poor Okie and Arkie families of 'Grapes of Wrath' fame" to the area in search of work.

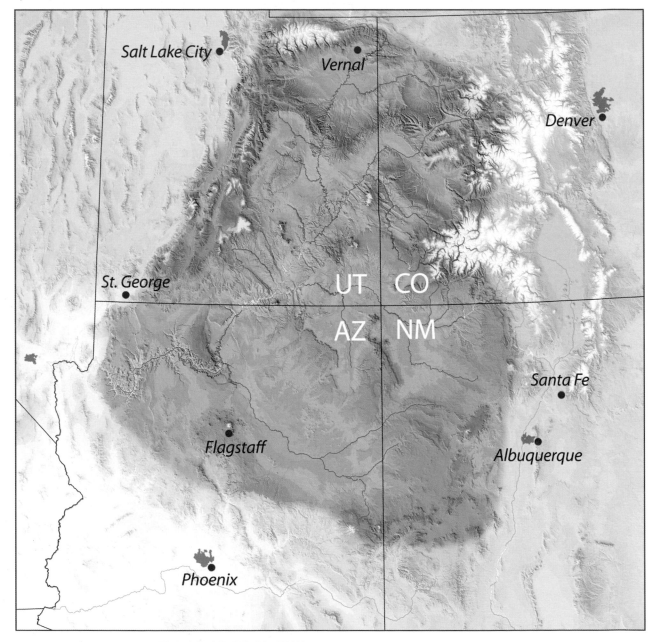

Salt Lake City

Vernal

Denver

St. George

UT   CO

AZ   NM

Santa Fe

Flagstaff

Albuquerque

Phoenix

THE COLORADO PLATEAU —COURTESY U.S. GEOLOGICAL SURVEY

Texan Marvin Gandy could not have been more delighted to see and work in the Grand Canyon. When he and his fellow enrollees arrived by train, he found the experience of standing on the edge of the canyon "just mind-boggling."

The exotic, beguiling, and in some ways intimidating scenery was just the beginning of the culture shock many of the boys experienced. Ed Braun, who came from Ohio to work near Green River, Utah, found the arid climate particularly challenging. "None of us were used to requiring a drink of water so frequently," he recalled, "especially while we were out on a job." Altitude and strong sun also had an impact on enrollees, many of whom came from substantially lower elevations and grayer climates.

CANYONLANDS NATIONAL PARK, UTAH

Their time in this most amazing landscape would leave a deep impression on many of the CCC boys—a lasting impression as meaningful as the work they did and the friends they made. For some, like Feltner, it became their new home. For others, it would remain a special place to bring their children and grandchildren and boast, "I worked here; I helped build that."

The Colorado Plateau is a vast and varied place that means many things to many people. It is a land of peaks, plateaus, and canyons, and home to an amazing variety of plants, animals, and human beings. In some places it is dry, dusty, and deeply furrowed. In others, it is mountainous and forested. It is rich with natural resources, including coal, petroleum, uranium, precious metals, and natural gas. But perhaps it is most rich in the myriad stories attached to its magnificent landforms—the stories of its distinctive geology laid open like the pages of a book, the stories of its prehistoric inhabitants, the early explorers and exploiters, scientists, trappers, artists, miners, homesteaders, ranchers, native people, and Mormon colonizers. When the CCC boys arrived on the plateau in the 1930s, they too added a new chapter to this storied land.

Pared down to its simplest definition the Colorado Plateau is approximately 140,000 square miles in the Four Corners region of Utah, Colorado, Arizona, and New Mexico. It is not a single formation, but a varied landscape united by its distinctive geology. It includes the areas drained by the Colorado River and its tributaries, including the Green, San Juan, and Little Colorado rivers. The Uinta Mountains of Utah and the Rocky Mountains of Colorado mark the northern and northeastern boundaries of the plateau. The Rio Grande Rift Valley in New Mexico defines the eastern boundary. The southern edge of the plateau spans the Mogollon Rim in Arizona and New Mexico's Datil section. The west edge is bordered by the Basin and Range Province in Utah. The Colorado Plateau can be divided into six sections, including the Grand Canyon Section, the High Plateaus, the Uinta Basin, Canyonlands, the Navajo Section, and the Datil Section of volcanic origin in New Mexico.

Within the Colorado Plateau are found soaring sandstone arches and fanciful hoodoos, towering temples of stone, laccolithic mountains and pine forests,

sprawling seas of slickrock, and picturesque buttes and pinnacles, such as those found in Monument Valley that have been the backdrops of western movies for decades. Yet, nowhere on the Colorado Plateau is the two-billion-year geologic history of the region more perfectly displayed than in the walls of the Grand Canyon.

Another unifying factor on the Colorado Plateau is its dry air and parched land. Precipitation is infrequent and sparse, averaging only about ten inches per year. Winter snows moisten the upper elevations, which reach above 12,000 feet, while the lower country crackles and splits under the blistering sun. Arroyos can lie dry for months on end, then fill bank to bank with the flooding fury of a sudden downpour.

Early in the twentieth century the region's beauty and scenic wonder so captured the hearts and imaginations of Americans that by the time the CCCs were organized, there were eighteen national parks and monuments on the Colorado

Plateau—seven in Arizona, six in Utah, three in Colorado, and two in New Mexico. Today there are nine national parks, sixteen national monuments, one national historical park, millions of acres of national forests, and many state parks and other protected lands on the plateau.

Much of what we see, access, and appreciate on these public lands today was made possible by the young men who left their boyhood homes in the 1930s and came to work in a strange and inspiring land called the Colorado Plateau.

The first Civilian Conservation Corps enrollment period opened April 1, 1933, with an ambitious goal but no real sense of how many might apply before it closed May 15. To qualify, young men had to be county residents listed on relief rolls as well as meet age and marital status requirements.

Arizona was a relatively new state in 1933, admitted to the Union just twenty-one years earlier, in February 1912. It contained vast undeveloped beauty, but the semi-arid landscape was in need of both conservation and development. The 1930 census count of 435,573 Arizonans, including large populations of Native Americans and Hispanics, entitled the state to 870 junior enrollees. Young, unemployed men who felt that earning any amount of money would be an improvement quickly filled the state's enrollment quota, and continued to exceed it by as much as 8 percent through the first two years of the CCC.

The state averaged thirty-one camps through the years of the CCC. With the small quota and vast federal landholdings, local men alone could not staff all the allocated CCC camps. As would prove true in all but Utah, the corps would have to import most of its workers from other parts of the country.

R. D. "Bo" Moorhead, the son of a Desdemona, Texas, cotton farmer, typified the men who came to Arizona. "Nobody was any poorer than we were," he recalled. "In 1935 my dad called me outside one night, me being the oldest of the family, and said, 'Son, somebody's got to go. You're the oldest.' And in a week to ten days' time, I was in the Grand Canyon." Moorhead said it was "hard" to join the CCC, particularly if the applicant's parents owned land. "You had to be almost destitute, which nearly everybody was," he recalled. "We had six boys, to this day I don't know how my dad fed us. We ate like a bunch of thresher hens."

For others, like Marvin Gandy, joining the CCC changed the direction of their lives. The eldest of seven children, Gandy started running with a bad crowd after his parents separated when he was seventeen. He quit school, tried in vain to find work, and finally started riding freight trains to widen his job search. He and the friends he acquired on the rails "planned to do some things that I would have wound up in jail [for] if we did them." Instead, he spent three years working "on the floor of the Grand Canyon."

Unlike Arizona, Utah did not have to look beyond its own borders for many CCC recruits. With a population of slightly more than a half million, Utah's initial enrollment quota was set at 1,000 unmarried men between ages eighteen and twenty-five. Four hundred applicants inundated the Salt Lake office the first day. By May 4, Salt Lake County had taken more than 4,000 applications for its 774 allotted positions. It was the same throughout the state, with applications exceeding quotas in every county. In addition to the 1,000 junior enrollees, Utah was authorized to hire 1,300 unemployed carpenters, lumbermen, miners, and others with outdoor experience, one of the largest such allotments in the program. These Local Experienced Men, or LEMs, would serve as project leaders and help the young, inexperienced CCC boys adapt to their new environment and outdoor working conditions. In its first year, out of the 5,500 CCC enrollees, supervisors, and LEMs working in the state, 4,000 were Utahns.

Records suggest the qualification guidelines were not applied evenly. Mark Baird was accepted because his employment would help his widowed mother and her six children, while an unsuccessful applicant claimed he was unfairly rejected because he had been unemployed for three years. Some applied out of sheer desperation and managed to skirt CCC rules. Don Penrod was the eighth of twelve children of a widowed mother, who had seven minor children still at home. At only sixteen years old and needing work to help his family, he lied about his age and was sent to Forest Service Camp 958. His first assignment was guard duty/fire watch, which proved "quite spooky" to a sixteen-year-old away from home for the first time.

One lucky applicant for the third enrollment period in 1934, Belden Lewis, wrote, "Can't sleep—I've been called, actually called to the CCCs! Just think! Zion National Park! I wonder what it is like? I wonder if they initiate? I wonder if the rest will treat me okay?"

The Eighth Corps area was allocated 24,000 men in 120 camps, including twenty in Arizona, twenty-five in Colorado and fifteen in New Mexico. The Ninth Corps area, which included Utah, had 459 camps in the first enrollment period. During the second enrollment, October 1933 to March 1934, the number dropped to 270. By then, many eastern states had developed their own projects and needed their enrollees.

Still, the Ninth Corps area had seventy-six more camps than the quota normally would have allowed. When the second enrollment period opened September 30, 1933, many boys reenlisted and almost all of the LEMs remained with the CCC. Utah was able to average 122 percent of its quota for the first, second, and third enrollment periods. In subsequent periods, more out-of-state enrollees joined the Utahns. Despite the high in-state enrollment, Utah's average of twenty-seven camps was the lowest of the Colorado Plateau states. Nonetheless, the state reached a high of forty-one camps in 1935 and never fell below thirty for the remainder of the program.

Lyall Wilson, from Lehi, Utah, started out with all Utahns, but eventually found himself assigned to a company of out-of-state boys near Cedar City. "These New York and Kentucky people didn't know one end of an axe or shovel from the other," he lamented, adding that despite their willingness to try, they were "doing more damage to each other with the axes and other tools than they were doing to the cedar trees and quaking aspen they had been cutting down." Supervisors teamed the Easterners with Utahns, who helped teach them the ways of the woods.

It was a cultural encounter that required understanding and patience. "These men were right off of the streets of a city and most of them had never known where their next meal was coming from. This explains their eating habits," Wilson explained. "When they learned to use their tools they were as good as any of us on the job. After we had worked with them for awhile we got to know them and their ways, we all learned to like and respect each other."

Being far from home in unfamiliar terrain and dramatically different climate—whether it was the heat of summer or cold of winter—sometimes proved overwhelming to enrollees. New Mexico received nearly 22,000 out-of-state enrollees, primarily from Texas, Oklahoma, and Pennsylvania. Those who had hoped to be assigned close to home found it especially difficult to adjust to those differences. If their numbers were great enough, the out-of-staters readily made their disapproval of their host state known to New Mexicans. Some also objected to having to work with, let alone be supervised by, Hispanics.

In the Ninth Corps area African Americans served with white LEMs in mixed camps under white officers and white technical service supervisors. With pressure from black leaders for African American officers to command segregated camps, President Roosevelt suggested that the War Department begin calling black reserve personnel as supervisors, medical staff, and chaplains.

On August 10, 1935, the War Department ordered corps area commanders to call up thirty-three black medical reserve officers and eight black chaplains for the African American camps. At best this was only token representation. In the Ninth Corps area, black CCCers continued to be assigned separate living quarters, latrines, and mess facilities. In 1940 the War Department began training and appointing black enrollees as junior officers in black camps, as well as appointing black reserve line officers to those camps. Black educational advisers were assigned to some African American camps, but they found it difficult to incorporate the white technical staff into the camp educational programs.

With 3,047 African Americans living in the state in 1930, Utah's quota was only ten. In reality, about half that number served at any point in time, and they were sent to camps in California. Community response to the black New Yorkers in Company 1256, which was working on the Kanab watershed near Alton, was typical in Utah. Local leaders told the CCCers to stay away from local church services unless they were invited, believing the boys to be an undesirable class of men. Some even characterized them as "Waterfront Boys" or "Coldwater Flat Boys." Residents, and even some enrollees, regarded them with fear and contempt, and Alton eventually requested that the camp be removed.

Colorado's first CCC camp was organized April 27, 1933, at Fort Logan, which was the administrative headquarters for Colorado and Wyoming. Indeed, Company 851 was established and assigned to a forest service camp just ten days after formation of the first CCC company in America. Their first project, to build a standard grade road seven miles from Minturn to the Mount of the Holy Cross, was a precursor to the major part CCC boys would take in western road construction. Through the nine and one-half years of the CCC, Colorado would boast the highest elevation camp, at 9,200 feet above sea level (the lowest was in California's Death Valley, at 270 below sea level) and the highest number of camps among the Colorado Plateau states, at thirty-seven.

With a population of slightly more than one million, Colorado had the highest enrollment quota—about 2,000—and the hardest time meeting it. In the first period, the state filled only 82 percent of its quota, and therefore came to rely even more on out-of-state enrollees. Men came from as far as New England, and as close as Texas to live and work in the Rocky Mountain state.

James C. Burnett was underage—only sixteen—and underweight when he signed up for the CCC in Wewoka, Oklahoma. The scrawny teenager couldn't report to his CCC camp in Mesa, Colorado, until he built up his strength and reached the minimum weight of 107 pounds. "I ate bananas and drank buttermilk and got up to ninety-eight pounds," he recalled, adding that the doctor remarked, "If he grows into those feet, he should make a pretty good CCC boy."

In 1933, Colorado had twenty-five widely scattered CCC camps, which presented an administrative problem, particularly with a swath of high peaks dividing the state. Two years later, forty camps were spread across the state on both sides of the mountains. To solve the geographical obstacles, in August

1935 the army split Colorado into east and west divisions along the Continental Divide, with headquarters for the Western Slope at Grand Junction.

Establishment of the Grand Junction district office generally coincided with a rapid increase in CCC camps, including several new Division of Grazing and Bureau of Reclamation camps in western Colorado. The district headquarters consisted of an administration building, a commissary, a garage, and warehouses for clothing and property, which became the central supply point for the west side of the mountains. The commissary stored dry and perishable food items. Fresh meat, smoked meats, eggs, and dairy products were kept in a large refrigerated room, while a root cellar preserved fresh vegetables, pickles, and vinegar.

The Army Quartermaster Corps provided the food, clothing, transportation, and most of the supplies that kept the camps operating, resulting in a net savings for the district. The finance officer handled payrolls and saw that the monthly deduction of $25 was sent home to enrollee families. In addition to twenty-six army officers, the headquarters employed sixty-one civilians to inventory and classify supplies, properly store goods, and dispense them to the twenty CCC camps that now graced western Colorado. Incoming camp officers also were trained at the headquarters complex.

CCC programs in Colorado were often touted as being among the best, partly because of the large number of technical personnel per camp and the practical training they offered in a variety of vocations. Enrollees were taught how to work on projects that were of immense practical value to the nation's land agencies, which in turn reversed a pattern of neglect. Stratton E. Van, a USDA Forest Service project superintendent, said, "If they eliminated now the stuff the CCC built, they would . . . eliminate 80 percent of the improvements

NAVAJO STONEMASONS
RESTORING ANCIENT
STRUCTURES AT CHACO
CANYON NATIONAL MONUMENT,
NOW CALLED CHACO CULTURE
NATIONAL HISTORICAL PARK,
NEW MEXICO —COURTESY
WESTERN ARCHAEOLOGICAL AND
CONSERVATION CENTER

on the forests. We've done well just to keep them maintained and add a little bit to it."

With more than one-third of its area owned by the federal government, New Mexico was well-suited to numerous CCC projects. But it was a relatively new state, its geography vast, with great uninhabited expanses. Securing CCC camps for such remote, isolated areas was a challenge. As a result, New Mexico had the lowest number of allotted camps among Colorado Plateau states at the inception of the CCC, and averaged thirty-two camps from 1933 to 1942. The state's enrollment quota was set at 750 men, not including enrollees in the CCC-ID. With the highest percentage of residents on relief in the country, the state always exceeded its CCC enrollment quota, but many of the state's enrollees served elsewhere in the Eighth Corps area, especially in Colorado. Even in 1941, as employment in the private sector increased in most of the country, two-thirds of New Mexico CCC enrollees had never held a job. The first CCC camps in the state were on forest service land southeast of the Colorado Plateau. The Soil Conservation Service and the Indian CCC-ID played a larger role in northwestern New Mexico's public works programs than anywhere else.

The state's 423,317 residents included 34,196 Native Americans, most of them Navajos. About half of the state's population was Hispanic, which perhaps prevented the kind of blatant discrimination suffered by African Americans in the CCC. By 1938-42, for example, Hispanics constituted more than 80 percent of New Mexico's enrollees and stayed in the corps an average of two enrollment periods, compared to one period for non-Hispanics. Despite friction with some out-of-state enrollees, Hispanics were never segregated in either separate camps or facilities within camps. Like so many other ethnic or geographic groups, however, they tended to form social groups with other Hispanics. Perhaps because of their limited educational backgrounds, few Hispanics served in the highest levels of leadership. Many did become foremen as well as leaders in recreational and social programs.

Within the Colorado Plateau, northwestern New Mexico has the least area and the fewest parks and monuments among the four states. As a result, the CCC programs there were more limited than in other plateau states. Activity on the plateau focused largely on preservation and stabilization of Ancestral Puebloan sites, at the region's two national monuments, Chaco Canyon (now known as Chaco Culture National Historical Park) and Aztec Ruins.

In the 1930s, the Navajos remained largely separate from the general population on their reservation, which occupies much of the Colorado Plateau in the state. The CCC-Indian Division was active among the Navajos, whose traditional lifestyle of raising goats and sheep drew particular interest from the Division of Grazing CCC program. Through the CCC-ID, Navajos also worked off the reservation at both Chaco Canyon and Aztec Ruins.

New Mexican Max Castillo enrolled in the CCC in his home state, but was assigned to Arizona. Orphaned at age eleven, Castillo bounced from one relative to another. "It was rough," he recalled decades later. "I went to school as far as I could go and could afford. And when I had to buy my books for the tenth grade, I couldn't go no more. So I joined the Cs."

As probably happened more often than not in small towns where enrollment officials knew their applicants, Castillo had a lucky break. Still five months shy of his eighteenth birthday, he lied about his age on the application. "One of the members of that board lived in Buffalo Gap, a little town I come from," Castillo recounted. "He knew exactly how old I was . . . but he just didn't take the second look because he knew we needed it." Castillo remained with the CCC for more than five years, working his way up from junior enrollee to foreman.

THE CCC IN NATIONAL FORESTS

For years the U.S. Department of Agriculture Forest Service had been short of funds and manpower for planting trees, improving timber stands, developing recreational facilities, fighting fires, building roads and trails, and other jobs related to conservation and development. With the opportunities offered by the CCC, its camps were often the first established and the last closed. Nationally, nearly three-quarters of all CCCers worked on Department of Agriculture (USDA) projects, the majority of them on national forests. In Arizona, the forest service directed more CCC work than any other single agency.

Although reforestation was a national priority for the CCC, most companies assigned to the Colorado Plateau focused more on firefighting, insect and disease control, road building, and recreational development. The relatively lower priority placed on planting seedling trees may have been in response to the region's semi-arid climate. Foresters today recognize the futility of trying to plant, protect, and nurture fledgling trees to maturity. The technical service agency planners may have recognized the same challenges in the 1930s, particularly in the face of existing drought conditions.

The typical fire season on the Colorado Plateau is early May to mid-July, the period before the summer monsoons, when little or no rain falls to quell lightning-caused fires. In the 1930s, with fires also started by sparks from locomotives, sawmill accidents, human carelessness, and even arson, there was great progress in reducing fire losses. The average number of fires per year declined as did the total acres lost to fire, in part due to rapid response by CCC crews. In most instances, they had access to bulldozers, a valuable tool in firefighting which allowed them to create firebreaks and contain fires more rapidly than could hand crews. The additional manpower available through the CCC and the boys' youthfulness and energy were key to improving fire containment.

In Utah, CCCers put in nearly 12,000 man-days fighting fires in 1934 alone, the worst fire year in the CCC's nine-and-a-half year history. Two years later, one CCC crew spent ten days fighting the 3,000-acre Wah Wah Mountain fire, one of the largest blazes fought in the state up to that time. The summer of 1940 was an especially bad fire season in Arizona, with more than one hundred fires on the Coconino National Forest alone. With dwindling CCC enrollment by then, the boys of the 3Cs could not combat the fires without help from volunteers recruited in Flagstaff, Jerome, and Winslow.

Learning to fight fires was the first training Everett Minteer and fellow enrollees received at the camp serving Wupatki, Sunset Crater, and Walnut Canyon national monuments in northern Arizona. "You had to clear everything out of the way, make like a road, best you can," he said, adding they had limited equipment for the job. "I thought I'd never survive it."

Three enrollees perished fighting fires in New Mexico, including one killed by a falling tree while cleaning up after a blaze west of Bandelier National Monument. CCC director Fechner honored the young man with a posthumous award for courage and meritorious service.

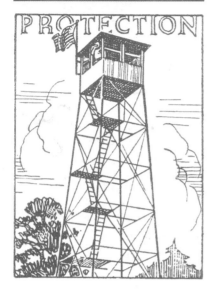

NATIONAL PARK SERVICE

Mission

The National Park Service preserves unimpaired the natural and cultural resources and values of the national park system for the enjoyment, education, and inspiration of this and future generations. The park service cooperates with partners to extend the benefits of natural and cultural resource conservation and outdoor recreation throughout this country and the world.

Beyond fighting fires, CCCers on the Colorado Plateau built fire lookout towers and administration buildings, including ranger stations, worked on soil and erosion control projects, and built trails and roads. Although most road-building was aimed at fire management, many routes cleared by the CCCers became forest roads, allowing people greater access to previously remote areas. On the Mogollon Rim, CCCers focused on a road which had started out as the General Crook Trail in 1871. They widened and otherwise improved it into what is now FR300, which traverses the forest, offering drivers splendid views along the way.

The Civilian Conservation Corps also provided manpower and equipment for the first large-scale development of recreation facilities in the forest service, including campgrounds and picnic areas. Controlling disease and insects that afflicted trees also occupied considerable time. Among Lyall Wilson's duties while working near Moon Lake in Utah was cutting infested trees. "These trees had a bark worm in them so they were cut down and used for a power and telephone line that we built. The bark and limbs from these trees were piled in a clearing and burned to kill the worms."

The isolation of many forest service camps led to higher than average rates of desertion, particularly among young enrollees. On the other hand, many of the men who started their careers as technical service supervisors went on to careers as rangers with the USDA Forest Service.

THE CCC IN NATIONAL PARKS AND MONUMENTS

The National Park Service, in the Department of the Interior, mirrored the plight of the country as the Great Depression tightened its grip on the nation. After its establishment in 1916, the park service focused its resources on development of the premier parks, those with extraordinary scenic value, especially if they could be reached by railroad. The park service and private concessionaires

32

built roads, hotels, and other amenities to accommodate growing numbers of tourists. Meanwhile, more remote parks and monuments received little attention. However, with shrinking budgets and dwindling recreational travel, the depression signaled the end of such business expansion. At the same time, the advent of public works programs presented an incomparable opportunity for development on a broader scale. Over the next decade, even some of the most remote monuments would receive at least some benefit from the CCC and other New Deal programs.

Louis Purvis knew he was far from his West Texas home when he arrived at the Grand Canyon. "I was so used to doing without food, I don't remember whether they fed us or not," he recalled. "Anyway, we pulled in out there in the parking area at the head of the South Kaibab Trail and met the people who were to lead us down or escort us down in the canyon. After he oriented us to the trail to a certain extent, he dismissed us. I was approached by three other boys about going over the hill [deserting] due to their first glimpse of the canyon, that being so different from what they were used to in West Texas."

Another Texan, Roy Lemons, was "seventeen years and four months of age" when he entered the CCC. He was deeply grateful for the chance to help support his family. "I came into the CCCs because it was a very destitute time. To put it very bluntly, for a number of years during the Depression my stomach was under the impression that my throat had been cut."

CCC WORKERS EXCAVATING RAMPART CAVE, GRAND CANYON NATIONAL PARK, ARIZONA
—Courtesy National Park Service

With about a quarter of the nation's CCC camps assigned to it, the park service chose camp locations, determined what work would be done, and furnished the equipment, technical planning, supervision, and transportation needed to accomplish it. The agency also oversaw projects in state parks. The CCC enabled the park service to catch up on badly needed construction and rehabilitation work, focusing on three major goals: conservation of natural resources, preservation of historical and archaeological resources, and development of recreational resources within parks and monuments. Some conservationists accused the park service of embracing recreation too readily, arguing that the agency should restrict its efforts to preserving unspoiled wilderness. However, the accusation did little to deter recreational development through the 1930s.

CCCers built campgrounds, trails, and bridges; they installed utility systems, repaired roads, and built dams and water supply systems; and they restored historic buildings, constructed visitor facilities, and built employee housing. In the natural environment, the men fought fires, planted and transplanted trees, controlled erosion, combated porcupines, and battled insects. They also worked on archaeological projects, surveying, excavating, and stabilizing sites.

SOIL CONSERVATION AND BUREAU OF RECLAMATION CAMPS

As drought conditions worsened, the nation's food supply was at stake. It became critical to add public works programs that could slow or prevent loss of top soil and improve delivery of irrigation water to farmers. Against a backdrop of debate over using the CCC and other public works programs on private lands and infrastructure, the Bureau of Reclamation and Soil Conservation Service tapped into the CCC labor pool. In the early enrollment periods, the forest service administered the relatively small number of programs charged with erosion control work, sometimes using project staff from state agencies and land grant colleges. Responsibility shifted to the newly created Soil Conservation Service in 1935, and the number of SCS and Bureau of Reclamation camps grew. Next to the forest service, the SCS had the most CCC camps in Arizona, but most were in the southern part of the state, in ranch country. Many CCCers assigned to SCS camps worked on those projects in the winter, then moved to forest service camps along the Mogollon Rim in the summer.

Both agencies focused on helping beleaguered farmers who lacked the resources to maintain irrigation ditches and dams, as they watched their precious soil disappear in ferocious windstorms. In order to calm the criticism of helping private irrigation districts and landowners, the Bureau of Reclamation also broadened its focus to include recreation development at its reservoirs. By 1937, local communities formed soil conservation districts in return for securing CCC camps to aid in carrying out their conservation programs.

Morris Grodsky worked on two Bureau of Reclamation projects in Colorado, the first near Grand Junction. "When the snows melted in late spring, our entire camp went by train to southwest Colorado," he recalled, adding that they stayed "in a camp in a remote backwoods area on the banks of the Los Pinos River, a wonderful rainbow trout stream." Their task was to clear trees from the valley, which soon would fill with water behind a new earthen dam. He noted that the resultant lake "would have a role in irrigation and recreation."

The two agencies had a limited number of camps on the plateau, but the majority of SCS work in particular was concentrated in the prairie states and farther east. In the West, SCS created several partnerships through the CCC-ID to improve land management practices. In times of disaster, including a flood in Colorado and heavy snows in Utah, Bureau of Reclamation CCCers helped restore damaged facilities and rescue stranded animals. By 1938, faced with continued criticism of using CCCers to benefit private irrigators, reclamation restricted further CCC work to those projects on federal lands that would directly benefit the government.

DIVISION OF GRAZING CAMPS

On June 28, 1934, Congress passed the Taylor Grazing Act, the first law regulating and controlling grazing on the nation's public domain. The law also created the Division of Grazing, within the Department of Interior, for the purpose of preventing overgrazing, rehabilitating overgrazed lands, working with livestock owners to stabilize the industry, and enforcing trespass regulations and range

DIXIE NATIONAL FOREST, UTAH

management practices. The CCC would play a key role in carrying out its program, through insect and rodent control, surveying and map-making, erosion and flood control, weed eradication, and construction of fencing, water developments, and stock driveways.

There were seven Division of Grazing camps by April 1935, and forty-five by the end of the 1936 fiscal year. In all, the ten western states had camps in fifty-eight grazing districts. In Arizona alone, grazing districts encompassed seven million acres.

Ed Braun was just shy of his eighteenth birthday when he boarded a train with 150 other CCC enrollees in Ohio, bound for a Division of Grazing camp in Utah's high desert. The prospect of seeing the region's herds of wild horses did little to offset the overwhelming isolation of the area. "We were met at the station by a barrack leader and his assistant leader," Braun recounted. "As our names were called, we formed a line and proceeded to follow him. After a half hour walk, we arrived at the camp. It was situated 500 miles from Nowhere surrounded by Nothing. There wasn't a tree as far as the eye could see."

DROUGHT RELIEF

By 1934 drought conditions had ravaged many areas of the western and central United States. The Colorado Plateau states qualified for much of the $50 million in drought relief funding earmarked for CCC work in the most devastated areas. As one of four federal agencies assigned to work on drought relief programs, the CCC was ordered to increase its enrollment so that it could carry out measures to conserve moisture, prevent wind erosion, and minimize effects of any future droughts.

A PROLONGED DROUGHT TURNED FERTILE SOIL TO DUST. —COURTESY FRANKLIN D. ROOSEVELT PRESIDENTIAL LIBRARY AND MUSEUM

Roy Lemons, who grew up in rural Texas, vividly recalled the drought conditions of the 1930s. "I would look to the north on a sunny morning which started off as one of the most cheerful good-looking days that you could imagine," he recalled. "By ten o'clock in the morning you could look to the north and you would see a dark cloud approaching and it looked like a very disastrous thunderstorm, but in an hour or two you were breathing dust as you had never seen before." Stuffing rags around windows and doors did little good as "the fine dust that was in the air entered the houses, your bedding, your clothes, and your food."

Early in July 1935, President Roosevelt authorized the immediate selection of 50,000 additional CCCers as an emergency measure due to drought conditions in the West. Quotas were based on the severity of the drought as well as the resultant unemployment. The men were to be selected from cities within the drought areas that had a population of 2,500 or more. Of the 50,000 men, 45,000 were to be standard enrollees between eighteen and twenty-five years old and LEMs, all selected in the usual manner. The other 5,000 slots were reserved for veterans selected by the Veterans Administration. Each camp was authorized to employ sixteen LEMs. In the twenty-two states that qualified for special funding, 174 new camps were set up and 308 existing camps each received fifty additional enrollees.

Utah's enrollment quota was increased from 1,000 men to more than 1,700 in order to deal with damaged land and provide employment in the hard-hit areas. Six camps were to be located in Utah to handle the nearly 75 percent increase in enrollment—three USDA Forest Service, one National Park Service (at Bryce in the summer and Zion in the winter), and two Bureau of Reclamation camps. One special company of World War I veterans was established at Veyo, and five additional companies were formed to handle most of these special enrollees.

The drought relief camps were authorized to continue through June 30, 1935, with the period of enrollment the same as existing camps. Corps area commanders would handle distribution of enrollees. The success of the work depended on the superintendents, many of whom were appointed because of skills and ability. These were considered good jobs since they paid $1,680 a year or up to $1,860 if the foreman had such technical skills as the ability to supervise engineering work. The technical service agency was authorized to retain key men such as leaders, assistant leaders, and machine operators to aid in the formation of new work companies.

Some got their jobs because of political influence, with each project superintendent and foreman expected to present written endorsement from the chairman of the county Democratic committee or from a Democratic member of Congress. No state was totally immune to political considerations in the choice of supervisors and foremen. Perhaps the regional forester in Region 2 of the USDA Forest Service, which included Colorado, was referring to such political appointments—and overstating his case—when he charged that political appointees had "left a wake of waste, drunkenness, and even crime," throughout the state's forested areas.

Chapter Three

CCC Camps on the Colorado Plateau

The first Civilian Conservation Corps legislation set a goal of enrolling 250,000 young, single men by mid-May 1933. They exceeded it, signing up 275,000 men and boys to work on the nation's public lands. Now the army had to prepare to transport, shelter, clothe, feed, and otherwise care for every one of them. Where possible, they hastily built simple wood barracks, furnished them with cots and footlockers, and erected whatever other structures were necessary for a functioning camp. There were kitchens and dining halls to be built, as well as latrines and recreation halls. Housing for the camp and technical service staff also would be needed. However, facing a July 1 deadline to have more than 1,000 camps operational, the army often had to settle for housing men in tents until more permanent structures could be built for them.

Meanwhile, the technical service agencies had to gather the machinery and tools necessary for the multitude of projects they envisioned CCCers undertaking. They had to determine how they would teach CCCers the tasks needed to carry out those projects, as well as identify the men who would supervise them and the vehicles that would transport them between camp and worksite.

It was a monumental undertaking, nowhere more so than on the Colorado Plateau, where remote locations and rugged terrain added to the challenge.

Colorado had some of the earliest camps in operation, while Utah's first camps were not fully occupied until mid-June 1933.

Throughout the country, enrollees had to be gathered together, given physicals, and put through conditioning to prepare them for heavy labor. For many, new experiences started in the course of the journey. Bill Waddell, who was among those first enrollees, rode a bus with other CCCers to Paris, Texas, where they were sent to a hotel and given rooms on the sixth floor. It was the tallest building Waddell had ever been in, and he'd never seen an elevator. "I watched those boys going in and pushing the button. I watched two or three of them, but I didn't want to ask. I didn't want to show my ignorance." Once he figured out how to operate it, Waddell "rode the elevator up and down awhile just to get accustomed to it."

R. L. Welch wasn't quite as lucky. He had to get from Abilene to Big Spring, Texas, on his own, for his CCC physical. Their examinations were finished twelve hours before the train's scheduled early morning departure. "None of us have any money to go to a hotel or anything, so we slept around the depots, in some boxcars—165 guys down there scattered sleeping everywhere."

One of the less pleasant aspects of preparations for the CCC was the need for immunization against diseases that might afflict the boys. Ed Braun remembered the Rocky Mountain Spotted Fever shots he and others received at the London, Ohio, processing camp. "Two medics were positioned about five feet from the door and as each man was given the shot, they walked to the two medics as their knees buckled and the medics caught them as they fell and helped them to a chair nearby." Others, like Lynn Atwood, were immunized when they arrived at their camps. He and his fellow enrollees had to stay in camp "for about a week . . . to make sure that everything went all right and that you weren't coming down with anything."

CAMP SET-UP

Throughout the Colorado Plateau, the army faced the daunting task of setting up what amounted to self-contained villages, often in remote locations. Getting the enrollees to the camps proved no less challenging, as Lyall Wilson recalled. It was late fall in 1934 when he and thirty-four others rode in the back of an open truck from Provo to Duchesne, Utah. The driver got lost, extending the trip by hours. When they finally arrived at their camp, there was snow in the air and the hot meal that awaited them had already been reheated a few times.

The next morning, they were lined up and told that anyone who wanted to back out of the CCC could return home the way they had come. A man standing next to

43

Wilson summed up the sentiments of the boys, "Hell, I'd work here for the next six months free before I'd make that trip again."

Yet no one could have had a more dramatic trip to camp than Louis Purvis and his companions as they descended the 7.2-mile South Kaibab Trail, a drop of 5,240 vertical feet, to the bottom of the Grand Canyon. They had gone about three-quarters of a mile when "the trail slid out between those two pack trains to a distance of about forty feet," isolating one pack train above and one below the break in the trail. Using rope strung between the two, the men had to climb over the ridge, then dangle over a 2,000-foot drop-off until they reached solid ground. "That caused me to take a rather firm hold on the rope as I ascended and descended over that ridge," Purvis recalled. The remainder of the trip was mild in comparison, and Purvis insisted, "I wasn't scared because all the other boys were going down there too, and we all laughed and had a good time going down, just like a picnic."

Bo Moorhead wasn't so sure about it being a picnic when he reached the bottom of the canyon in 1935. They were loaded, ten at a time, into a tram to cross the river. On the far side, the tram stopped seventy-five feet above the ground, and from there they had to climb down a rope ladder. The tram became their daily conveyance across the river, between camp and their work site. "It was real slow. It probably took it fifteen [or] twenty minutes to get us across and then let us down," he recalled.

At Washington, Utah, temporary living quarters were set up in an old cotton mill. To prepare for the company, twenty-seven men arrived in September. They removed machinery, leaving gaping holes in the floor and roof. They hooked into the city water system and built an outside shower east of the mill. A great deal of clean-up was necessary to rid the site of trash. While cleaning up the trash, the boys encountered numerous snakes, including sidewinders, but no one was injured. While at the mill, the men slept in army jungle hammocks with netting to protect them from flies so thick that folded newspapers were set afire and run up and down the walls to drive them out at night. The one comfort for the boys was a swimming pool across the street. The owners, Id and Caddie Neilson, made an agreement for the CCC boys to use it. In exchange, the army paid $25 per month and the boys cleaned the pool once a week.

The Dalton Wells Camp near Moab, Utah, was barely inhabitable when the first enrollees arrived in October 1935. Water had to be hauled from Moab to the Division of Grazing camp until a well was drilled. Trucks and cars became so mired in the unstable sand that they had to cover walks, roads, and parking areas with shale. Once completed, the wooden camp structures had tarpaper roofs, board sides, and windows spaced four feet apart. The barracks' wooden plank floors were not insulated until the summer of 1939. There were electric lights, when the generator worked.

Many of the first CCCers were disappointed with conditions at their new camps as well as the transportation used to get them there, especially when they had to live in tents instead of barracks. Others had no chairs to sit on while eating. Sanitation facilities were limited, as were supplies.

"They did the best they could with what they had. Our first beds were army cots with straw mattresses, wool army blankets and no sheets. It is not hard to picture the discomfort of some who were allergic to wool—especially in Colorado in June and July," recalled Thurlow R. Pitts, who was among the first enrollees in Colorado, assigned to work at Colorado National Monument west of Grand Junction. "We were issued Army clothing of 1918 vintage. Trousers and shirts were of wool, and the trouser legs were so pegged it was hard to get some of the boys' feet through the pant leg hem." The men had to sew gussets into the pants seams, or find someone else who would.

Two years later, when Ernest Lee Burns went to work at the same national monument, the six-foot-one, twenty-one-year-old was "disappointed" with his ill-fitting uniform. "I walked in the supply room, and he said, 'What size shoes do you wear?' I told him. He set them up there. He threw me a barracks bag and said, 'Your clothes are all in here.' . . . instead of a twenty-eight [inch] waist, I had a thirty-eight waist. . . . It struck me about here and instead of being 28/36, they was 38/29." The men did some "switching and trading," and still had to find someone to sew gussets into the narrow pants legs.

Typically, a camp included two hundred enrollees with twenty-five LEMs, usually four military officers, the necessary technical staff to supervise work projects, and, in later years, an educational advisor. In reality, though, jobs often required sending small groups of men to spike, or side, camps where they would live in tents, usually with a single supervisor. The trade-off for simpler accommodations was a less regimented lifestyle, and many men came to appreciate the assignment. Many CCCers also found themselves shifting locations with the seasons. At the Grand Canyon, some men spent winters working in the bottom of the canyon, and summers on the North Rim.

Pitts found that conditions improved in the course of the summer that first year, even though the men continued to live in tents on wood platforms. Food was both more varied and better prepared, and the work crews became better organized. The men also had more and better equipment to do their jobs. By November, like many CCCers who started out in such temporary camps, they were moved to more permanent quarters, with five forty-man barracks, a mess hall, and a bathhouse "with a concrete floor, so no more splinters in our big toes." The latrine was still "quite a trek," but Pitts considered the new camp a "Taj Majal" compared to their dusty tents. The men had steel army cots with "real cotton mattresses" instead of the covers they'd had to stuff with locally produced straw, which Pitts pointed out had "never won any prizes at the county fair."

The first permanent camp at Colorado National Monument typified the amenities of CCC camps, with its 100-by-20-foot barracks,

INTERIOR OF MESS HALL AT MESA VERDE NATIONAL PARK, COLORADO —COURTESY NATIONAL PARK SERVICE

INTERIOR OF BARRACKS AT CEDAR BREAKS NATIONAL MONUMENT, UTAH —COURTESY UTAH STATE HISTORICAL SOCIETY

47

mess hall, and bathhouse. Many also had a blacksmith shop, infirmary, and an administration building. Some camps had lawns, and most had stone walkways and a flag pole. Skilled laborers were paid to set up camps, although CCCers installed telephone lines and built restrooms. The roughly built wood buildings were usually unpainted. One building, or sometimes a series of small cabins, provided quarters for the officers, the project supervisors, and later the camp educational advisor—some with their families.

The kitchen and dining hall were in the largest building, which also often housed the recreation room. In more permanent camps the rough wood barracks had bathroom facilities attached. Some lucky camps had separate bathhouses. More permanent camps also had sheds for trucks, road machinery, and storage.

The buildings were heated with wood- and coal-burning stoves. The uninsulated barracks could be cold or warm, depending on where men had their bunks relative to the stove. "It was too warm in the wintertime, but you had to take the bad with the good," Hobart Feltner recalled. "And of course the feller down at the other end, he got cold."

Taj Mahal or not, the Colorado National Monument facilities paled in comparison to a Bureau of Reclamation camp near Grand Junction. The landscaped camp had trees, grass, flowers, and shrubs. Interiors of the buildings were painted in pale pastel shades—even the window sills—and pictures decorated the walls of the recreation and mess halls. Even the furnishings were new, rather than the more common military cast-offs. Another Reclamation camp near Montrose also enjoyed nicer than average amenities. Built in mid-1935, the forty-man barracks were lined with plasterboard. Large easy chairs, writing desks, a pool table, magazine racks, pictures on the walls, and even curtains at the windows gave it a homier touch than most camps had.

Few CCCers were that lucky. After living in an abandoned cotton mill for awhile, the boys in Washington, Utah, were moved to a regular camp, complete with four barracks, a mess hall, an administration building, and infirmary. The old cotton mill continued to house the clerk's office and living quarters. The mess hall consisted of thirty to forty tables with benches, a large kitchen, and a built-in storage area which included a large, insulated ice box. The four wooden barracks each had forty double bunk beds, one heating stove with a water tank, and two fresh water taps, one at each end of the building. There were two shower stalls in a separate building and one sixty-hole chemical latrine, also in a separate building.

The wood structures in CCC camps were susceptible to fire, as the men of Company 3843 near Montrose, Colorado, found out on April 7, 1936, when their recreation hall burned down. The CCCers formed a bucket brigade, but were unable to save the structure or its contents. Fire was a hazard at tent camps as well, with sparks from chimneys landing on tent roofs and igniting the fabric. Men stood watch at tent camps to make sure all embers were extinguished and no tents set afire. The men who periodically were assigned to sew patches over burned holes in tent roofs became quite proficient at the task, lending some tents the appearance of patchwork quilts.

Hobart Feltner appreciated the furnace that kept the supply of hot water flowing in the group shower room at his Henrieville, Utah, camp. "We had everything there at this camp," he recalled. "If a guy got to where he wouldn't bath or nothin' and got to stinkin' a little, some of these big boys would take him down there and strip him off and soap him up, and take one of these ol', we called them GI brushes, with them ol' bristles on them . . . they bathed after that."

Camps had to be located near ample water and wood supplies and in proximity to the work projects. By 1935, more care was taken to make sure that camps were built to withstand winter temperatures. Winter work projects often were limited and required some planning. In Division of Grazing camps it was a good time to work on erosion control and spring and water development. Some camps were closed down during months of extreme weather and the men were sent to other locations.

CAMP LIFE

Life in the camps was healthy, thanks to hard work in the outdoors, plenty of basic food, and the camaraderie of other young men. They learned to get up and go to bed at scheduled times, make their own beds, scrub the barracks,

HIGH-ELEVATION PONDEROSA FORESTS AT COCONINO NATIONAL FOREST, ARIZONA

clean latrines, and live in an all-male camp. Upon a new group's arrival, camp administrators told the boys the CCC was giving them an opportunity. They, in turn, were required to uphold the reputation of the company as a courteous, clean-cut, manly group of boys.

The Mount Elden Camp in northern Arizona offered "lots of fresh air," according to Pennsylvanian Albert Spudy, who spent five months there. The boys were encouraged to keep barracks windows open when weather permitted, and air out their bedding regularly. "You slept without any clothes on, in between two good, clean sheets. I never heard of anybody—*anybody*, the whole time I was in the 3Cs—that got sick over exposure to the cold air or colds or anything. The way of doing things was always clean."

The day started early in CCC camps, usually with a bugle sounding reveille at 6 a.m. Lacking a bugler, the camp at Green River, Utah, improvised with a record player attached to a public address system. "That could blow you out of the sack," Ed Braun recalled. In other camps, an officer walked through the barracks calling to the boys to get up, some brusquely and others with a bit of masculine humor. The day often started with an inspection of the barracks by one of the army officers.

Joseph Michalsky described a typical day at the Walnut Canyon National Monument camp. "Well, get up at six o'clock in the morning. Get over to the washrooms, bathrooms, come back and have breakfast. Eight o'clock would roll around and you would board the trucks and go to work on the road till four o'clock in the afternoon. Four o'clock the trucks would pick you back up and bring you back to camp."

Michalsky's routine was the norm at most camps. The men would make their cots and straighten their belongings, clean up and, for those who needed to, shave. They'd head to the mess hall for breakfast, then leave the world of the army-run camp to spend the day working under the watchful eyes of their technical service supervisors. Some stayed behind to work in camp while most rode back and forth between camp and work on open trucks. At the end of the day they returned to camp, cleaned up, ate dinner, then had the evening to themselves. Lights went out at 10:00 or 10:30 p.m., although some camp commanders allowed men to stay up past that time. The weekends were free time, with the exception of required Saturday morning chores in some camps. Toward the late 1930s, some camps also conducted routine "close order" drills, either after work or on Saturday mornings. At the Mount Elden Camp, the men substituted sticks for rifles in the drills.

In camp, the army staff not only had separate living quarters, but also enjoyed special privileges. Robert Ashe, educational advisor at Grand Canyon, had an orderly to make his bed and clean his quarters. The orderly also waited on the staff at meals in a small dining room that was separated from the main dining hall by a partition.

As the men at Colorado National Monument had found, clothing was basically army issue. Winter clothes included khaki wool pants and shirt, wool shorts, a heavy wool sweater, brogans, a wool coat, a melton jacket, a wool hat with earflaps, and snowpacs. The rubber shoes had leather tops coated with a greasy compound that was supposedly waterproof and warm, but when temperatures were low they provided little warmth. Summer work clothes included denims, pants, shirt, and gloves.

The men also received military shaving kits when they arrived. Lyall Wilson's was in a metal box that he thought "looked like it was left over from World War I with a round of shaving soap that was hard as flint and a piece of chrome coated metal that served as a mirror." After men used up such personal hygiene items, they had to purchase replacements at the camp canteen.

One enrollee noted that on his first day in camp the boys worked on cleaning up the yard. They were given information and introduced to the work they would be doing, but did not receive clothes until the second day. Since his own shoes were thin, he hoped new shoes would be issued soon. At the end of the second day, those whose last names began with letters A to H got their clothes. The third day, I to Z received clothing.

Many boys were discouraged and homesick upon arrival, enough so that some returned home before they even took the oath. Others complained of bunks being too hard, and of waiting in long lines for food or to wash their mess kits. They sometimes complained about rules that did not seem to make sense. For example, everyone but the leaders was required to serve KP duty, which involved getting up at 4:30 a.m. and working from 5:00 a.m. to 9:30 p.m. Many considered it "a long day in hell."

Some of the men missed such amenities of home as flush toilets, which were a rarity in the camps. The supply of straw to be stuffed into mattress ticking was inconsistent, and some men were so tired that they simply slept on the hard bunks. At least one National Park Service camp—and likely many others—had to do continuous battle with bedbugs, much to the discomfort and displeasure of the enrollees. Others complained about having to listen to lectures, participate in safety drills, and endure safety inspections.

For many of the men who had not known when they might eat again, three meals a day in the CCC was a relief. Ed Braun deemed the food "excellent," noting that it was "far better and more nourishing than most of the young men were used to at the home they left." Decades later, Braun still could conjure up vivid memories of his favorite pineapple fritters. At Bo Moorhead's camp in Grand Canyon National Park, the men went on strike to protest the inadequate amount of food they received. Within hours, two army officers arrived from another camp and took care of the situation. "I don't know what happened, but the food was great from then on," Moorhead recalled.

At night, Lyall Wilson assembled lunches for eighty men who would be working far from their Utah camp all day—160 sandwiches, plus fruit, cookies, and "other goodies." In the morning he put everything in large wooden boxes outside the mess hall, then went back inside to eat his breakfast. One enrollee reported a lunch menu in his camp included stew, baked pork with apple sauce, squash, sweet potatoes, cocoa, and Jell-O with plenty of everything. The same day's dinner consisted of corn bread, cheese, pickles, milk, potato salad, celery, and pie. His comment was "not bad, eh?"

At Mesa Verde National Park, the army insisted on serving hot lunches to crews working more than seven miles from headquarters. In response, the park service established a central lunch station with twelve campground tables and a protective canvas cover. In the summer the park service had to drive about half of the CCC workforce to and from their jobs and the central lunch station. Later a second lunch station was established about twenty miles from headquarters for a crew of fifty to sixty men working on the east side truck trail.

The park service considered the costly system both complicated and cumbersome, and asserted that in the summer the men would prefer cold meats, cheese, and peanut butter and jelly sandwiches along with thermos jugs of hot coffee. They wanted to shift the delivery cost to the army, which could take cold lunches to the men at their job sites, saving both time and money for the park service. The army resisted the suggestion and won, as it usually did in controversies among the agencies involved in the CCC program.

The logistics of supplying a camp with food or any other needed supplies were particularly challenging at the Grand Canyon, where Company 818 spent the winter at the bottom of a 7.2-mile trail, a location they called "the hole." The army's 7th Pack Train located at Yaki Point (with home station at Fort Huachuca, Arizona) carried all supplies except water by pack mule from the trailhead to the canyon floor. Regular army and civilian packers ran a string of ten saddle mules and fifty pack mules. When snow became too deep for safety, men had to clear the trail so the pack trains could get through. The camp always tried to keep fifteen days' supply on hand for emergency situations since the trail could be blocked by slides for days at a time. When that happened, supplies were brought down the Bright Angel Trail and across the Tonto Platform to the Kaibab Trail, then across the river and on to the camp. The mules made five trips a week, carrying loads of about 200 pounds each. The average train had two sections, each with ten mules and two packers. In severe weather three sections would make up a train, with one conveying 3,000 pounds of coal and the others carrying mail and food.

Despite the farming background of many enrollees, the fruit and vegetables that were an essential part of their diet were not grown at the camps, according to Robert Ashe, the educational advisor at Grand Canyon's South Rim Camp. Rather, produce was brought in by truck once or twice a week. The mess sergeant had a food allowance, which sometimes ran low before the end of the month. "Some of the meals near the end of the month were a little skimpy, but they weren't bad," Ashe recalled. "The average boy gained, I think, fifteen pounds in the first four months they were in camp."

BUREAU OF LAND MANAGEMENT

Mission

It is the mission of the Bureau of Land Management to sustain the health, diversity, and productivity of the public lands for the use and enjoyment of present and future generations.

In 1939 the Division of Grazing was renamed the U. S. Grazing Service and is now a program of the Bureau of Land Management.

HIGH-ELEVATION SUN
EXPOSURE BECAME A SAFETY
ISSUE FOR CCC WORKERS.
—COURTESY UTAH STATE
HISTORICAL SOCIETY

The CCC monitored enrollees' weight and general condition and kept detailed records, to track the effects of adequate nutrition and physical labor on their health. On average, the boys gained eleven and one-half pounds. It was, for at least some of the boys, a higher level of care than they had received in quite awhile, if ever. Many camps had small infirmaries, and if not their own doctor, then one who visited them regularly.

One health issue proved especially troublesome on the Colorado Plateau: sun damage. Enrollees shed their shirts when working in warm weather, unaware that sun exposure could be more damaging at high altitude. After one enrollee developed pneumonia and died as the result of a severe sunburn, sun tanning became a subject of weekly safety meetings. Enrollees were warned of the danger and of limited medical knowledge concerning the value of lotions, creams, and ointments. They were instructed to tan gradually—five minutes the first day, then ten the second, and so on. The boys were warned to cover up whenever their skin began to feel hot, and those with fair skin were advised against trying to tan at all.

Another health issue, venereal disease, affected some CCCers in the southern and eastern regions as well as the Eighth Corps area, which included Arizona, New Mexico, and Colorado. It was uncommon in Utah, though, and overall the rate of occurrence was only about one-third that of the army. When it occurred, the enrollee was treated and then discharged from the CCC. To help prevent venereal disease, lectures were given that some, tongue-in-cheek, termed "enlightening."

Caring for the men in the bottom of the Grand Canyon was a concern for camp officials and inspectors. It would take fifteen hours and twenty men to evacuate a man from the canyon to a hospital. Physicians were assigned to camp and there was both a camp infirmary and a camp hospital, set up in a leased room at the Phantom Ranch. Patients were treated in the hospital for pneumonia, scarlet fever, influenza, mumps, measles, minor accidents, and emergencies. If major surgery was needed, the man would have to be evacuated.

Marvin Gandy, a Texan who served in Company 818 from 1934 to 1937, was the first passenger on the "ambulance mule" used for evacuating someone from the camp. "We come up with the idea of a big pack mule and lash a stretcher on the pack mule's back," he recalled. "We put the sandbag on the stretcher and walked him up and down the trail. Then a few weeks later in November, I come down with an attack of appendicitis, and I was lashed on that mule's back and hauled out to the South Rim. . . . It was pretty rough. The old stretcher was giving it this [flapping hands up and down] and I don't remember how long it took us. It must have been a good three [or] four hours, I guess."

Canvas bands secured the 110-pound litter to the mule, with the patient's head placed above the mule's ears and his feet over the animal's tail. One man would lead while two others walked in front and two behind to steady the litter. Men like Gandy who had the displeasure

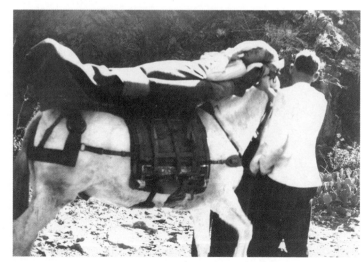

EVACUATION BY MULE FROM PHANTOM RANCH, GRAND CANYON NATIONAL PARK, ARIZONA —Courtesy National Park Service

of coming out on the litter equated it to being on a ship in a heavy storm or in an automobile traveling fast on flat tires. At intervals the party would rest and if necessary another mule would carry the load for a while. Thirty-four men were carried out on the mule litter over the years, taking an average of four hours from camp to rim. All thirty-four recovered and returned to their camp duties.

Despite great effort to protect the health and safety of CCCers, some inevitably died, either on the job or during their leisure time. Morris Grodsky's good friend, Vic Tenhoff, drowned in a lake, and Grodsky remained convinced it was the result of foul play though it was ruled an accident after an investigation. In 1939, Mesa Verde's Company 1843 suffered two deaths in a week. Assistant Leader James R. McRay was killed in an accident the first week of February 1939. Within a few days, Charles D. Skipworth, a facilitating pump operator died of natural causes during the night, at the bunkhouse. In northern Arizona, a truck carrying CCCers to a remote work site went out of control and overturned, killing one enrollee. Everett Minteer, one of the few who weren't injured in the accident, recalled it vividly. "Everywhere I looked, there was people laying on the ground, ain't moving. . . . I was scared to death."

Throughout the country, seventy-nine men died fighting fires, and in all, the fatality rate was 2.25 per 1,000 enrollees through the nine and one-half years the CCC operated. Safety training remained an important focus but could not prevent all deaths, accidental or otherwise.

Thoughts of death and injury were far from the minds of most CCCers, who particularly looked forward to their time away from work. Permanent camps had small canteens where the men could purchase candy, tobacco, and personal items with the $5 per month they received from the CCC. A recreation hall also provided furnishings and equipment for their leisure time. Ashe recalled buying used typewriters for the CCCers on his own, and charging the men 25¢ to use them or take lessons on them. "I never did get my money out of them. When I left, I left them there. But that was a way to get some equipment," he recalled.

The vast majority of CCCers relied on CCC vehicles or public transportation—either paid or unpaid—to get around. However, the first men at Colorado National Monument, who all were from the immediate area, were frustrated that they could not keep personal vehicles at the camp. Leroy Lewis recalled that vehicles were allowed until they moved to their winter camp in late 1933. Lewis was not surprised when "some enterprising civilian" offered private parking at the base of the cliff, and charged $3 per month to use it, "10 percent of total pay, and 60 percent of what was received at the pay table!" After a few times up and down the steep ladders from the parking area to the camp, the few who owned vehicles decided to carpool or "worked other schemes to keep our jalopies available."

SIDE CAMPS

Throughout the years the technical services often established spike camps (also known as fly, side, or spur camps) for conservation work. By eliminating long daily commutes to distant work sites, temporary camps made it possible to accomplish the greatest possible amount of conservation work with small, self-sustaining detachments. Technical service officials were in charge of the camps, which were located as much as sixty or more miles from the main camp, often over crude roads. In the beginning, only 10 percent of enrollees could be sent to a side camp, and for no more than five days. The restriction was lifted by mid-August 1933 when permanent side camps were authorized.

George Lockwood, a bulldozer "grease monkey," and two other enrollees who operated bulldozers worked by themselves at a Division of Grazing spike camp about two or three hours' drive from their main camp. A supervisor would come out twice a week to check on them, but they were otherwise on their own. "On Monday morning we loaded up supplies (groceries, fuel, oil etc.) for the coming week," he recalled. "We lived in a tent for five days a week then on Friday afternoon we returned to the main camp for the weekend."

Their dirt-floored tent was equipped with cots and footlockers for clothing and personal effects. Other than the supervisor's periodic visits, they "never saw any life while out on the job." Lockwood noted that other larger spike camps were more permanent, complete with temporary barracks and mess halls.

The number of side camps was limited by the capacity of the technical service agency to provide leadership, tents, transportation, and kitchen equipment. These camps also provided work for additional LEMs, and assignments were rotated to help keep morale high.

Enrollees generally reported enjoying side camps. Some suggested that camp commanders sent only their best enrollees to side camps and kept the unruly men in the main camp. An army officer accompanied groups of more than twenty-five men, and the military retained veto power over establishment of any individual side camp.

LEISURE TIME

Teaching young men new skills and sending money home to their families were the CCC's main objectives, but the program also sought to influence their physical, moral, and spiritual welfare. After 4:00 p.m., when the boys returned from work, they were on their own until the next morning. Leisure time activities were organized to keep them entertained, broaden their range of experience, and give them outlets for youthful exuberance.

Enrollees were allowed to have a radio, camera, musical instrument, and other items if they could afford them. Where possible, mail service was provided on a daily basis and was highly anticipated. Utahn Belden Lewis remarked, "No mail for me. It's sure discouraging to see others getting news from home when I don't get a word."

Recreation and traveling libraries were available from the beginning, and increased from one enrollment period to the next. Organized team sports gave the men an outlet for vigorous play, and sports competitions with other CCC companies were welcome diversions from day-to-day life in the camp. Some of those who had musical talents staged concerts. Even remote camps managed to stage periodic movie showings, projecting films onto bed sheets strung up for the occasion. More than one hundred enrollees in Company 818 watched the first movie ever shown in the bottom of the Grand Canyon—*Romance in Manhattan*—after a mule train hauled the film and equipment down to them.

Despite their isolation in winter months, the boys of Company 818 had a camp library where they could check out books and read. Some played volleyball and threw footballs around. Once they had a recreation hall completed, they had tables where they could play checkers, chess, and cards. The camp library had many hometown newspapers donated by enrollees who had received them by mail through the Kanab, Utah, post office. They enjoyed musical entertainment from the first, and when the swimming pool was completed in the fall of 1934, swimming became a popular recreational activity. In the fall of 1934 and spring of 1935 recreational facilities were enlarged and boxing and wrestling programs were introduced. A ping pong table was constructed inside the recreation hall and ping pong tournaments became popular.

For those camps that were close enough to a community, there were dances and church suppers. Some camps even staged their own parties, inviting girls from nearby towns. Rivalry over the affections of local girls sometimes

VOLLEYBALL AT MESA VERDE NATIONAL PARK, COLORADO
—Courtesy National Park Service

FIELD DAY AT PHANTOM RANCH, GRAND CANYON NATIONAL PARK
—Courtesy National Park Service

fostered conflicts between CCCers and local boys. Hostility and fighting were more common where ethnic differences entered the picture. In southern and eastern New Mexico, off the Colorado Plateau, businesses displayed signs barring "Mexicans," despite the state's large Hispanic population. On the whole, however, local communities and CCCers developed a rapport born of mutual benefit. The boys had a place to go away from camp, and the communities benefited from their spending.

Most permanent camps had athletic fields and some community and church leagues invited CCC teams to participate. Camps often had intramural competition among teams organized by barracks, home county, state, or even by work crew. Competition included baseball, basketball, races, boxing, wrestling, horseshoes, volleyball, and tugs-of-war. Camp regulations prohibited tackle football, but boys at the Washington, Utah, camp were playing using a canteen for a ball in a large barn loft when one of the boys was injured in a fall to some support beams below. Injuries to two boys playing football at Mesa Verde reinforced the need for the ban.

At Mesa Verde, with the exception of basketball, sports were curtailed during the winter because of potentially hazardous driving conditions. The nearest basketball facility that could be used was at Cortez, approximately thirty miles over a winding, cliff-hugging road from the two camps in the park. Even so, the Company 861 team went undefeated in the sub-district. Unfortunately, at the

CCC BAND AT GRAND CANYON NATIONAL PARK —Courtesy National Park Service

time of the district tournament at Grand Junction, the company was unable to participate because they were quarantined for scarlet fever. A work project the following spring added another recreational option for CCCers as well as park employees. When there was a lull in work while new arrivals went through conditioning, the boys of 861 were able to use a tennis court they had just refurbished.

With an excellent volleyball team, boxing, and "hard baseball," Louis Purvis said he and his campmates always "had plenty to do" when Company 818 moved to their summer camp on the North Rim of the Grand Canyon. Robert Ashe recalled having a pool table, which had been purchased with canteen proceeds, in the South Rim recreation hall. Athletic equipment also was purchased with profits from the sales of "candy and stuff."

63

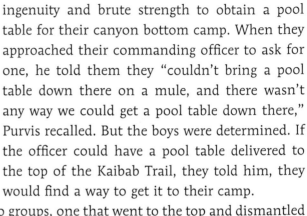

The boys of Company 818 applied legendary ingenuity and brute strength to obtain a pool table for their canyon bottom camp. When they approached their commanding officer to ask for one, he told them they "couldn't bring a pool table down there on a mule, and there wasn't any way we could get a pool table down there," Purvis recalled. But the boys were determined. If the officer could have a pool table delivered to the top of the Kaibab Trail, they told him, they would find a way to get it to their camp.

CACTUS IN BLOOM

Fifty boys divided into two groups, one that went to the top and dismantled the table—which included three 150-pound sections of slate—and the other which waited to take over at the halfway point. They carried it piece by piece to the bottom, with four of them needed to haul each piece of slate. "There's always somebody in line to see who was next" to play at the table, Purvis recalled with special pleasure. "So we played pool all winter."

Others enjoyed exploring the area around their camps. CCCers at Mesa Verde organized weekend trips to archaeological sites within the park, while Ed Braun recalled "roaming around the desert chasing little critters" in Utah. Jake Barranca liked to explore the Grand Canyon, looking at "rocks and all that, animals, see what I could see, flowers. Because I used to love cactus in bloom and all that." One of his fondest memories was of watching eagles, both in flight and at their nesting sites. Over the course of two weeks, he watched one eagle build a nest in the canyon's inner gorge. As he peeked into the nest one day and spied one chick and an egg, he noticed "the eagle start[ed] circling around and circling around making all kinds of noise. So I got out of there quick. Huge bird."

Men who had musical instruments would lead friends in songs from home, like the "good old hillbilly songs" George Lockwood and his fellow Kentuckians loved. An enterprising civilian in Arizona rented "regular movies" for a month at a time, then made the rounds of CCC camps, charging the boys 10¢ for the picture show.

Monumental News, published by Camp NM-1-C at Colorado National Monument, included a recurring feature that encouraged boys to better themselves by reading. The March 1939 issue included a description of the camp's new library, which included shelves of books, racks of magazines and newspapers and new tables. "Look neat when you come to read," the newspaper advised, adding "maybe the fellow next to you will enjoy it more if you act like a gentleman."

BALD EAGLES IN
PONDEROSA PINE

In addition to the books, reference material, magazines, and newspapers available in the camp library, enrollees could request books through a circulating library. On the twenty-fifth of each month camps would receive new books of fiction as well as a supply of textbooks and reference material. One enrollee commented, "I hope I finish that book within the allotted time. It sure is a neat one. The whole library is made up of new books of the best description."

Many camps published newspapers like *Monumental News*, which tell much about life in the CCC. They were published weekly, semi-monthly, or monthly by enrollees with assistance from educational advisors. Articles generally dealt

DEDICATION OF MIDVIEW DAM

SEPT. 10, 1937

CCC Reflections
NEWSLETTER, ZION
NATIONAL PARK
COLLECTION
—MICHAEL PLYLER PHOTO

with camp projects and educational opportunities. Jokes, poetry, stories, cartoons, project updates, and camp news also were included. Most were mimeographed and they often changed names and format with changes in the companies or camps. Companies with a large number of Hispanics sometimes printed their newspapers in both English and Spanish.

At Zion National Park, in addition to the *Zion Zephyr*, Company 3238 from New York published *The Carry On* monthly. The side camp at Cedar Breaks published *See Der Breaks News*, while Zion's Bridge Mountain Camp published *Park Post*. Encouraged by their educational advisor, the boys of Company 861 at Mesa Verde purchased a handset printing press and began publishing the only handset-printed newspaper in the entire Eighth Corps area.

Enrollees received enough stationery to write two letters per week. Those who wrote more had to purchase the additional paper. The pursuit of hobbies, letter-writing, educational classes, and organized trips filled many leisure hours. Arranged field trips were usually taken on Saturdays or holidays. From Zion National Park in 1934, Company 962 was taken to Las Vegas and Boulder Dam (renamed Hoover Dam in 1947) for a weekend field trip. Some boys complained that they nearly froze to death in the back of the trucks. Division of Grazing boys near Vernal had ready access to Dinosaur National Monument for their outings. Boys from the Orderville Camp frequently made trips to Zion and Bryce Canyon National Parks.

Dances, either in nearby communities or at the camp, proved to be one of the most popular leisure time activities among the CCCers. To be sure, there were community members who worried about the behavior of boys from far-off places, as well as adverse effects on local employment. Out of concern for possible negative influences, the Blanding, Utah, Commercial Club arranged a meeting between CCC officials and a local Mormon leader. Cigarettes, liquor, and questionable behavior would not be welcome in town, especially at dances, the church leader warned, adding that anyone with dishonorable motives had better stay away from the local girls.

Camp officers frequently offered equally stern warnings to their young charges before sending them off to town. During their summers on the Grand Canyon's North Rim, when they made trips to Kanab, Utah, officers from Company 818 put troublemakers in the truck, where they had to wait until everyone was ready to return to camp. The boys at Mount Elden Camp in northern Arizona were grounded for months if they drank too much. As further punishment, some even had to dig holes in camp after working all day. Louis Purvis attended dances in Kanab, Utah, in the pavilion if weather was good, and the church if it wasn't. Parents accompanied their sons and daughters to the gatherings. "They set there on those benches and watched the kids have a big time," he recalled. "I think that was good."

Lyall Wilson recalled his experience at the Moon Lake Camp on the Ashley National Forest. Officers let the enrollees use army trucks once or twice a month to attend dances in nearby towns. On one occasion, the men spruced up their mess hall and staged a dance for people from the surrounding area. "We decorated the hall and hired an orchestra," Wilson recalled, adding camp trucks were dispatched to pick up people who didn't have transportation. "For

PATCH, ZION NATIONAL PARK COLLECTION —MICHAEL PLYLER PHOTO

67

the people who had their own cars we had a parking lot all cleaned and lighted for them. It was a huge success and we talked about this dance and the girls we had met for days after."

After his transfer, the people of St. George, Utah, offered Wilson and his fellow Utahns a warm welcome, inviting them to the church soon after their arrival. "We all shaved, bathed in a small stream of water that ran just below the camp, put on our best clothes and were sitting on the church steps at least a half hour early," Wilson recalled. "The townspeople started coming with home-made cakes, fresh green salads, and big pots of Boston baked beans, along with homemade bread and butter. They all smiled and greeted us like old friends."

The locals learned that most CCC boys did nothing worse than local boys did, and stopped discouraging their visits to town. Some attitudes also changed in response to the economic benefits that accrued to towns located near CCC camps. In some small towns the coming of the CCC also meant that previously nonexistent medical services became available.

At Washington, Utah, many fears were allayed when, on the first Sunday, a good many of the camp boys showed up at church in the local Church of Jesus Christ of Latter-day Saints (LDS) Ward. The townspeople then welcomed them at public affairs, church dances, and other activities. After dances many of the boys were invited into homes for dinner. The local people continued to be very hospitable and many of the boys who attended church and town dances ended up marrying local girls. A number of Arizona CCCers reported similarly warm treatment in neighboring communities.

Civic organizations in Montrose, Colorado, developed close ties with the boys from Camp 3841, a Bureau of Reclamation camp. Local clubs provided entertainment for the boys and the Colorado National Guard Armory was used for dances, boxing, basketball, and such. Many of the boys attended services at local churches and always felt welcome. Several of the CCC boys even volunteered to help build the Montrose community swimming pool.

Good relations with the community were conspicuously advanced by two other events. First, two truckloads with twenty-five CCC boys each were traveling in town when they met a funeral cortege. The drivers pulled the trucks to the curb and the boys unloaded and stood at attention with bare heads as the procession passed. Second, on a Saturday night in June 1936 several CCCers were attending a dance when a car crash occurred nearby, killing one occupant, a young woman. James Benham, of Company 3841, quickly administered first aid to the critically injured driver, saving his life.

Trips to other CCC camps for boxing matches and basketball, softball, baseball, and volleyball games, even horseshoe tossing, also provided a welcome change of scenery. Robert Ashe recalled driving his baseball team to the North Rim camp one day, playing the next morning, staying another night and then returning to their own camp. "It had to be on the boys' time. Once in awhile, we would get some of them excused from work so we could take them somewhere, but most of the time we didn't." The long trips to Flagstaff or the North Rim were especially tough on the boys in the winter, when they would sometimes lie down on the floor of the open truck in an effort to stay warm.

Wayne Blackburn, an LEM at Capitol Reef who was married and shared a small home in Richfield, Utah, with another CCC couple, was called out of the audience at a boxing match with his buddy. What ensued reads more like a free-for-all than a boxing match: "Keith was a fightin' and I looked around to see him and he had his hands full, too. Finally he got away from his [opponent] and come over and hit one of mine right in the ear and he fell over. So I done

the same thing to his man and they throwed the towel in. Ha! Ha! Ha! So we won that match. They give us five dollars for that fight."

Even for an LEM, an extra $5 was a welcome sum. For the junior enrollees, it was all they received from their monthly earnings. The balance of their $30 per month—raised to $50 in later years—was sent home to their families. With their shelter, food, and clothing provided for them, $5 was generally enough to get by. Some enrollees recalled a savings plan in the later years of the CCC, with as much as $8 per month set aside for them and paid out when they left the program. Others recalled that they were allowed to keep $7 or $8 of their pay in later years.

On payday, the men received a coupon book with 5¢ tickets that could be used for purchases in the canteen. In numerous camps, one or more enterprising enrollees applied their skills to earn additional pay. Morris Grodsky became the camp barber in his spare time, taking over from "some guy who was a real hair butcher." He charged 25¢ a haircut, and soon became "a wealthy man in our rock bottom economy." Others would iron fellow enrollees' shirts for a nickel each, or wash their clothes for anywhere from a dime to a quarter per item. Those who had cameras took advantage of the darkroom facilities at their Grand Canyon Camp, developing and printing photos for fellow CCCers. At the Mount Elden Camp, enrollees could pay 25¢ a month for someone else to take their turn at KP duty. Others received money from their families, at least once in awhile. Poker games, which often went on past lights out, filled some men's pockets and emptied others' despite a prohibition against gambling. Between paydays the poker players often wagered with canteen tickets.

Depending on how close their camp was to a town, some men could go to movies or do their weekend shopping outside of the camp, including buying liquor, whether from bootleggers or stores. One enrollee recalled being warned that anyone found with liquor would be sent home, but when he and the entire kitchen crew were found with a jug of wine, they laughed off the threat, knowing the camp could not get along without them. Marvin Gandy was given the task of buying liquor for the officers of his camp. "On payday morning, it's eight o'clock, my day's work was to hike out of the canyon out the South Kaibab Trail and hitchhike down the village and get twelve pints of Old Corky, 50¢ a pint, about the rottenest whiskey, and be back down at four o'clock."

Special occasions such as Labor Day, Halloween, Thanksgiving, Christmas, and New Years provided opportunities for celebrations and sometimes leave to visit home. Enrollees were entitled to one day leave for each month of service. In a six-month enrollment period an enrollee could therefore accumulate one six-day leave. At first, some enrollees hitchhiked home, and one recalled using his leave to take long trips on freight trains, even though CCC district regulations and state law prohibited the practice. Emergency leaves were granted in case of family sickness or deaths. Those who stayed in camp for holidays liked it because there usually were only about fifty men left. They got better food, hot showers, no lines to wait in, and less noise in the evenings. They also could spend time outdoors hiking, swimming, or doing whatever they liked.

In October 1934 the Zion Camp gave the discharged boys a big send-off. They had an extra special supper with chicken and pie. Afterward they put on an impromptu show with music and song. "The whole thing went over fine. A real heartfelt spirit pervaded," Belden Lewis recalled.

EDUCATIONAL PROGRAMS

Some enrollees finished high school before joining the CCC, but the majority had quit school, often to find work so they could help support their families. The average CCCer Robert Ashe worked with at the Grand Canyon had completed fifth or sixth grade. "If we got a high school graduate, that was

CIVILIAN CONSERVATION CORPS

U.C. 584461

Unit Certificate

THIS CERTIFIES THAT *Dwight Paul Barnard* of Company *962* has satisfactorily completed *14* hours of instruction in *Cooking* and is therefore granted this Certificate.

F.X. Legree
Project Superintendent.

Edward Kwahe
Company Commander.

Von H. Robertson
Camp Educational Adviser.

Date *March 30, 1940* Place *Springdale, Utah*

GPO 6—9671

UNIT CERTIFICATE ISSUED AT ZION NATIONAL PARK
—MICHAEL PLYLER PHOTO

unusual. And I don't think we ever had more than two or three high school graduates out of 150 boys," Ashe recalled. Although he seldom had more than a few illiterate enrollees in his camp, Ashe was aware of one camp in southern Arizona that had few boys who could write their names, let alone read. "At that time we didn't have any kind of literature to teach adults reading . . . so we had to improvise. We used some early elementary, first grade reading material, you might say. Well, Dick and Jane, who wants to hear Dick and Jane?"

Morris Grodsky was the solitary high school graduate among the CCCers at his camp near Grand Junction. By then the education program was in full swing and Grodsky was made an assistant, teaching the three Rs to "a number of truly illiterate guys from Oklahoma. . . . I must admit that it gave me real pleasure to see these guys begin to spell out their names and simple sentences."

In its nine and a half years, the CCC taught more than 40,000 young men to read and write. Beyond enhancing literacy, the CCC also taught a broad range of academic and vocational subjects to eager students.

Early on, President Roosevelt decided to increase education to a systematic level by adding a civilian educational adviser to the staff of every camp, but with education under the control of the army. The arrangement left education to company commanders, with generally negative results. A revised plan called for the Office of Education to select and appoint the educational personnel, although the educational advisors remained responsible to the company commander, and could be removed by the corps area commander.

Educational advisers were assigned starting in February 1934, with most of the staffing completed by mid-summer. John B. Griffin, president of San Bernardino Junior College, was appointed the first educational advisor for the Ninth Corps area and directed selection of camp educational advisors. At first many were assigned to serve two or sometimes even three camps. Thereafter, with each annual appropriation, the number of educational advisers increased and eventually equaled one per camp.

The educational adviser was in charge of all camp educational activities, aided by two enrollee leaders who were appointed on his recommendation. The designated leaders were paid $45 per month to assist the camp commander and educational adviser. Enrollees were encouraged to take classes, but could not be required to do so. In addition, the advisers also were expected to assist in establishing a viable recreation program featuring athletics.

Ashe said few camps had basketball courts or football fields. While he was helping out at a forest service camp in Globe, Arizona, he tried to arrange evening activities for the boys. "They didn't have any night classes and [the superintendent] wasn't interested in cooperating in any way. And I thought, 'well, maybe we could get them in a basketball league or something,' but they weren't interested in accommodating the boys."

In 1935 camps received only $100 per year, beyond salaries, for the educational program. It was raised to $240 for educational supplies the next year, slightly more than one dollar per man per year. Money for the program was allotted to the War Department in a lump sum, with the annual budget at first limited to $2.5 million. Education eventually had an annual budget of about $5 million. Ashe had to find creative ways to make up for budget shortfalls, including the purchase of those used typewriters so his boys could learn to type. Canteen profits were used to purchase a sixteen-millimeter projector so they could show educational films.

Whenever the camp was short-staffed, Ashe also had to run the canteen. He would order candy, cigarettes, shaving supplies, razor blades, and such from a

Flagstaff business, which delivered them to the camp every other week. The financial records of the canteen were audited twice a year, which proved frustrating to Ashe, who recalled how auditors would scrutinize the records "nine different ways."

A good educational advisor had to be a superman. He was expected to help every enrollee make the most of his capabilities. It was his responsibility to set up sixteen to twenty classes that would appeal to young men sitting in a classroom after a hard day's work. He had to find camp personnel or local school teachers to staff the classes and file frequent reports for the camp commander and district educational officers. He also served as a counselor, coordinator, and liaison between the army, the technical services, and the boys. He acted as the camp public relations spokesman, keeping the local newspapers supplied with articles. He had to do all of this with very little power, inadequate supplies and facilities, and often in the face of an unsympathetic camp leader.

Although he was a civilian, the educational advisor wore a military-style uniform. He was paid $1,980 per year and had the use of a camp car and driver, free lodging, and meals at cost. Most were employed through educational institutions or from the ranks of the CCC. Rules held that he was to be endorsed by the state superintendent of public instruction and be unemployed. However, the unemployment requirement was not strictly observed, as some educators resigned teaching positions to work in the CCC. By 1938 all educational

BELDEN LEWIS DIARY, ZION NATIONAL PARK COLLECTION
—Michael Plyler photo

advisors were expected to have at least a bachelor's degree and some high school teaching experience.

Robert Ashe was interviewed by a CCC official who complimented him on his qualifications, grades, credentials, and his background in sports, which was considered essential. But those factors alone weren't enough to secure the admittedly "political" job, he learned. Ashe fortunately had studied under the state's only U.S. representative, at Arizona State University. "How about your senator?" the interviewer asked. Although Ashe didn't know either senator, he was able to secure reference letters from both along with the congressman, and landed the job, starting in January 1936. He taught photography, reading, and government, and had twenty-one unpaid teachers on his staff.

Each month, the educational advisor had to file a report listing the courses, with the grade level, the name of the instructor, the number of class meetings, and the average attendance for each. Academic courses generally included English, mathematics, government, journalism, psychology, and nature study. Vocational courses included auto mechanics, radio, baking, cooking, landscape gardening, and photography. The business program included bookkeeping and salesmanship. General courses included first aid, singing, safety, personal hygiene, and leadership.

Most classes were offered in the evening. First aid was very popular because boys had to have a first aid certificate to become an assistant leader. Leadership was another popular course. In the Ninth Corps area, correspondence courses were available, administered by the Bureau of Vocational Rehabilitation under the California Department of Education. Forty institutions across the country offered extension work to CCC enrollees, but the Ninth Corps area had more correspondence courses than all other corps areas combined.

PATCH, ZION NATIONAL
PARK COLLECTION
—MICHAEL PLYLER photo

Like Ashe, the educational advisor generally taught classes himself and also recruited local elementary teachers to help out, some on a voluntary basis and others for meager pay. Sadie Avery, of Moab, taught history, reading, writing, and arithmetic to seventy-two southern boys, several of whom were illiterate and few of whom had gone beyond the fourth grade. She described them as "real sweet boys." They all smoked until she asked them to quit for her sake. In response, they all went to the door, threw out their cigarettes, and never smoked in class again. Other teachers related poignant stories of teaching homesick southern boys to write their names and tell time. It was the goal to teach each illiterate enrollee to read a newspaper and write a letter within three months of beginning literacy training.

The camps never equaled the public school system in academic instruction, although about 30,000 instructors were teaching about 50,000 courses nation-wide by 1937. The legislation that year also provided that an enrollee could be given a leave of absence from the CCC for as much as a year in order to attend regular school. Many left the CCC to return to school. Annually, there would be a slow but steady drop in enrollees each fall as a new school year resumed.

Ultimately, it was up to the enrollees to take advantage of the educational offerings. Everett Minteer was one of many who later regretted not doing so. "Very few" took classes at the Mount Elden Camp in northern Arizona, where he served in 1939–40. He personally considered himself a "dummy" for passing up the opportunity.

The Ninth Corps area had the highest average grade completion of all corps areas, perhaps because of the high educational attainment of the Utah enrollees. The average Utah CCC boy had completed 11.2 years of school. Those boys in the Ninth Corps area who came from the Second Corps area had an average of 10.0 years of school, the Seventh Corps boys 9.2 and those from the Fifth Corps 9.0. Company 962, the all-Utah Camp NP-3 at Zion and Bryce, reported in 1936 that all but two of its members had received some high school education.

The director of CCC education selected advisors and prepared texts and teaching materials under guidance of the Office of Education. The War Department was responsible for purchasing, allotting funds, and the overall success of the program. The director's office coordinated the program and held final authority over the content of materials. Rather than have a detailed program imposed on the camps, the needs and desires of the enrollees became central to the educational program. A broad-based program of literacy

training, academic, vocational, and on-the-job education generally prevailed.

Education became strongly integrated into enrollees' leisure time activities, at least in part because the educational advisors also were responsible for recreation programs. Nationwide about 85 percent of enrollees participated in some kind of educational activity taught by 3,500 teachers, 10,000 technical service personnel, 6,500 enrollees, and 4,500 army officers.

When replacements joined a camp, the educational advisor would interview them to determine what previous training and education they had through the

CCC up to that point. He also would identify their vocational goals, advise them to take classes to support their goals, and structure classes toward those goals. Each enrollee was encouraged to take twelve hours of instruction weekly, so convenient scheduling became quite important. On-the-job training and vocational training were particularly emphasized, since they had the greatest potential for equipping CCCers with the skills they would need when they returned to civilian life.

Albert Spudy, who was assigned to Walnut Canyon National Monument, recalled an array of building trades options at his camp. "You had a chance of taking carpentry, bricklaying. There wasn't a whole lot electrical going on, but we did make a big model home, like . . . an oversized bird house which I thought after we got done that it could make a big martin house," he said. "I was involved in the carpentry because . . . my time wasn't long enough to take in the stone mason or bricklaying."

Boys at the Division of Grazing camp at Pipe Spring National Monument had a wide selection of classes. Those taking journalism published a twice-monthly camp newspaper, *The Pipe Post*. Three classes were offered each day, Monday through Friday, at elementary (reading and writing), high school (journalism, vocal music, history, shorthand), and college (physiology and psychology). The boys also could study baking, cooking, construction, photography, use of explosive powder, typewriting, and how to care for and use tools and trucks. The vocational courses were especially popular, while informal sessions in woodworking, drama, nature study, discussion groups, and safety meetings also attracted participants.

Hundreds of men completed high school and some took college courses through the CCC education program. Morale stayed higher and desertions lower in camps with well-organized programs. Some camps reported that 100 percent of the men were enrolled in at least one course. In New Mexico, more than one-third of teachers were enrollees themselves—a model that proved particularly necessary in more remote camps where it was difficult to attract teachers. The CCC's own *Manual for Instructors in Civilian Conservation Corps Camps*, which was distributed in 1935, encouraged teachers to foster critical thinking and share experiences with one another.

Camps like those at Grand Canyon also focused on courses related to their immediate environment. Lynn Atwood recalled studying the geology, biology, and geography of the canyon for about a month when he first arrived. For four hours a day, they learned "all the plants, animals, any of the Indian ruins, anything like that that we may be asked about later on."

In later years, CCC enrollee and LEM turnover reflected improving employment conditions. By 1936 many camps were experiencing a shortage of men and large turnover at the end of each enrollment period. In 1936, Division of Grazing Camp 10-C out of Montrose, Colorado, saw sixteen LEMs resign over a three-month period to accept other employment. The history of camps throughout the country was similar, with many boys coming and going all of the time.

BLACKSMITH SHOP, GRAND CANYON NATIONAL PARK
—Courtesy National Park Service

80

Rapid turnover necessitated almost constant attention to first aid training. All leaders, assistant leaders, many foremen, and all truck drivers were to be trained and given Red Cross cards authorizing them to handle first aid cases. On more than one occasion first aid training paid dividends in lives saved. Thomas "Shorty" Howell, from Company 3843 in Colorado, decided to take a swim in the fast-moving waters of the South Canal and was swept downstream. As he passed through two tunnels and over a drop, another enrollee, George Curds, ran about a mile along the bank until he found a point where he could reach Howell. Thanks to his first aid training, Curds was able to pull Howell from the water and revive him.

CCC CARPENTERS, GRAND CANYON NATIONAL PARK
—COURTESY NATIONAL PARK SERVICE

With limited supplies and thus a constraint on the number of formal classes they could offer, the Grand Canyon camps concentrated on those that were most vital to national defense and morale-building. The goal was better attendance, better classes, and better teaching, with an emphasis on instruction in citizenship. Nonetheless, administrators took great pride in vocational offerings, urging enrollees to make career decisions and learn the associated skills. Training was available in car, truck, caterpillar, and grader maintenance and overhaul. Carpentry and woodworking classes were taught with emphasis on construction work: house building, cabinet work, upholstery, and sign making. On-the-job instruction was available in electricity, painting, plumbing, truck driving, and janitorial, clerical, trail building, and reconnaissance-archaeology work.

By 1940, more than 90 percent of enrollees in most camps were taking courses. The worsening world situation with war in Europe in late 1939–41 led to an increased emphasis on vocational training. The CCC educational program now placed even greater emphasis on curbing illiteracy, improving on-the-job training, and preparing the enrollees to work with their hands at skilled occupations. Commanders and educational advisors organized more vocational classes and established special schools to train enrollees in needed skills. By the middle of 1941, CCC education mainly focused on the needs of national defense.

RELIGIOUS LIFE IN THE CCC

As was traditional in the military, the opportunity to participate in religious services was considered an essential element of life in CCC camps. Services were infrequent since the Army reserve officers or contract ministers responsible for them often served seven or eight camps. In some instances, local volunteer clergy helped out.

Most seemed to have the respect of the men. For example, Chaplain Curtis, who was assigned to the Zion camps, was described as, "a really fine man with a good personality." He would typically start with community singing, speak briefly, then close with a "touching" prayer. Rather than sermonizing, chaplains were encouraged to give uplifting, non-sectarian moral exhortations, teaching the boys to be honest. Chaplains usually met with the boys in the recreation hall.

Various preachers came to Bo Moorhead's camp on the Grand Canyon's North Rim, possibly from Kanab and Jacob Lake. "There was always some kind of religious service to go to," Moorhead recalled. About 15 to 25 percent of the men participated, representing a variety of faiths. Fewer chaplains reached them during their months in the canyon bottom. Father Albey reportedly conducted religious services December 4 and 5, 1934, and Chaplain Freye presented a special Christmas program, as well as leading services on December 13.

Before provisions were made for educational advisors in 1934, the chaplain handled many tasks later assigned to the advisor, organizing clubs, encouraging vocational guidance activities, assisting in finding work for those being discharged, and organizing recreational activities. Contract clergymen received $30 a month and transportation expenses. Volunteers served without the $30 stipend.

At Pipe Spring National Monument in the remote Arizona Strip, the district chaplain conducted church services twice a month—inter-denominational and Catholic. In addition, the LDS church offered two programs each month. In nearby Utah, The Church of Jesus Christ of Latter-day Saints was the predominant faith, introducing many out-of-state boys to Mormonism. Several married Mormon girls. Religious affiliation in the camps was generally diverse. The Vernal Camp, made up of boys from the Fifth Corps area, had 130 Protestants and 27 Catholics. The Bridge Mountain Camp at Zion, made up of Utah boys, had only one Catholic. Many of the Utahns were members of the predominant church and participated in local church plays, dances, and athletic events. The Bridge Mountain boys from Zion were actively involved in LDS dramatic activities at Springdale where they participated in putting on four or five plays a year. Camps with out-of-state enrollees had more difficulties being accepted into community activities in Utah. Community leaders and religious leaders of most denominations worried about the lack of moral training in the camps and about the potential moral decline among young men away from home and under the influence of peers.

CCC DISCIPLINE

Order was maintained in the camps with firmness and a clear idea of the consequences for breaking rules. Few enrollees had ever been subjected to military discipline, and, predictably, some bowed to it more readily than others. At one camp, leaders who participated in a food strike were informed they had just lost their jobs—a serious blow because of the resultant reduction in pay. Others felt there was safety in numbers and confidently rebelled in the belief that the army couldn't send all of them home. It depended on the camp commander whether the gamble paid off or not.

Penalties were generally quite light, but ranged from admonition to discharge from the CCC. Sometimes men lost privileges or were assigned specific camp duties for a time rather than regular work. Pay could be suspended for up to three days per month. Those guilty of criminal offenses were usually given dishonorable discharges and sent home. Desertion or continuous misconduct could bring discharge, and if men refused to work it usually resulted in a discharge.

Hobart Feltner said it was pretty straightforward in his Utah camp. "You did what they said. 'Cause you knew you had to. If you got to messin' around and didn't do what you's s'pose to, you went home."

Misbehavior away from the camp was equally likely to invoke consequences. When the CCC boys attended town dances, fights occasionally broke out, as they also did during the work day. Leaders and foremen stopped them immediately and at night in camp the combatants would settle their disagreement with boxing gloves.

There were consequences for poor performance on the job as well. If the behavior persisted, boys were advised in writing that they would not be allowed to re-enroll in the corps. In that case, they received honorable discharges but no recommendation on their ability or conduct.

Company 3844, assigned to a Division of Grazing camp near Redvale, Colorado, established a form of self-government with a mayor-council system as a governing body. Members were chosen by popular vote and meetings were signaled by ringing a bell. The system was designed to stimulate interest in camp affairs, give the boys a hand in company administration, provide citizenship education, and promote confidence among the boys.

A mayor, chosen by the enrollees, presided over the eight-member council—one councilman for each twenty-five enrollees. A clerk chosen by the council kept minutes. The senior leader automatically became the chief of police, responsible for assuring that all decisions of the council were carried out.

Each Monday night the company would assemble to conduct business, hear complaints and recommend punishment to those who disobeyed rules and regulations. Punishment was usually extra duties. The council functioned at the pleasure of the commanding officer who had to be present at all meetings. Regulations would not allow him to delegate authority and so he had to approve all punishments. The most serious offenses were handled only by him, according to regulations. The mayor-council system seemed to work well and added to the morale of the company.

Although rules prohibited enrolling anyone with a criminal record, some found their way into the corps nonetheless, particularly juvenile offenders. One foreman said he had five confessed murderers in his crew, including one who reputedly had killed three times in his native Kentucky. Robert Ashe noticed increasing discipline problems in the two years he served as an educational advisor in Arizona. The new enrollees were "lower class," and "a bit lower in educational level," he explained, adding that some had been given a choice by judges: go to jail or join the CCC. The most troubled boys wasted little time getting into trouble once they arrived in camp. The commanding officer would give them a chance to explain themselves in a formal hearing, but often would "bust them right out, give them a ticket home." Most enrollees understood that if the master sergeant asked them to do something, "they'd better darned sure do it, or he'd report them to the [commanding officer]." Some boys would be in so much trouble that rather than face the consequences, they would "go over the hill" as deserters.

At any given time, more than a thousand of the CCCers in Utah were from out of state, most of them from New York, Virginia, Kentucky, North Carolina, and West Virginia. The mixing of farm boys from Kentucky and West Virginia with city boys from Ohio and Indiana in Utah camps resulted in an abnormally high number of camp disturbances and fights. For criminal offenses, enrollees were usually given dishonorable discharges. At Leeds Camp SCS-7, a twenty-two-year-old Kentucky enrollee sold wine to a seventeen-year-old CCC boy, who became drunk, fell into an irrigation ditch, and drowned. The sheriff's department investigated the incident and brought charges against the Kentuckian, who was discharged from the CCC. An enrollee at Vernal drew a five-day jail sentence for disturbing the peace, then was discharged and returned to Kentucky.

On a visit to Cedar City, an enrollee from the spike camp at Cedar Breaks was put in jail for drunkenness. Two friends broke him out and in the process freed two other prisoners. At the sheriff's urging, the camp commander determined who helped the enrollee escape and sent them both to the judge. The boys were fined all the money they had in their pockets, prompting Sammy Taylor to write a song about the incident.

I'm a stranger in your city, My name is Charlie Flynn
I got drunk in town one night, and the sheriff ran me in,
I've got no money to pay my fine, no one to go my bail,
So I got soaked for ninety days in the Cedar City jail.

Oh, Hurry, Mr. Captain; Captain, bring back the key,
Hurry, Mr. Captain; give me my liberty.

Oh, what a bunch of hoodlums, the worst you ever saw.
All robbers, thieves, and burglars, all breakers of the law.
They all sang songs the whole night through; their curses fell like hell,
I'll bless the day when they take me away from the Cedar City jail.

In 1936, the Utah Liquor Commission clamped down on the sale of liquor to minors in the camps. To help curb underage drinking they ordered officials to provide liquor stores with the names of all minors. But when the boys wanted to drink, they found ways to obtain liquor. When foremen were close to the enrollees, they often took care of the matter with the army officers.

Some misbehavior brought stern lectures. On a Friday in August 1934, a water fight broke out in the barracks at Zion. The next day the participants received a good talking-to. Later, when some boys went AWOL for about four hours, they also received a stern lecture. A camp captain received a letter from a lady in Springdale complaining about boys smoking, cursing, and disturbing the peace. He chewed them out and told them they would have to observe rules governing behavior while on leave—or else.

When government property was damaged or destroyed the responsible party was expected to pay for it, with the money withheld from paychecks if necessary. Sometimes threats were used to correct misconduct. When Springdale began charging the CCC boys 40¢ for dances, the boys of Camp 964 at Zion decided to boycott. Two boys defied the boycott and went anyway, provoking the rest of the barrack into taking all their clothes and making them walk back to camp naked.

In the fall of 1937, members of Mesa Verde's Company 861 repeatedly cut holes in new tarps on the stake trucks that were used to transport workers to job sites. Administrators warned that those riding in the truck would be assessed for the total purchase price of new tarps, from $19 to $22.60 per tarp. On January 3, 1938, when new holes were found in five tarps, the boys were denied the use of any CCC trucks for recreational purposes until the damaged tarps were replaced.

In another incident, on April 21, 1939, truck driver Bishop Cash apprehended two enrollees, members of the highway maintenance crew, as they attempted to put dirt in a truck gas tank. After a hearing before the headquarters equipment operator, the boys were fined $2 and classified as AWOL for the day of the incident. Chief Ranger Frank J. Pena considered the incident a deliberate act of sabotage rather than mischief, and took issue with the punishment. As civilians, however, the CCCers could not be subjected to military discipline. The army had to exercise leadership more by persuasion than by command and harsh discipline.

An enrollee in the Mount Elden Camp in northern Arizona took a vehicle without authorization and later returned to camp without it. He told the custodian he had taken monument garbage for disposal and instead of returning immediately to the monument, he had driven to the home of a girlfriend. The couple then drove to a movie theater, where they left the truck parked outside. When they returned, the truck had been stolen. The truck was found a couple of days later, prompting the young man to change his story.

He had taken the truck for a joy ride and on his return the lights failed, at which point he struck a bank of loose gravel on a curve and overturned. He got the truck upright and began driving back to camp when he ran out of gas about three miles from his girlfriend's home. At that point, he left the truck and walked.

The sheriff was notified and arrested the enrollee, who pleaded guilty in a Justice of the Peace court and was sentenced to serve sixty days in the county jail. There had not been a comparable case in the Eighth Corps area. After serving his sixty days for unauthorized use of government property the enrollee was discharged without an attempt to collect damages.

Boys nearing the end of their enrollment period could become somewhat impervious to the threats of discipline. In northern Arizona, the Pipe Spring National Monument custodian reported CCCers were gathering cactus and museum artifacts as souvenirs, carving their names or initials on historic buildings, killing snakes for their skins, even mailing lizards home. "There are one or two who have been raised out in the open that can't see any good for any living snake or smaller animal, only to practice on with a rifle or rock," Leonard Heaton wrote in his report. "I might confess that I was that way till I began to study the life and use of wild animals to man, and this has mostly all happened since I have been working for the National Park Service." He hoped the CCC boys would learn the same lesson.

Discipline challenges increased when, with the improving economy, the enrollment age was extended in September 1935 to include seventeen- to twenty-eight-year-olds. Half of those enrolled in the fall of 1935 and the spring of 1936 were either seventeen or eighteen years old. In July 1937, the maximum age was reduced to twenty-three, where it stayed for the remainder of the program. As a result, about 75 percent of the new enrollees were under twenty-one, and two years later only 3 percent were twenty-three.

Including the younger boys greatly increased desertion rates and discipline problems. Perhaps, also, enrollees in 1935 and 1936 were not being scrutinized as closely as they had been previously because the relief agencies were dealing with a greater number of applicants during that time.

Urban enrollees had the greatest difficulty adjusting to the vast, sparsely settled plateau country and were more likely to act out their displeasure than boys from the West. In New Mexico, a disproportionate number of enrollees from east of the Mississippi River were dishonorably discharged. A 1939 study of CCC enrollees from Pittsburgh, Philadelphia, and eight other cities found that 27.3 percent were dishonorably discharged, compared to a national rate of 17.5 percent. Problems cited at various New Mexico camps included trouble-making, bad language, and unwillingness to work. Camp newspapers editorialized against gripe sessions, encouraging a positive attitude instead. Those who wrote letters of complaint, and particularly those whose families joined in their protests, generally garnered quick responses—and sometimes transfers to camps closer to home.

Camp disturbances over the quantity or quality of food were not uncommon. At Zion, boys in Company 964 complained about "slim eats for breakfast and dinner," but acknowledged that supper was "pretty good." Although 78¢ was allocated per man, per day for meals, they asserted that the cooks were spending only 48¢. Chaplain Lowell Bennion tried to cheer up the boys, telling them their camp was well-off compared to most others, but the boys were not persuaded. Later, when one small plate of bacon was placed on each breakfast table for eight hungry enrollees, shouting and threats led to an order to clear the mess hall. The CCCers defiantly stayed. Not long afterward, the captain was replaced by a new commanding officer who imposed more stringent restrictions on the camp.

Many of the enrollees at Zion believed the cooks were taking food to Springdale and Rockville and trading it for Dixie wine. Some burned their straw ticks in protest and a few wrote to corps officials. An army captain who was dispatched from Fort Douglas to investigate promised to deal with the complaints. The camp captain, on the other hand, was less sympathetic. He maintained the variety of food was better than the boys generally got at home and good enough to fill their stomachs. Some felt the captain was responsible for the "slim eats," alleging he was holding out on them. The men spread rumors that $900 had been saved on the mess fund and the captain was pocketing a 10 percent commission on the savings. The quantity of food suddenly increased, and meals were described as decidedly better. Other such rebellions had far less satisfying results for the enrollees who participated in them. In one case, one hundred enrollees went out on strike over job conditions. All received immediate discharges.

The men themselves contrived ways of keeping one another in line as well. Those who failed to make up their cots sometimes found them overturned outside the barracks. Short-sheeting—turning up a bottom sheet so a boy could not get into his bed—was a popular trick or way of getting even. Some also created initiation rituals for new arrivals. At one camp, they had to run a gauntlet of the old-timers, who struck them with sticks or whatever was available. At another, they were sent into the boxing ring to face particularly skilled boxers.

Thomas "Toddy" Wozniak was sent from Connecticut to a CCC camp near Blanding, Utah. "When a guy came, they'd want to break him in! They'd strip him down and throw him in a cold shower," he recalled. "They had these G. I. brushes, and they'd rub him down with one of them till he was red as a beet."

Chapter Four

CCC PROJECTS ON THE COLORADO PLATEAU

In the beginning, teenage boys and young men signed on with the CCC without knowing much about the kind of work they'd be doing. "Conservation" was a vague concept in the minds of most enrollees who were just looking for a job and a place to live. A city boy from the East would be hard-pressed to envision the work that awaited him in the high desert or deep canyons of northern Arizona. Neither could Utahns anticipate building a road through treacherous terrain to finally connect a remote town in their state with the outside world. Unless they were recruited specifically for the task—as some later were—enrollees couldn't know that they might learn to carve wooden furniture or hammer tin into light fixtures and mirror frames, let alone quarry stone, then build offices and homes with it. And those who had never seen snow could hardly anticipate that they would be helping rescue families and livestock stranded by a blizzard. As they stepped off the trains and trucks that brought them to the Colorado Plateau, they surely arrived with the full gamut of emotions, from excitement to trepidation, over what work lay ahead for them.

Some had aspirations of learning to operate heavy equipment, and had a chance at it if they ended up on road-building crews. It was a job that crossed agency lines, a part of the plan whether they were in a forest service or a National

—COURTESY DOUG LEEN, RANGER DOUG ENTERPRISES

Park Service camp. But many would find the backbreaking work of building road involved less equipment and more hard labor, and at times, more than a little danger. The same would hold true for some trail-building projects.

The CCC was not established to cultivate artistic or scholarly talents, but it did precisely that in numerous national parks and monuments on the plateau. Some enrollees would learn not only building trades, but also decorative arts and even museum science. Those who were interested could even help repair and act as guides to prehistoric archaeological sites.

Not surprisingly, some boys took to the work more readily than others. Those from rural America were more accustomed to hard physical labor than the ones from cities. Brooklyn native Bo Montella had no idea how to wield an axe when he was assigned to cut cedar posts at a spike camp in southeastern Utah. Although the foreman laughed at the boys' awkwardness at first, each was soon cutting thirty-five to fifty posts a day. In Southwest Colorado, one enrollee lamented being stuck typing endless reports while his friends got to shoot porcupines and cut down trees. Another reveled in the relative ease of his office job. In the end, few got to choose their work, but most took satisfaction from what they did.

At his forest service camp in northern Arizona, Max Castillo and other new arrivals were quickly divided into work crews. Then, one by one, officials told the groups, "You go to the telephone crew. You go to the porcupine crew. You go to the soil erosion, pine tree planting, and whatever," Castillo recalled. He was pleased when he was told he would be "on the road."

The technical service agencies decided what work would be done by CCC crews. At first it consisted mainly of road and trail construction, campground improvement, insect control, and extension of telephone lines. Later, range reseeding and erosion control under the Soil Conservation Service and the Division of Grazing were added, along with irrigation works under the Bureau of Reclamation. Each enrollment period, National Park Service superintendents submitted work project proposals to their Washington office, which prioritized them. The CCCers often proved to be so efficient that projects took far less time than anticipated.

Soon a system of project review was instituted through which all proposed CCC projects were to be approved by landscape architects, engineers, historians, archaeologists, and wildlife experts. The professionals judged the appropriateness of each project and rejected those they believed might cause irretrievable loss of natural and cultural resources.

HARVESTING ASPEN LOGS AT GRAND CANYON NATIONAL PARK, NORTH RIM
—COURTESY NATIONAL PARK SERVICE

Whatever work they would be doing, the first order of business, after new arrivals got settled in camp, was whatever job training the technical service agency deemed necessary. Supervisors broke each job into a number of simple steps and each enrollee went through the task step-by-step until he understood how to accomplish it. The forest service gave enrollees a pamphlet entitled "Woodsmanship for the CCC," which explained with text and illustrations how to use an axe or crosscut saw safely and how to recognize potential hazards. For many, though, training occurred in the course of their work.

Hasty development had its shortcomings, despite the enthusiastic response by enrollees. In the beginning, the program did not have enough supervisory personnel to staff the rapidly proliferating CCC camps. Adequate, experienced direction was needed for the untrained young men. Hugh Calkins, at the southwestern regional forest service headquarters in Albuquerque, wired forestry schools in the West seeking recommendations of about eighty men who could be hired as supervisors. Numerous trained foresters, who were recent graduates of forestry schools, served as CCC camp supervisors. Many later transferred to the forest service as full-time employees in Arizona and New Mexico.

Louis Purvis was apprehensive when a supervisor assigned him to a trail-building crew in the Grand Canyon:

> Well, I protested. I said, "Mr. Seavey, I have never done any hard rock mining." I didn't know what hard rocks were. I was totally uninformed as to any method of hard rock mining. He looked at me and kind of smiled and said, "Mr. Purvis?" and I said, "Yes, sir?"
>
> He said, "You know how to crank up an air compressor, don't you?"
>
> I said, "Yes, sir."
>
> He said, "Do you know how to connect up a hose on a compressor?"

I said, "Yes."

"Well," he said, "you can connect a jackhammer to the hose, can't you?"

And I said, "Yeah."

He said, "I'll tell you what you do. You go over there and crank up that compressor, connect up the hose to the jackhammer, and drill a hole. And then when you get the hole drilled, load it. Pack it with the same stuff you load it with and just blow hell out of it."

That was the instruction that I got to take over [the] face of the cliff on the river trail.

Pennsylvanian Joseph Cmar and his tree-cutting crewmates got explicit directions on how to do their job. A ranger told them which trees to cut, how to cut them, where he wanted them to fall, and what would be done with them. "We wanted no injuries," he explained, "because there were other men working in the area, and he wanted it to fall in a place where they could cut it into lengths, then drag it to another place where they would split it into rails." Another crew then used the rails to construct a boundary fence.

Men who were unhappy with their first job assignment sometimes were able to change, as Lynn Atwood was. "One of the jobs I had was building a fence around the national park, South Rim. That was part of it, lasted, oh, I don't know, too long," he recalled. "You get kind of bored with that job and go on another one. Next job was putting in a telephone down the canyon. Got bored with that job, changed jobs. The weather, you didn't like the weather, so you got a different job."

Hobart Feltner started out building roads, but eventually became a cook. He loved the freedom it offered him. "I put it on my application back in Fort Knox . . . I knew how to cook some stuff anyway. And so six months was all

I spent on the road, building roads and things and then I got in the kitchen." Army regulations required that cooks alternate work days and free days, a schedule he loved even though it admittedly gave him "too much time to play around." Feltner met a local girl during all that free time, and when he married her, he had to leave the CCC.

Meredith Guillet cataloged and made drawings of items from the cliff dwellings of Mesa Verde and tried to put together the pieces of broken pots, like a jigsaw puzzle. The men in one CCC-Indian Division mobile camp became experts in archaeological stabilization, and worked at numerous sites around the Southwest. While at Chaco Canyon, they tried in vain to stabilize a boulder that loomed over Pueblo Bonito to keep it from falling on the ancient structure. Alas, in spite of their efforts, Threatening Rock eventually fell while the men were eating lunch. At other cultural resource sites, CCCers learned how to excavate and stabilize the ancient structures, and talk to visitors about the ruins and their original inhabitants.

ROAD BUILDING

Many CCCers found themselves working on some form of road or trail construction. They built high-quality roads to open up the forest stands for timber harvest and recreation access, as well as truck trails or fire roads, and considerably improved early-day wagon roads.

The work mixed intensive hand labor with the use of heavy machinery and trucks. Young men were kept busy cutting posts, sawing and chopping stakes, and digging holes and trenches with picks, shovels, and crowbars. On one occasion four enrollees using only picks and crowbars moved a three-ton rock eight feet off a truck trail. Some piled riprap on reservoir faces and streams, while others used heavy machinery to build, cut, and blast roads and trails. Bulldozers and tractors could move large amounts of dirt and rock in a reasonable time, but there were more roads to build than equipment to build them. Those chosen to operate or maintain heavy machinery gained valuable training, often guided by supervisors who were experienced construction hands.

Road construction involved much more than leveling ground. Hillside roads, or dugways, required cutting into the bank and using the removed material to extend the flat surface, often with bulldozers. "Cat skinning" was regarded as one of the best assignments because it usually relieved a man of KP duty. Two men were assigned to a crew, the driver and a helper who did the greasing and could also operate the Cat if needed. Many road-building camps had two Cats which often worked two shifts, so that eight enrollees were assigned to a company's Cat crew.

The jackhammer was another important road-building tool, powered by one hundred pounds of air pressure generated by a compressor. Hundreds of cubic yards of rock had to be broken up with jackhammers and moved away when building roads and trails. Horses and scrapers also were used, along with hand-tools.

Castillo had wanted to operate a jackhammer since he was a young boy. "So I asked the superintendent for a jackhammer job. He said, 'Buddy, you're too small,' which I was. I only weighed 130 pounds," he recalled. Undeterred, he kept asking the supervisor for a chance, and the supervisor kept refusing. Finally, he got his chance when one of the jackhammer operators became ill. "From there on, I was there for three years."

ROAD TO BOULDER, UTAH

Boulder, Utah, sits in the midst of a broad, fertile valley in south central Utah. It is a lovely place, lined with lush grasses and laced with tall cottonwoods, quiet testimony to the precious moisture contained in its soil. But for the thirty-five families that called it home in the 1930s, Boulder was, above all, isolated—surrounded by some of the Colorado Plateau's most tortured terrain. Only pack mules could bring goods and mail into or out of the town, following a path from Escalante across fins and knobs of deeply eroded, petrified sand dunes. The solitary vehicle in town, a small truck, had been dismantled and carried in by mule train, piece by piece, and then reassembled.

Amasa and Roseanna Lyman knew the territory when they decided to leave Grover, thirty miles to the north, and take up residence in the valley in 1889. They journeyed by wagon over 11,000-foot Boulder Mountain, cutting through dense stands of aspen and ponderosa pine and picking their way across seemingly impassable rock fields. The valley proved to be a fine place to raise cattle, and others followed. Despite its lush beauty, though, Boulder was hemmed in. To the north lay the mountain over which the Lymans had journeyed. To the west and south lay mile upon mile of bare, twisted, deeply furrowed slickrock. To the east, the earth's crust was fractured, thrust up into miles of unbroken cliffs. The CCCers who built the first roads to Boulder must have wondered, as they scrambled over vast expanses of solid rock, built bridges over deep, narrow canyons, and clung to the flanks of a sprawling, boulder-strewn mountain, why anyone would choose to live at their yet-unseen destination.

Over the span of eight years, from 1933 to 1941, the boys from two forest service camps on the Powell National Forest opened access to Boulder. The Camp F-19 boys started six miles south of Grover, building a road around the east side of Boulder Mountain where thick stands of aspen carpet its upper slopes, and rock outcrops and water-worn lava boulders dot the surface. They were aided in 1936 by Works Progress Administration men who improved the road so that it could be used year-round.

Wayne Blackburn remembered building the road around Boulder Mountain as being hard but satisfying work. "It was just a trail, you couldn't hardly travel it and we made a pretty good road from Singletree clear to Wildcat ranger station," despite having only one Caterpillar for the job, he recalled. He described having to churn drill large rocks, with two men using an eight- to ten-foot drill. "Then we would pound them up and down and go all the way along with that drill with a sharp drill on the end. Then we would have a big long spoon to dip the rock shavings out of the rock. It was a slow job."

Meanwhile, the boys from Camp F-18 started from the west side of the Navajo Sandstone slickrock. Instead of trees and boulders, they confronted dangerously steep rock slopes. Eons of flowing water had carved the layers of sandstone into sharp, narrow ridges splayed across the land like gnarled fingers pointing south. Travelling east across them required repeatedly going down into drainages and up over the ridges between them. It was small wonder that only sure-footed mules could traverse the difficult terrain.

Starting nineteen miles north of Escalante, the CCCers zigzagged their way across three north-south drainages. Over the length of the thirty-eight-mile route, CCCers put in twenty-two bridges, none more harrowing than the Hell's Backbone Bridge over a 109-foot-deep crevasse that bisected the narrow ridge. The depth of the crevasse paled in comparison to the sheer, 1,500-foot drop-offs into Sand Canyon and Death Hollow to each side of the ridge. All necessary supplies, including lumber, cement, and sand, were packed in by mules. The boys, from what they affectionately called the "Hungry Creek Camp," finished the Hell's Backbone connection before they left in October 1933 for winter camp in California. Although Boulder now had its first auto road, it was only passable in dry weather. The slickrock lived up to its name when rain fell, rendering the road impassable.

The CCCers went on to build a third road to Boulder, skirting southeast from Escalante, then north across less formidable slickrock to Calf Creek. The road includes one stretch along a narrow hogback from which the boys could look west over the rocky expanse to the cliffs of the Escalante Rim. It must have been a breathtaking sight and a source of substantial pride for them to look back across miles of undulating rock to where they had started, and finally, east to their destination, Boulder.

On April 3, 1940, the CCC boys celebrated firing the final blast in this twenty-nine-mile stretch of road. On June 21, 1940, the road was completed and dedicated, making possible the first year-round automobile service to Boulder and ending mule train mail delivery. Although it is sometimes referred to as the "Million Dollar Road to Boulder," the more southerly route actually cost just over $1,700 for materials. The expenses were shared by the forest service, the District Five Grazing Unit, and the Garfield County Commission. Much of the road is within the present-day Grand Staircase–Escalante National Monument that was proclaimed in 1996.

The CCCers opened up other remote areas in south central Utah as well. On Cedar Mountain the CCC built a road up Second Lefthand Canyon over the summit to Castle Creek, to connect with another CCC-built road from Cedar Breaks to Brian Head and Panguitch Lake. They also built a road up Strawberry Valley to the Strawberry Point Lookout. On the Powell National Forest, they built a road up the East Fork of the Sevier River to the Tropic Reservoir. The road from Utah Highway 24 to the Aquarius ranger station was improved and construction started on the road through The Gap to Cyclone Lake. After

1935, WPA (ERA) crews built several other road improvements on the forests of Utah's Colorado Plateau area.

COLORADO NATIONAL MONUMENT'S RIM ROCK DRIVE

As its name implies, Rim Rock Drive clings to the northern edge of the Uncompaghre Plateau, tracing the outlines of sheer-walled tributary canyons high above the Colorado River. A bird might cover the distance from east to west in a mere eight miles, but for those dependent on wheeled vehicles, it is a twenty-two-mile drive across the 20,457-acre monument, which was established in 1911.

The first section of road into the monument—the aptly named Serpent's Trail—was completed in 1925, climbing the cliffs at the east end of the monument past Cold Shivers Point. In the early 1930s, National Park Service engineers designed an east-west road which would offer visitors optimal views of the spec-

BUILDING RIM ROCK DRIVE, COLORADO NATIONAL MONUMENT —Courtesy National Park Service

tacular rock formations along the edge of the plateau. About fifty men from Mesa County began work November 21, 1931, near the center of the Rim Rock Drive, building west toward Fruita Canyon. With limited resources, Mesa County meanwhile improved the Serpent's Trail and constructed four miles of roadway from the Glade Park store to the monument boundary.

A CCC tent camp, NM-1-C, opened in May 1933, and was filled with the twenty-six LEMs and fifty enrollees from the surrounding area who were designated

Company 824. The following month they reached full strength with the arrival of young men from neighboring counties. Their trucks and compressors arrived as well, filling the narrow ledge where their camp was perched, amid rock formations known as the Coke Ovens.

Thurlow R. Pitts, among the first group of CCCers put to work at the monument in 1933, had hiked and climbed in the canyons since he was a boy. "The traverse of the Trail of the Serpent was an experience in both directions [with] fifty or more switchback turns." The chance to actually live and work in that beautiful place, was, quite simply, "most enjoyable."

Leroy Lewis was in Company 824 as well. Armed with shovels, sledgehammers, and crowbars, the boys' first job was to improve the entrance road so "regular trucks" could be driven to the camp. "Work gloves had not arrived, and there were plenty of blisters. Sore arms were also in order, as all the men were given numerous inoculations with wicked looking syringes that mounted humongous needles," Lewis recalled many years later. The superintendent's solution for their sore arms "was to swing a twelve-pound sledgehammer at that never-ending supply of rocks!"

Working toward the north, compressors powered jackhammers that were used to drill into the rock, some boring as deep as sixteen feet into the solid rock. Dynamite and black powder were tamped into the holes, and men took cover to the warning of "fire in the hole." Small mine cars carried rock on tracks to areas where fill was needed, and dump trucks hauled away the excess fractured rock. Clint Shoffner was a muleskinner on the project. It was relatively good duty in comparison to wielding a sledgehammer, as he had done in the beginning—except for dealing with a stubborn mule. "[They] would set the rails up there up where they were cutting out a hill," Shoffner recalled. "Then, with the mule I would hook onto that car and haul it down and dump it to get rid of the fill. Then I would pull the car back and the boys would fill it up again."

Pitts recalled that some of the road cuts and fill areas required months of hand labor. Schoffner said rather than having heavy equipment, "the front-end loader was your two hands." As they worked, supervisors reminded the CCCers they were in a national monument, and it was everyone's responsibility to keep it as natural as possible.

It was rough work. Pitts recalled "walking and working in blasted Colorado stone" in his army issue shoes. "After a few days the stitching that held the soles on parted company with the shoe uppers, and we found ourselves with shoe strings and uppers in fair shape but no soles or heels. Socks were the next to go." One officer gave him an old, oversized pair of oxfords, which he "appreciated" very much.

On November 9, everyone moved to their permanent camp, NM-2-C, at the Saddle Horn. But excitement among the boys of Company 824 at their new accommodations was dampened when only a month later, on December 12, 1933, nine local construction workers were killed in an area known as the Half

Tunnel. Only two days before the accident, CCCers had been pulled off the job because they did not yet have masks to protect against rock dust.

The road design called for an open-sided "tunnel" in the sheer cliff. About twenty men from nearby Glade Park were blasting small sections of rock and then clearing the debris by hand from under the overhanging rock. After each shot was fired the men usually waited about twenty minutes to begin clearing. They were working in what was considered a safe area when a powder charge fired by a CCC crew on the other side of the canyon apparently dislodged part of the overhang. Six men were crushed in the cave-in, including one who was partially buried and rescued, but died later that night. Three others jumped over a 300-foot cliff to escape being crushed, and died of their injuries. The victims ranged in age from nineteen to sixty years old.

It was a devastating blow to everyone working on the road. Pitts, who had been switched from operating a jackhammer to driving a truck, had driven through the work area an hour before. He was in camp when the doctor arrived with the only survivor and asked for his help. "All went well until he opened his eyes and called me by my first name," Pitts recalled. "I was the next casualty, when upon coming to, I found myself outside under the shade of a juniper tree, and someone else had taken over as the doctor's assistant."

Lewis recalled that it took only a few days to clear the rock, but "the families of those who were crushed by the rock, or thrown to their deaths over the 300-foot cliff, took much, much longer to heal." Despite a coroner's inquest ruling that the accident was "unavoidable," continued rumors and questions prompted a grand jury investigation and public hearing. It was finally agreed, even by disgruntled workers, that the supervisors and foremen were blameless, although suggestions lingered that the powder man had not been as careful as he needed to be, nor had the foreman in charge of the local workers.

By March 1936 enrollment in the camps shrunk to 160 men each, cutting into the effectiveness of their road building. Even so, by June 7, 1937, twenty miles of the drive, including two tunnels, were opened to visitors. Up to then, only a few hundred people visited the monument annually. In 1937, 20,000 people were able to view its magnificent canyons and rock formations.

CARVING THE COLORADO RIVER TRAIL OUT OF SOLID ROCK, GRAND CANYON NATIONAL PARK. —COURTESY NATIONAL PARK SERVICE

Lewis epitomizes the men's pride in their accomplishments: "We were a CCC showcase, one of the most successful of the many 'alphabet' projects."

TRAIL BUILDING

CCCers cut new trails and improved old ones in national parks and monuments throughout the Colorado Plateau, often segment by segment from one enrollment period to the next. In the majority of instances, they rode trucks to the work site each day and returned to the relative comfort of their camps by evening. The men used hand tools—picks, sledgehammers, and shovels—for most trails, then hoed and raked them to control weeds.

Louis Purvis recalled walking five miles down from the Grand Canyon's North Rim every working day during the summer, doing a "day's work" and hiking back to camp. They built dry walls, hauled material for resurfacing the trail, and built drains—"whatever you do to maintain the trails."

But some more challenging trails required the type of equipment used in building roads, and just getting to the job site proved as challenging as building

107

IN SPITE OF THE HARSH WORKING CONDITIONS, NO LIVES WERE LOST DURING THE CONSTRUCTION OF THE COLORADO RIVER TRAIL.
—Courtesy National Park Service

the trails themselves. One project in particular stretched the creativity, strength, and will of supervisors and workers alike.

COLORADO RIVER TRAIL IN THE GRAND CANYON

The most spectacular and hazardous of any trail work was along the two-mile length of the Colorado River Trail. It connects the Kaibab rim-to-rim trail with the Bright Angel Trail, which runs from the South Rim to the river. With the two trails linked, hikers would not only gain access to new canyon vistas, but also have an alternative way out if a rock slide blocked one route.

Most of the Colorado River Trail was blasted out of solid rock, from Pipe Creek to the foot of the Bright Angel Trail and to the Kaibab suspension bridge—the only bridge across the canyon for 180 miles. The four-and-one-half-foot-wide trail clung to the cliff face, which at points plunged 500 feet straight down to the river. The path was steep as well, up to a 15 percent grade. At the most dangerous points, they built a wall on the outside edge of the trail.

Work started on the Colorado River Trail in December 1933, with a crew of seven enrollees working under foreman D. Alton Frost, at the junction of the River Trail and the South Kaibab Trail. Another crew of about thirty enrollees, under Charles Fisk and Guy Simple, had to cross the river on a CCC-installed tram and start work about a half mile down the gorge. By May when the camp was moved to the North Rim, they had completed about 3,500 feet of trail. In October 1934, the trail work resumed.

Picks and shovels were no match for the solid rock. As Louis Purvis had learned, the project called for hard-rock mining equipment. He not only had to learn how to operate a jackhammer, he had to figure out how to get a 2,000-pound compressor from the South Rim to the work site. It "sounded like another man-sized job" to him, but Purvis agreed. He rounded up about fifty men and they hiked out of the canyon. Making their way through the Corkscrew switchbacks to the foot of the Bright Angel Trail, "we assigned two men to the tongue and half of them in front and half of them in the rear," he recalled. "Part of the time, those in front were pulling, and the rest of the time, those in the rear was holding back." In all, CCCers hauled five compressors down the trail and took three of them across the river on the tramway. Bo Moorhead recalled being "one of them boys that was one of them mules" who helped haul compressors up and down the trail.

A TWO-MILE TRAIL WAS CHISELED OUT OF SCHIST TO CONNECT THE BRIGHT ANGEL AND KAIBAB TRAILS AND PROVIDE ACCESS TO THE FOOTBRIDGE ACROSS THE COLORADO RIVER. —COURTESY NATIONAL PARK SERVICE

In the fall of 1934 and spring of 1935, they built the most difficult portions of the trail. About one mile was through black schist, the hardest rock in the Grand Canyon. Blacksmith George Shields had to temper steel to drill this rock. One eight-foot hole required from two to six hours of steady drilling, using anywhere from twenty to sixty-five bits and twenty to forty sticks of powder. Ten Ingersoll jackhammers were employed on the trail, the boys often dangling from ropes over sheer ledges to use them.

Purvis, who spent three years with the CCC, appreciated supervisors' encouragement as he learned how to drill and blast rock. Initially, he was discouraged when one blast made very little noise. "Well, I'm sure there was a look of disappointment on my face, but I said, 'Well, it just didn't make a whole lot of noise.' And [the supervisor] said, 'The noise is wasted energy. You did a good job.' That coming from an old hard-rock miner and the project superintendent did a whole lot for my ego. That man is responsible for me overcoming the inferiority complex that I'd been suffering with all my life."

Watchful project supervisors and foremen insisted on rigid adherence to safety measures, and although there were no fatalities on the trail construction project, there were accidents and close calls. Moorhead was responsible for "mucking" behind the jackhammer operators and odd jobs—"things anybody could do." One day as he stood watching the jackhammer operators in a "pretty rough place, right up over a big whirlpool" in the river below, he felt a "nudge" to move. "I took one step forward and [a] big rock weighing four to five hundred pounds fell" where he had been standing. It was, he said, one of "several" similar experiences he had on the trail.

Morris Birdwell, said part of the trail "slid off" while he was working on it from 1933 to 1934. He and others "blasted out around" the slide area, then climbed out of the canyon. "We got out to the top and our clothes was froze, solid ice. They told us to get in the bathroom as soon as we get here and take a shower and put on dry clothes," he said, adding "We all did and nobody got sick."

Moorhead and Birdwell's experiences pale in comparison to an accident that sent two men careening over the side of the trail. Three boys, secured by ropes, were working on the ledge when the cliff broke away along a seam in the rock. One boy's rope held and he suffered only minor injuries. But falling rock cut ropes holding the other two boys, Williams and Blade.

"The first fall was about forty feet, and then there was a slide of ten or fifteen feet, and then another drop of about sixty feet," Purvis recalled, adding everyone was surprised and curious about the men's ability to survive the fall. "We came to the conclusion that they were falling on falling rock, and this first slide slowed them down, and then the next slide they fell on falling rock."

Purvis was in the rescue party that climbed down to the river. "We went down this long sandbar type thing until we got to the cliff, then we took to boulders and waded in the river," he said, adding they were wary of quicksand as they made their way. They found one of the men on a rock beside the river, and the second fifteen feet above him, both unconscious and suffering from shock. "When the other [rescuers] got there I told them to pull off all their clothes except the necessities. . . . We kept them warm with the kids' clothes until we got there with the litters, and we kept them wrapped up as we painstakingly took them out."

Badly bruised and cut, the two injured boys were carried by stretchers to the camp hospital. Despite his dark skin, Blade—an African American—was indistinguishable from his companion because of the extent of their injuries. Doctor Aaron Berger skillfully sewed up the many bad cuts, but Purvis recalled that they

"had a lot of ugly scars" when they returned to camp six weeks later. "You could tell that they had been through the mill," he said. Blade chose to leave the camp after his recovery, but Williams stayed and helped finish the trail.

When temperatures became too hot to work in "the hole," the company hiked out to the North Rim, where they spent the summer. In late September they returned to complete the final two-tenths of a mile of the trail. It opened January 20, 1936, with "Shorty" Yarberry, a Fred Harvey packer, taking the first mule train over it—a string of ten mules carrying hay.

Forty thousand pounds of powder were used in constructing the Colorado River Trail, together with thousands of electrical caps, 10,000 jack bits and more than 20,000 commercial bits. Thousands of feet of rope, many wheelbarrows, shovels, and unknown gallons of gasoline and oil and thousands of man hours went into its construction. Today it stands as a monument to the Civilian Conservation Corps.

Despite—and perhaps because of—the grueling work and challenging living conditions, the men who built the Colorado River Trail took special pride in their accomplishment. Nick Duncan had lost both his parents by the time he joined the CCC in 1933, so he was especially appreciative of the opportunity to run a jackhammer on the trail project. The following year, he was promoted to foreman. At the time, and years later, he had a "good feeling" about his work in the canyon. "You had to take a lot of chances and that sort of thing," he recalled. "It gave me a feeling of worthiness and confidence in myself which I never had before."

Work on another less spectacular and less challenging trail began in November 1933. Known as the Clear Creek Trail, the route ascended the Bright Angel Gorge by switchbacks until it reached the Tonto Platform on the north side of the river. From there, it crossed the plateau and wound its way to Clear Creek. The first part of this trail was also through solid rock and compressor-driven jackhammers were needed to drill into the rock in preparation for blasting. Although it took 10,000 pounds of explosives to construct, most of the trail is relatively level as it crosses the Tonto Platform. When it was completed April 19, 1935, the nine-mile trail opened up new vistas in the canyon, led to numerous Indian ruins, and opened Clear Creek to fishermen.

Jake Barranca recalled staying at Indian Garden while they worked on the Tonto Trail. Getting to and from the work site took up the majority of the day, "three hours going, work two hours, and three hours coming."

The fact that the trail led to Indian ruins and opened Clear Creek to fishermen was probably well known to the CCC boys. They did considerable pot hunting in the archaeological sites along the trail and also fished in Clear Creek during closed seasons, much to the consternation of park service officials who could not keep a close watch on such a remote camp.

FOREST MANAGEMENT AND INFRASTRUCTURE DEVELOPMENT

CCCers in forest service camps found that they were expected to do much more than be lumberjacks. They also learned to quarry and dress stone, then use it to construct administrative and residential buildings, parking areas, retaining and culvert walls, and curbing. They built ranger and guard stations, sheds, lookout towers, and other structures, ranging from 2,000-square-foot warehouses to small storage buildings. On Utah's Dixie and Powell national forests (now combined), the CCC constructed fifty-one buildings at a cost of $119,000.

Although they planted fewer trees than elsewhere in the country, enrollees on the plateau improved the health of timber stands by removing diseased or damaged trees as well as less valuable species. In the summer of 1936 a crew of forty-one boys was assigned exclusively to timber stand improvement work on the Powell National Forest.

The first CCCers who were sent from nearby communities to what became known simply as Schultz Pass Camp on the Coconino National Forest faced the most primitive of accommodations. There was little more than a single water faucet when they arrived in May 1933—no hot water, no showers, and only tents and straw-stuffed mattresses. Nonetheless, the boys had a full complement of tasks: construction of a road from Fort Valley (Highway 180) to U. S. Highway 89, twig blight eradication, timberland improvement, porcupine control, drainage control, dam construction, roadside clean-up, mapping and surveying, fire suppression, and construction for a local ski area.

The skiing industry was in its infancy as the CCC was formed. People from the Flagstaff area had taken to skiing on some of the hills at the base of the San Francisco Peaks when a timber staff officer arrived from Colorado in 1934. Ed Groesbeck decided CCCers should work on construction of Snowbowl Road, and by 1939, sixty men from the camp were assigned to the project. By the fall of 1940 they started building a log lodge, ninety-five feet long and twenty-five feet wide, with a glass observation porch, lounge, lunch room, and storage facilities. The forest service footed the $20,000 bill for the lodge, which was reputedly cold all the time in spite of three fireplaces. Although it burned down in February 1952, the CCC-built lodge helped give birth to the Arizona Snowbowl ski area.

Schultz Pass boys also worked on two nursery projects. They built a two-and-one-half-mile water line to the Fort Valley Experimental Forest Station, which had been started in 1908. In 1936, a half mile up the Snowbowl road, CCCers built a 200,000-gallon reservoir and a half mile of underground pipe to supply water for the Leroux Nursery. They planted seeds, cleared rocks from the soil, made flood control ditches, and strung telephone and power lines to the nursery. By June 1939, twenty-five boys transplanted a million ponderosa that had been started from seed in 1936. Another 750,000 pine seedlings planted in 1938 were reportedly growing "nicely." Small trees from the nursery were used to restore forests that had been damaged by heavy logging and fire in the 1890s.

In the opinion of the U.S. Biological Survey, next to fire, porcupines were "the greatest single enemy of the pine forests of northern Arizona." It became a goal of the CCC, therefore, to eradicate the prickly creatures through hunting or poisoning. The Porky Crew saturated blocks of wood with a strychnine salt formula, then nailed them to tree branches at least ten feet above ground and marked the trees with spots of white paint. Hunting seemed to be the favorite pastime, though. A crew of six men shot seventy-five porcupines in Walnut Canyon in one day. One amusing story in the camp newspaper, *Echo of the Peaks*, told of a CCC enrollee who was twenty feet up a tree when his limb broke and down he came "without the aid of a parachute." The enrollee subsequently found it "a bit painful sitting down."

When Alan Wilkerson was an enrollee at the Schultz Pass Camp, from about May to December of 1941, the primary job was constructing forest roads. He said during that time the camp was 75 percent Hispanic, which led to much friction. Earlier inspection reports (until 1937) had listed the camp as white and there did not seem to be any ethnic strife. Gangs were forming by the time Wilkerson was there, he said, and men typically hung around with their own crowd and tried to stay out of fights. By then there were no camp newspapers, no sports, and no education classes, yet he still had a good time and loved being there.

BELOW AND FACING: STRINGING PHONE WIRES ACROSS THE GRAND CANYON —COURTESY NATIONAL PARK SERVICE

TELEPHONE SERVICE

CCCers were instrumental in improving not only transportation through road building, but also communications through extending telephone lines across the rugged, sparsely populated Colorado Plateau. Nationwide, CCCers strung 89,000 miles of telephone line. None of the individual projects was more challenging than the line across the Grand Canyon.

THE TRANS-CANYON TELEPHONE LINE

A trans-canyon telephone line was installed by the CCC at the Grand Canyon. This line improved upon an earlier system that had been put in place to facilitate administrative communication between the inner canyon and the rims and to help reduce response time in the event of inner-canyon emergencies.

William T. Coulter, considered by some to be the father of Grand Canyon's telephone line system, worked with Company 847 to extend the line from the South Rim to the Colorado River. Then, working with Nick Duncan's Company 818 crew, they extended the line from the river to Roaring Springs. The third leg was accomplished with the help of Louis Purvis and his Company 818 crew, from Roaring Springs to Bright Angel Point and the North Rim ranger station. Coulter also supervised extension of the line to Hermits Rest and Desert View.

In October 1934 Company 847 arrived on the South Rim and their camp became known as NP-4-A. Their campsite was near Grand Canyon Village, where they could provide the manpower for the park service to begin the trans-canyon telephone line in November 1934. They started at Indian Garden and progressed toward the river. A fly camp from Company 847 was assigned this difficult portion of the line. In the winter, work was done in the lower canyon, with the upper levels left for summer. The side-camp

crew constructed the line from Indian Garden to the South Rim. By spring of 1935 the camp moved out, with the line to the South Rim 90 percent complete. The last 10 percent was completed after the fly camp moved from the canyon.

In addition to their trail-building, the boys of Company 818 also worked on the line, replacing old, crystallized tree-to-tree telephone wire with new wire on more permanent metal poles. The new line was built along the new Colorado River Trail, then from the Phantom Ranch to the North Rim over some difficult terrain. As if to repeat their daring trail construction activities, the boys had to dangle from ropes over 300- to 400-foot ledges in places. They completed the line to the North Rim in September 1935 and later ran it twenty more miles to the park's north entrance station.

DRILLING TO SET POLES FOR TRANS-CANYON PHONE LINE, GRAND CANYON NATIONAL PARK
—COURTESY NATIONAL PARK SERVICE

Duncan, Purvis, and others spoke at the October 6, 1986, ceremony commemorating placement of the trans-canyon telephone line on the National Register of Historic Places. Duncan praised the CCCers who helped build it. "They really done an honest job, and it's not to my credit that it got in there. It's the boys that really done the work," he said, recalling the challenges they faced. "We had to go around corners. We had to duck back and forth across the canyon and over the creek to get through that narrow box canyon, because . . . in some places that thing isn't over fifty

118

[or] sixty feet wide. We had to really look to find places that we could put poles, where we could hang on long enough to drill the holes. And that was the hardest part of the whole job was drilling a hole up on the wall where you just barely could hang on with a drill in one hand and a double jack in the other."

CONSTRUCTION AND DECORATIVE ARTS
REBUILDING THE PAINTED DESERT INN AND SIMILAR PROJECTS

The Painted Desert Inn, now a museum for Petrified Forest National Monument, stands today as a testament to CCCers' ability to learn and apply new skills. With its thick stucco walls, hammered-tin light fixtures and mirror frames, painted glass skylights, and carved wood furniture, it is the embodiment of Pueblo Revival and Spanish Colonial styles.

Herbert David Lore operated the "Stone Tree House" on the site five miles from Route 66 through the 1920s, serving meals, selling Native American arts and crafts, and taking visitors on tours of the surrounding petrified forest. By the mid-1930s, the building was sorely in need of repairs. Visitation had declined with the Depression and its remote location, compelling Lore to sell his inn and surrounding land to the National Park Service in 1936, for $59,400. The master of the Pueblo Revival style, NPS architect Lyle Bennett, created an entirely new design for the structure. Bennett's building and furniture designs also were the foundations for CCC projects at Bandelier and White Sands national monuments and Mesa Verde National Park.

With only limited park service funding available to carry out Bennett's plans, NPS officials turned to the CCC. Over the span of three years, 1937–40, hundreds of CCCers restored and expanded the building, doing everything from excavation to finish work. They not only quarried the stone, but also crafted the light fixtures and painted the intricately detailed skylights. They installed wiring,

plumbing, and the heating system, and added guest rooms, entrance, restrooms, dining room, and shade porch to the building. They even made the furniture and display cabinets by hand, carved and painted the beams, posts, and corbels, and built a twenty-five-by-ninety-six-foot storage building.

At the end of the enrollment period in September 1937, company strength dropped to fifty-one men. As would happen throughout the project, new men had to be trained in the skilled work that was required. During the cold winter weather of 1937–38, they employed a novel approach for installing concrete slabs. They piled sand and rock over scrap culvert pipes placed under the slab forms, and set coal fires twenty-four hours prior to the pour. They maintained a watch for five days to keep the fires burning until the cement cured.

Initially, the men assigned to the Painted Desert Inn project could work only six hours a day because of travel time from Rainbow Forest. The army and some enrollees began constructing a new CCC camp at the original Rio Puerco site in August 1937 to replace the more distant one. The new camp, completed in April 1938, was more central, less than ten miles from the inn, and offered better facilities.

The inn had structural problems caused by underlying clay, making it necessary to shore up and rebuild entire walls. Guided by skilled masons, CCC enrollees learned to cut stone and lay up walls, using mortar sand they dug and screened from local washes. Some walls had to be braced while they removed faulty sections by hand and replaced them with sound stone and mortar. They built all the walls up to the second floor height at the same time, to provide a full building area for construction of the upper level floors. When they were finished with the walls, they removed the original hip roof and replaced much of the existing sub-floor.

Bennett had designed the ceilings to mimic those of Pueblo structures, using peeled log vigas topped by half-round log crossbeams, all supported by posts and carved corbels. A crew of fifteen enrollees spent six weeks at the Los Burros CCC

camp at Pinetop cutting and preparing 680 pine logs ranging in length from six to twenty-four feet for the vigas, posts, and corbels. In addition, CCCers split 4,300 aspen poles from the White Mountain Indian Reservation and laid them across the vigas. They then added insulation, with slope boards over that, followed by solid tongue and groove sheathing, and finally hot tar and pea gravel.

By the end of 1938 all flooring was installed and the inn was near completion. In January 1939, a new group of enrollees arrived from Philadelphia and went to work constructing flagstone walks and terraces on the grounds. The CCCers were taken off the inn project in July, August, and September, but began working on furniture and fixtures in October. Although they worked from Bennett's designs, the CCCers had to muster substantial artistic skills to finish the inn's distinctive architectural touches.

Two CCCers painted Bennett's designs on glass skylights, mimicking decorations on pottery from Mesa Verde. Some made hammered tin wall sconces, chandeliers, and mirror frames based on Mexican designs. Others handcrafted chairs and tables for use in the dining and lunch rooms and swivel stools for the soda fountain, decorating them with notches, scallops, and painted floral and bird designs. Enrollees sandblasted contractor-made door and window frames so they would appear aged. Others scored the concrete floors, then painted Native American blanket designs on them.

By the summer of 1940, the inn was finished and it opened for business July 4. Only two and a half years later, it closed because of the war, and did not reopen until 1946, when the Fred Harvey Company took over its operation. After that, several murals were added by a noted Hopi artist, Fred Kabotie. With The Harvey Company's departure in 1963, the inn had accommodated its last overnight guests. Now on the National Register of Historic Places, the Painted

Desert Inn recently underwent extensive renovations and reopened in 2006 as a museum and bookstore.

Visitors to Bandelier National Monument's Frijoles Canyon Lodge will find similar architectural details. The monument was devoid of infrastructure for visitors when the first CCCers arrived. Enrollees started by building a road to the canyon bottom, then constructed thirty-two buildings—the largest collection of CCC structures in the National Park Service. Guided by skilled craftsmen, the boys learned to carve intricately detailed wood furniture, including chairs, tables, bed frames, dressers, stools, benches, and even couches. They learned to hammer tin into fanciful light fixtures, table lamps, and mirror frames, using a combination of southwestern and Spanish colonial motifs. The one-story lodge offered overnight accommodations until 1976 and now serves as administrative headquarters for the monument. The lobby of the former lodge is now a gift shop.

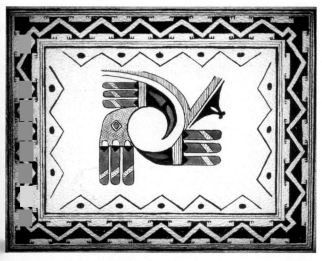

ONE OF SEVERAL DESIGNS FOR SKYLIGHTS AT THE PAINTED DESERT INN —COURTESY NATIONAL PARK SERVICE

Bennett's influence is visible at Mesa Verde, particularly in the furnishings and light fixtures of the museum overlooking Spruce Tree House. However, three-time superintendent Jesse Nusbaum also exerted considerable influence on the architecture of the park, creating his distinct version of Modern Pueblo Revival style. CCCers built numerous structures, including staff residences and an addition to the museum. Unlike those at Painted Desert and Bandelier, the Mesa Verde structures are built of sandstone quarried in the park, without stucco overlay.

Kenny Ross hired on as an LEM at Mesa Verde expressly to work at the museum. He recalled how closely Jesse Nusbaum monitored construction of the museum addition. "He showed them exactly where he planned the walls," Ross said, adding Nusbaum did a "lot of fussing" if things weren't just as he intended them to be.

John McNamara said he and the other CCCers who worked on quarrying stone and building with it "earned every damn bit of money" they got. Retaining walls around parking lots, curbing, an amphitheater, and even drainage channels all were made with dressed sandstone cut in the park. "They would drill holes, put steel wedges and double jack it out. About twenty of us at a certain command would swing and it only took a couple of swings before the whole block fell out," McNamara recalled. Stone masons did the actual cutting of stone into blocks, then CCCers loaded the blocks onto trucks to be hauled to building sites.

In Utah's Zion National Park, boys from the 3Cs expressed their creativity in entrance and directional signs and outstanding rock work. They built the heating plant, comfort stations, employee cabins, a dormitory, an addition on the administration building, curbing, the old museum with its reptile pit, stone borders on walkways, fireplaces, the irrigation ditch at Pine Creek, the Oak Creek Bridge, and stone walls, as well as the checking stations and ranger cabins at Oak Creek.

ARCHAEOLOGICAL STABILIZATION AND INTERPRETATION
MESA VERDE MUSEUM AND DIORAMAS

For one CCCer, his stint at Mesa Verde National Park became the foundation of a long, distinguished career in the National Park Service. Meredith Guillet had grown up in southwest Colorado, the son of a trader. Thanks to his father's business, the young man spoke both Navajo and Ute. But it wasn't his linguistic abilities that brought him to Mesa Verde in the summer of 1934. It was his skills as an artist.

Guillet left college in 1930 to work in the park as a rod man, surveying sewer lines. Locked into the crushing 1930s Depression, he left and, as so many others did, "rode trains to fruit harvests, potato harvests, and so forth for a couple of years."

He returned in 1934 at the suggestion of then Acting Superintendent Paul Franke, who had been his superintendent of schools when Guillet was in high school. "I'm sort of an artist and he wondered if I would come to work." The CCCers were building a substantial addition to the park's museum, and Franke wanted Guillet to help, particularly in designing and building a diorama of Step House.

L TO R: MEREDITH GUILLET, PAUL FRANKE, AND KENNY ROSS WORKING ON STEP HOUSE DIORAMA, MESA VERDE NATIONAL PARK, COLORADO —COURTESY NATIONAL PARK SERVICE

The twenty-three-year-old said yes, but he didn't get to start on the diorama right away. Mesa Verde was burning—one major and four smaller fires scorched 4,400 acres. So before he could officially enroll, he and three other newcomers were rushed to fight the fire. "We started down there and saw spot fires burning, and no one there had much experience working fires."

When they finally reached the main fires, they learned that Navajos were bringing sandwiches on horseback. Rather

than fighting the fire, he turned his attention to helping feed everyone. "I speak Navajo, so I finally worked with the Navajos who were breaking a road in so we could get some food." We eventually had to feed about 1,400 people. It was an inauspicious beginning, and they dubbed their temporary living accommodations "camp filthy but nasty."

With the fires under control, Guillet officially enrolled in the CCC. But he couldn't yet go to work at the museum. First, he had to make "a vegetative map of Mesa Verde," traversing every mesa top and canyon of the park. Years later, when he retired as superintendent of Mesa Verde, he recalled that task. "I guess you can say that I'm the only superintendent of a park that ever went over every doggone foot of the park. . . . I knew every bit of ground of Mesa Verde National Park. We went into ruins that no one had been in for a long time."

Finally, with the survey completed, he could go to work on a contribution that continues to educate and entertain museum visitors today. After working on pottery repair, he delved into cataloging and drawing everything in the collections. Then came the task for which Franke had recruited him. The museum already had one diorama depicting the earliest inhabitants of the area, based on an Arizona site called White Dog Cave. Renowned archaeologist Earl Morris came to Mesa Verde and took Guillet with him to visit Step House, where the young CCCer "made pencil sketches and drawings of everything."

Back at the museum Guillet went to work on the Step House diorama, which would depict the earliest inhabitants of the alcove rather than the later cliff dwellers. "Paul R. [Franke] said it had to be in perspective. Kenny Ross worked with me, I modeled the figures and he helped with the framework."

As they continued their work, Guillet was promoted to assistant leader, earning $36 a month. Franke vowed to get a special appropriation to keep the diorama project going, but was unable to. "He couldn't, so I went to work for my dad at the trading post," Guillet recalled.

Other CCCers would go on to build the remaining dioramas, bringing the total to five. At one time, as many as eight men worked on them. Ross, Guillet, and those who followed them demonstrated remarkable attention to detail, from the intricate and authentic designs on baskets and pottery to a bit of whimsy in the final diorama. In the midst of a miniature Spruce Tree House, a perplexed kiva builder finds one log has been cut too short and cannot reach from one pilaster to the next. Over the decades, the head-scratching Ancestral Puebloan has brought a smile to countless observant museum visitors.

A COMPLETED DIORAMA
—Courtesy National Park Service

After his time with the CCC, Guillet worked at a number of trading posts before being hired as a seasonal National Park Service ranger in 1942. The young artist grew into a passionate protector of public lands on the Colorado Plateau as well as a respecter of the region's diverse cultural traditions.

For the next thirty years, he served as custodian, then superintendent in numerous national parks and monuments. His understanding of Navajo language and culture were especially valuable during his years at Canyon de Chelly National Monument, where he worked through the 1940s and again in the 1960s. The benefits of his advocacy for cross-cultural cooperation between the federal government and the Navajo Nation remain evident today.

Guillet closed out his park service career where it had started, at Mesa Verde. During his six years there as park superintendent, he not only focused on programs and infrastructure within the park, but also on the park's neighbors to the south. He believed that developing the rich archaeological resources on the Ute Reservation would not only take tourist pressure off Mesa Verde, but also provide an economic boost to the tribe. Out of his efforts grew the Ute Mountain Tribal Park, which today offers guided tours through the Mancos Canyon and side canyons to lesser known vestiges of Ancestral Puebloan occupation.

As he reflected on his long career, Guillet said he took special pride in overseeing the extension of the road on Wetherill Mesa, and particularly fostering "good rapport with the Ute Tribe, good personal feelings."

BEN WETHERILL AND THE CCC

No names are more closely associated with early investigations of Ancestral Puebloan sites on the Colorado Plateau than the Wetherill family. John Wetherill, third of the five brothers often credited with "discovering" Cliff Palace at Mesa Verde, went on to be the first custodian of Navajo National Monument in northeast Arizona. His son, Ben, was hired by Ansel Hall—then chief naturalist for the National Park Service and another luminary in exploration and development of the plateau—to run an archaeological project in Zion National Park.

In 1933, Ben Wetherill and fourteen LEMs attached to a CCC company explored, documented and excavated sites in Parunuweap Canyon in 1933. In the span of six months, Wetherill and his crew identified and recorded nearly one hundred archaeological sites both in and outside the national park. They excavated or dug test holes in ten sites.

Wetherill continued to work on weekends, documenting sites as far away as the North Rim of the Grand Canyon and the site of Boulder Dam in southeastern Nevada. They finished their field work by mid-1934 and returned to Zion and Bryce Canyon national parks to work on other CCC projects. By May 1935, with funding for the archaeological work exhausted, Wetherill left the CCC to work, along with his father, on Hall's Rainbow Bridge–Monument Valley expedition.

At Chaco Canyon National Monument one tribe of Native Americans cared for the remains of another's long-since vacated settlement. An all-Navajo CCC crew worked on repairing and stabilizing the prehistoric structures that were crumbling from centuries of exposure to the elements and decades of minimally regulated excavation. Navajos became skilled stonemasons as well as sought-after experts in archaeological excavation. Even today, descendants of CCC stonemasons work in archaeological stabilization at Chaco and elsewhere on the plateau. In later years, a regular, permanent camp spent slightly more than two years in the monument, working on stabilization as well as erosion control and road and fence construction.

DIVISION OF GRAZING AND DROUGHT RELIEF

Although their role was minimal in the early years of the CCC, by the mid-1930s, the Division of Grazing, Bureau of Reclamation, and Soil Conservation

Service were active as technical service agencies on the Colorado Plateau. Typically, their work focused on counteracting the effects from years of poor agricultural practices and minimal upkeep of irrigation canals and ditches. CCCers often were put to work building roads—including one across Utah which a former CCCer proudly said is now supplanted by Interstate 70.

Each new Division of Grazing camp was authorized to purchase eight trucks per camp or one truck to each twenty-five men. In order to help farmers who were severely impacted by the drought as much as possible, tractor use was to be limited and farmers' teams were to be hired in place of tractors as often as practical. The CCC was willing to spend more money and have less efficiency in order to give assistance to drought-stricken farmers.

Like the campaign against porcupines on national forests and in some national parks, some Division of Grazing projects focused on eradicating rodents that threatened public lands. But Division of Grazing boys also found themselves battling fierce winter storms to rescue livestock and people, even a newborn baby.

Ed Braun was assigned to a Division of Grazing company near Green River, Utah. "Our primary duties involved wildlife management in the Southwest to help preserve the grasslands . . . for use of grazing herds," he recalled. "At the time there was an abundant supply of kangaroo rats that were eating the vegetation needed by the wild horse herds that roamed the area. The solution was to poison the rats."

In groups of about fifty, the CCCers were trucked out into the desert, where they formed a line, arms spread out and fingertips touching with the man on each side. The men carried canvas bags of poisoned oats, which they threw to the ground with every other step. "We killed thousands of rats," Braun recalled, adding, "The government found out the hard way that there were a lot of hungry mouths between the rats and the wild horses. We took a major link out of the food chain."

The CCCers then moved on to building water retention ponds for the wild horses. At sites that were thirty to forty miles from camp, they collected rock which they used as riprap to line water holes. They often had to use hammers, picks, and crowbars to break "huge boulders" into manageable size. It was, Braun believed, the "hardest" job in the CCC. "At the time though, we didn't really think too much of it. We were young, strong and healthy. In six months we were able to convert eighteen pounds of flab into twenty pounds of muscle."

As the work crews spread out across the desert, Braun was intrigued by the way sound reverberated through the dry air. "Being from the Midwest, I had never experienced [echoes] before," he recalled. "You could watch one guy 200 yards away, swing the sledge hammer and watch it 'bounce' off the rock, quietly back on his shoulder. Then you would hear the ding of the hammer. It was a very interesting experience in the speed of sound."

George Lockwood also worked near Green River, breaking up rock to clear livestock trails, then using the rock to line an earthen dam. Supervised by local ranchers "with experience," they double-jacked holes in the rock, then packed them with dynamite, blasting caps, and wire leading to a detonator. "It was remarkable to watch the rocks blow up."

WINTER RESCUES

The summer's drought must have been a distant memory for the boys in southwestern Utah Division of Grazing camps in the winter of 1936–37, when blizzards threatened rural families and their livestock. Crews from the Henrieville Camp, DG-33, cleared 585 miles of roads and trails that winter, as well as hauling thirty-four loads of feed to stranded herds. It took twelve truckloads to move animals that couldn't survive the storm where they were. Men from the Cedar City Camp used a bulldozer and tractor to clear roads to Newcastle, Enterprise, and other small towns, west of their camp and just off the plateau.

The cold spell began December 27 and continued to January 27. During that time, there was no break in the weather. Sub-zero temperatures ranged from ten below to thirty-eight degrees below zero, with two to four feet of snow covering the ground and much more where it drifted. Lyall Wilson took leave over Christmas 1936 to go home to Lehi, Utah, and marry his sweetheart, then returned to his camp at Cedar City to finish out his enlistment. Regular work had been suspended for the holiday, so it was quiet around camp until the wind howled out of the north and it started snowing. "It snowed for a good week to ten days. When it wasn't snowing the wind would blow like crazy. It went on like this without a letup," he recalled.

When the storm finally broke, the area was buried in snow. All the roads were closed, and state and county equipment was completely inadequate for the task of clearing them. Stockmen received an emergency allocation of $25,000 to keep CCC equipment rolling. CCC road crews worked day and night to clear roads and keep them open. After four days of working to clear a road in Emery County, a Castle Dale crew was within one mile of their objective when another storm filled the road. They had to start again.

At Cedar City, area stockmen volunteered a "sheep camp," a wagon sheepherders use as living quarters in remote locations, and the CCC assigned a bulldozer to pull it and a Caterpillar tractor. A foreman familiar with the area and roads accompanied three CCCers on the rescue mission. The boys had to take turns driving the tractor, a "warm weather machine" with no side curtains or windshield. "The fan seemed to pick up all the loose snow and blow it right back in our faces," Wilson recalled. Each man drove for half an hour at most, then changed places with another so he could warm up in the sheepherder's wagon. Stockmen provided fuel to heat the wagon, and coffee to warm chilled bodies along the way.

They first cleared streets within Cedar City, and quickly realized "it wasn't going to be a Sunday school picnic. The drifts were as high as the Cat in some places and a hundred foot long." They had to unhook the wagon each time they needed to break through a drift, then reattach it. A line of pickup trucks and cattle trucks followed them, carrying food for livestock and the herders tending to them. One truck carried gas and oil for the tractor.

"We made better time than we had hoped for when we first started out but it was still a slow, cold journey," Wilson wrote. As they cleared access to farmhouses along the way, trucks would drop out to take care of animals and people. Others joined the parade, which persevered through the night, despite the challenges of staying on the road with only a single light on the tractor to guide them.

The next day they passed a farmhouse where a woman had given birth during the storm. "The husband had helped her and took care of things as well as he could," Wilson recalled. "As soon as we passed their house we could see them loading her and the baby into their car and take off for Cedar City as fast as they could."

Finally, at the end of the second day, they stopped to rest, although someone had to start the Cat engine every hour through the night to keep it from freezing up. By the third night, they reached Enterprise, about forty miles southwest of Cedar City. They were met with "a hero's welcome . . . with all the homemade goodies we could eat." A couple of stockmen gave the CCCers "a little hard stuff to liven things up a little."

After resting for a day, they made some repairs on the tractor, "a 1934 model which only travelled about three miles an hour in first gear, which we used most of the way coming to Enterprise." The foreman went ahead, leaving the three CCCers on their own for the return trip. It was, Wilson recalled, "the longest, coldest ride I have ever had in my life." Temperatures had dropped, and driving eight to ten miles an hour in high gear made it even colder in the open tractor. "If we hadn't of been so young and dumb I don't think we would have made it," he added. They reached camp that night and bed "had never felt better" to them.

Even in the St. George area, it proved impossible to keep roads open. Stockmen asked Camp DG-45 at St. George to send a relief expedition to Little Tank, on the Arizona Strip fifty-two miles away. A Caterpillar tractor, along with eight CCC trucks and four private trucks loaded with cottonseed cake and grain headed south into northern Arizona. In two days, they travelled twenty-eight miles, making about a mile an hour. The progress then slowed to three miles a day. They found people out of food and cattle starving. In eight days they travelled fifty-two miles, then returned to St. George only to repeat the trip with eleven CCC trucks and eleven private trucks. In thirteen days of continuous travel with tractor operators working in shifts, they reached Mt. Trumbull to bring feed to two cattle herds. Then it began to rain and the relief crews had to struggle back on muddy roads, often getting stuck along the way.

Chapter Five

CCC ACHIEVEMENTS ON THE COLORADO PLATEAU

The CCC instilled confidence in shaky young men. It saved them from the streets, or a life on the rails. It taught them job skills they could apply in the working world. It clothed and sheltered them—albeit sometimes rather uncomfortably so—and fed them. It even entertained them, and for those who chose to participate, educated them. Lifelong friendships grew out of the close living and working circumstances. Some met girls, fell in love, and ended up staying on the plateau. The impact of the program on the boys and young men who participated is as varied as they themselves were, but undeniable no matter where they came from or where they went afterward.

What about this beautiful, sometimes harsh environment they came to? How much of a mark did *they* leave on *it*? Certainly, not every company made as remarkable a contribution as those who built roads to isolated towns or into dramatic, seldom seen mountains and canyons. Many labored in anonymity, the results of their work long-since obliterated, or now such a long-standing part of the environment that few stop to wonder how a fence got where it is, or who might have cut the stone that lines a sidewalk.

What is as unmistakable as the impact of their experience on the CCCers, is the realization that every visitor to national forests, parks, and monuments enjoys

DIXIE NATIONAL FOREST, UTAH

the fruits of their labors. Hike down into Bryce Canyon, and you're likely to tread on a trail built by CCCers. Picnic or camp in a national forest, and at least some of the comforts you find there were provided by CCCers. Attend an evening campfire program and the amphitheater you sit in may have been built by CCCers. Stop to rest on a bench and it could have been carved by a CCCer. They may have built the boat ramp on your favorite high mountain reservoir, or stabilized the irrigation canal that carries water to your favorite peach orchard. Their work is seldom "signed," and therefore easily overlooked, but cannot be underestimated.

FOREST SERVICE ACHIEVEMENTS

The USDA Forest Service was established not only to manage the nation's forests but also to protect its watershed. Decades of heavy timber cutting had left slopes exposed and susceptible to erosion. When it rained, the soil, rock, and debris washing off denuded hillsides choked the nation's streams and rivers, in turn threatening agriculture. Unlike the mission of preservation in national parks and monuments, national forests were to be used, their resources managed for sustained yield. Against that backdrop, the primary purpose of the CCC was to provide employment to young men through fighting fires, planting trees, thinning timber stands, halting soil erosion, and controlling floods.

The program accomplished those assignments, and also contributed significantly to expansion and maintenance of trails, roads, highways, dams, bridges, buildings, campgrounds, and picnic areas. The CCC made it possible to accomplish decades worth of recreational improvements in a few years, tremendously enlarging forest inventory of such tangible assets as campgrounds, structures, dams, bridges, and trails. Even roads initially built for fire control became valuable recreational resources, leading to camps, hiking trails, private in-holdings, and previously inaccessible sites such as rock quarries.

Arizona was allotted seventeen forest service camps, including four on the Colorado Plateau. Although the number varied from year to year, in 1935 at the peak of enrollment, the state had twenty-two forest service camps. As CCC crews completed projects, their camps often were moved or disbanded.

KAIBAB AND COCONINO NATIONAL FORESTS, ARIZONA

The Kaibab and Coconino national forests in northern Arizona had both experienced the effects of the Great Depression on the lumber industry. Many mills closed, orders were canceled, and shipments dropped drastically from 1929 levels. Fewer forest workers and loggers were needed, causing high unemployment in the area's logging industry. When the CCC was created, many unemployed forest workers and loggers protested that "eastern boys" brought in to staff the camps would take the forest jobs that were rightfully theirs. The opportunities for work as Local Experienced Men (LEMs), however, went far toward allaying those concerns.

The forests were in urgent need of clearing, thinning, planting, and fire prevention and suppression. Fires had been frequent on both forests, although the generally low rainfall amounts limited the grass and ground fuels that led to more intense forest fires in some other areas of the country. Traditionally, firefighting equipment was simple: axes, shovels, mattocks, and rakes that were kept in a central location and distributed to firefighters. Fire losses on both the national forests dropped to new lows through the 1930s with the development of new trails, fire towers, and firebreaks. Furthermore, the CCC boys became a trained firefighting corps for the forest service.

The Coconino National Forest was home to one of the first forest service camps on the southwestern part of the Colorado Plateau. Boys at the Woods Spring Camp, two hundred enrollees from Texas, worked on a variety of projects, including thinning a stand of ponderosa pine and replacing a telephone line to Flagstaff. A small crew poisoned porcupines. In the fall the camp moved to Sedona where the boys constructed erosion control check dams, and began a long tradition of building and repairing roads. They developed campgrounds by making and installing tables, benches, fireplaces, and outdoor toilets, and putting in water systems. The CCC on both the Kaibab and Coconino national forests worked to eradicate white pine blister rust in ponderosa pines, as well as twig blight and pine beetles.

PLANTING TREES AFTER A FIRE
—COURTESY NATIONAL PARK SERVICE

On both national forests, professional landscape architects and engineers were employed to design structures and supervise the plentiful CCC labor force. They built bathhouses, shelters, amphitheaters, and playgrounds on all four districts—Peaks, Mormon Lake, Red Rock, and Mogollon Rim—of the Coconino National Forest.

Young men from Scranton, Pennsylvania, were unskilled in the use of forest tools and conservation work when they arrived at the Coconino's Camp F-32-A. With the guidance of competent supervisors, they became enthusiastic about their camp, their work, and the CCC. One crew made rustic signs to mark trails, roads, and points of interest on the Sedona district of the forest. The boys decided to work longer days so they could travel to the various locations and install their signs. The camp commander approved, and the crew took "camp time" to place the signs during the week.

Most of the boys assigned to forest service camps on Arizona's Colorado Plateau were from the Eighth and Third Corps areas. From 1933 to 1942 nine forest service camps were located in the Flagstaff area. The Williams, Arizona, area had five forest service camps between May 1933 and May 1940. Holbrook had the Springerville Camp, established in May 1940, and Winslow had two camps established in April and June 1939. Boys from each of these camps built forest roads, trails, bridges, picnic shelters, restrooms, forest service ranger stations, sheds, warehouses, and public recreation sites. Stone masonry and log buildings constructed in what was termed "rustic architecture" predominated. The nearby communities benefited directly, as each camp spent about $5,000 a month on supplies and other necessities.

Some boys at the Schultz Pass Camp on the Coconino were sent to Lockett Meadow—now the site of a campground and trailhead to the Inner Basin of the San Francisco Peaks. There they were to begin building a road, as the first step in laying a new water line to Flagstaff. The road likely continues to be used as a hiking trail today. Although they were reluctant to work at the 9,000-foot elevation initially, those who volunteered raved about the beauty of the place and the clear, brisk air.

The two and one-half miles of water line Schultz Pass boys built to the Fort Valley Experimental Forest Station remains in use today. As for the trees they nurtured from seed at the Leroux Nursery, entire forests exist today because of their work, not only in northern Arizona, but in New Mexico as well. The boys themselves predicted the future benefits of their work in the May 1940 issue of the *Coconino Sun*. Three-year-old seedlings had grown six to eight inches tall, with nine-inch roots, the story reported, adding, "About the year 2087, and for thirty years thereafter, they will go to the mills to become lumber, if there is any use left in the world for lumber at that time. Perhaps they will not become lumber at all, but will simply serve as part of the watershed; perhaps they will be appreciated then only for their aesthetic value."

Another notable project had CCC workers seine fish from Lake Mary on the Coconino, transport them to other lakes, and then plug cracks, holes, and faults in the lakebed with clay and concrete. By stopping the bad leaks, they restored the lake so that it would hold water and remain a favorite camping and fishing spot.

On the Kaibab National Forest the CCC improved fishing, undertook game studies, did erosion control work with check dams and gully plugs, and sprayed, cut, and burned infected trees to control insects and disease. They built new ranger stations, warehouses, and sheds, and opened access to many forest areas with new roads and trails. Some summer side camp crews were assigned rodent control work, trail construction, drift fence construction, weed eradication, forest reseeding, and campground improvement. The CCC also assisted in research activity by fencing designated areas, then helping to compare fenced and grazed plats. Repairs and improvements to the east-west road along the Mogollon Rim were among the most significant road-building endeavors on the forests of the Colorado Plateau.

Twenty forest service camps were approved for Utah. The Manti, Dixie, Powell, and LaSal national forests, all located at least in part on the Colorado Plateau. Each received two camps in the first enrollment period. Some camps were made up entirely of boys from other states, some had all Utah boys, and some were mixed. Boys from Virginia set up the first forest service camp in the Uinta Basin. They put in cattle guards and built fences, but their main work was road construction. At Joe's Valley west of Orangeville, Camp F-10 was made up entirely of youth from Emery, Carbon, Sanpete, and Salt Lake counties. Twelve miles to the south was the Ferron Camp, F-11, made up of Utah and Virginia boys who lived together in square, six-man tents.

At Warner ranger station, a nucleus of Company 1345 arrived from Fort Monroe, Virginia. Two trucks from Moab took the one hundred men to a temporary camp at Dill's Knoll on Brumley Creek in San Juan County. The camp reached its full strength with the addition of one hundred Utahns. Their main work was constructing a road along Brumley Ridge. Except for a spike camp of fifty men who remained to complete the road, the enrollees were transferred to Moab for the winter.

Dixie National Forest had two camps during the first enrollment period, at Duck Creek and Pine Valley. The Duck Creek Camp, F-16, was a tent camp established in June 1933. A few weeks later it was relocated three-fourths of a mile closer to Duck Creek Springs, about five miles east of Navajo Lake, with thirty-five tents in a long row facing the creek. Their first project was construction of a road from Duck Creek to Mammoth Creek. They built a bridge across Mammoth Creek, using cobblestones and cement for the buttresses and pillars and pine logs for stringers. For more than seventy years, this bridge remained in service.

The men of Camp F-16 also poisoned rock chucks (marmots), and put in pipelines, fences, and phone lines. At the Duck Creek Campground, they put in fireplaces, stoves, and signs. They also dug trenches for water lines and cleared roads and trails. A detail was assigned to design, build, and set out poison salt licks to control porcupines. One of their major projects was taking over the construction of a recreation area at Duck Creek, from the Cedar City Chamber of Commerce. The CCC put in a large amphitheater, cleared sixty acres of land for the park, and finished a baseball diamond.

At Pine Valley, Camp F-17 began with a cadre of boys from Virginia, which was augmented with enough Utah men to bring the camp up to its two-hundred-man quota. The boys lived in thirty-six tents with wooden floors as they built roads, put in culverts and fences, and did much of the work at the Pine Valley recreational park, where they piled firewood and constructed bulletin boards, latrines, tables, drinking fountains, and a 330-seat amphitheater.

In May 1933, Pine Lake was the only improved campground on the Powell National Forest and there were only five on the Dixie. The campgrounds CCCers developed often included shelters, toilet facilities, picnic tables, fireplaces, parking lots, water systems, garbage bins, and playgrounds. They also made directional signs for visitors. At the conclusion of the CCC in July 1942, there were fifteen completed campgrounds with 450 new individual camping units on the two forests that were consolidated in the 1940s to constitute what is today the Dixie National Forest. The cost of those improvements was about $260,000.

Many projects were designed to repair damage done by years of overgrazing and erosion. The CCC boys moved wildlife from overpopulated areas. They also did the first significant planting and reseeding on the Dixie National Forest, reseeding more than 8,500 acres between 1933 and1935 alone. The CCC boys also constructed many allotment and drift fences for controlling and managing livestock.

One month into the second enrollment period, in October 1933, most of the Utah forest service camps were closed and the boys moved to lower elevations, sometimes to camps run by other technical service agencies. In the winter of 1933-34 Utah had eleven camps of all kinds, ten located in the warmer climates of the Colorado Plateau. Washington County had six of the ten, including camps at Santa Clara, St. George, Washington, LaVerkin, Leeds, and Zion National Park. Later, additional camps were added at Hurricane and Veyo.

The Leeds Camp had a short but significant history. The CCCers built a recreation area at Oak Grove and a road to it from Leeds. They also worked on a loop road from Leeds to St. George via Oak Grove and Diamond Valley. In the spring the company was transferred to Idaho and the camp temporarily abandoned. Later, the campsite was taken over by a Soil Conservation Service company.

Before the Soil Conservation Service was established and took over flood and erosion control projects in 1935, many forest service projects focused on those issues. In November 1934, the boys from Duck Creek Camp were sent to St. George to work on flood control along the Virgin River and the Santa Clara and LaVerkin Creeks. They constructed fences, built a diversion dam two hundred feet long and thirty-three feet high on the Santa Clara River to impound irrigation water, and remodeled the Cottonwood ranger station. They also built a road north from Diamond Valley to Oak Grove, to intersect the road being built by the men from Camp F-24 at Leeds. Many of the dams and spillways they erected are still visible today, including a big spillway above Indian Farms on the Santa Clara Creek and many pilings throughout the St. George fields. That April, part of the camp was assigned to help build a campsite at Oak Grove. Each year, about the middle of June, when the snow was gone from the Duck Creek Camp area, the company would transfer back there.

The main work of the Washington, Utah, camp was flood control—building small dams and long jetties into the Virgin River south of town to protect farm lands from river floods. To construct jetties, they placed large willows on the sand, then rolled out steel mesh wire in five-foot widths on the willows. They then built a stone wall five feet wide at the bottom, four feet on the top, and five feet in height. From rock piles that contained various species of scorpions and large centipedes, they hand-loaded lava rocks for the walls onto flatbed trucks. Finally, they put steel-mesh wire over the rock wall, all at an angle to the river.

Another jetty design used large cedar posts set into the river on an angle downstream, with steel-mesh wire strung from post to post to catch the trash and divert water to the center of the channel. CCCers cut the posts, then dragged them to trucks using horses leased from local farmers. Sometimes young boys were paid to ride the horses. A block-long corral was built northeast of the camp, to keep and feed horses. Each morning riders would lead out a string of six or seven horses to the cutting sites. Since the cedar posts were being set in sand, they attached a small water pump to a small fire hose, and placed the hose nozzle at the base of the post. The force of the water sank the post deep into the sand, then the nozzle would be jerked away and the sand would wash in and set the post.

COLORADO'S NATIONAL FORESTS

Western Colorado had a total of fourteen forest service camps over the years, some of them occupied by more than one company. CCCers worked at such remote locations as Grand Mesa, a soaring landform southeast of Grand Junction, and Lone Dome in the southwest corner of the state.

The state's first CCC camp was on the east side of the Continental Divide, well outside the Colorado Plateau, but demonstrated the important role western states with large federal land holdings would play in CCC activities. This forest service camp was organized April 27, 1933, and became the forerunner in trail construction through challenging, remote terrain. A fly camp was established at timberline in July, from which CCCers built a trail to the top of Notch Mountain and constructed a shelter and lookout at the 13,224-foot summit. All water, cement, sand, timbers, and supplies for the structures had to be carried by horses. A small sled was improvised to transport thirty-six-foot-long timbers to the top. At each of the thirty-four switchbacks of the trail they had to remove the load and reverse the sled to make the turn.

In 1934, because of persistent dry conditions in the West, several new drought relief camps were established, seven of them in Colorado. Some were USDA Forest Service Camps, and others were Division of Grazing, National Park Service, or Soil Conservation Service camps. Company 1842 was a forest service drought relief camp set up at the summit of Columbine Pass in the Uncompahgre National Forest, thirty-five miles southwest of Delta. Two years later the company, which originally had 184 enrollees, experienced a complete turnover except for five men who had been promoted to the rank of leader. This company constructed various range improvements including drift fences to aid in distribution of livestock. They reseeded overgrazed range, built reservoirs, developed springs, and grubbed larkspur. Road-building activities included surfacing, widening, and constructing roads to make the forest more accessible to users.

The boys also maintained roads and telephone lines. They cut and burned ponderosa pines infested with Black Hills beetles over a 125,000-acre area. The enrollees spent much time fighting forest fires and they even helped out in Norwood when the theater caught fire. In Colorado's Montezuma National Forest, men were employed in building fire breaks or reconfiguring roads to reduce grades to 6 percent or less.

As for New Mexico, the state had national forest camps, but none on the Colorado Plateau. In all the plateau states, some CCC companies were shifted from one agency to another, going from a state park to a national forest designation, for example. When that happened, the company would receive all new technical service support from the appropriate agency.

Throughout the plateau, city boys assigned to forest service camps found the experience new and exciting. Most had never seen a forest fire, and knew nothing about how to suppress one. Under the guidance of trained forest service supervisors, they learned. Whatever the work, the main key to a camp's success was pride in the company and in the work.

DIVISION OF GRAZING, SOIL CONSERVATION SERVICE, AND BUREAU OF RECLAMATION ACHIEVEMENTS

At the time of the Civilian Conservation Corps, the federal government managed 80 percent of the land in southeast Utah's Grand County. The primary assignment of Division of Grazing camps was to work on water projects to aid drought-stricken livestock owners.

Dalton Wells, located thirty miles south of Moab, was suffering from a combination of over-grazing, soil erosion, and disastrous flooding when Camp DG-32 was set up there in October 1935. The Dry Valley Camp, near Blanding, Utah, had a full-time well driller whose rig was kept busy. The enrollees also built roads, fabricated corrals and water troughs, and undertook reseeding projects designed to improve the range. That often entailed establishing stock driveways, trails, and springs, as well as constructing reservoirs, corrals, bridges, and pipelines. The men at Dalton Wells also lined the west side of Courthouse Wash with riprap and worked to eradicate prairie dogs and jack rabbits. Today such eradication programs would be impossible, but in the 1930s every blade of grass was seen as important for stockmen on the drought-parched ranges, so killing prairie dogs, kangaroo rats, and rabbits provoked little concern. Ironically, experts today would contend that rodent suppression actually caused more predator pressure on sheep. By March 1942 fewer than thirty men remained in the Dry Valley Camp. They were given the option of transferring to a camp in Wyoming or being discharged. All chose discharge, with most returning to their homes in eastern states.

The CCCers from a Division of Grazing camp, DG-9-C near Durango, Colorado, built several truck trails, reservoirs, dams, and stock drives, which helped ranchers save time and resources when moving their cattle and sheep. Their rodent and weed eradication work also provided an important service.

Although Pipe Spring had been established as a national monument in 1923, a Division of Grazing camp took up residence there in 1936. The ensuing four years were filled with frustration for the caretaker, frequent turnover of

Mission

The mission of the Bureau of Reclamation is to manage, develop, and protect water and related resources in an environmentally and economically sound manner in the interest of the American public.

VISION STATEMENT

Through leadership, use of technical expertise, efficient operations, responsive customer service and the creativity of people, Reclamation will seek to protect local economies and preserve natural resources and ecosystems through the effective use of water.

army personnel, and a succession of unfinished projects on the monument. In the especially harsh environment of the Arizona Strip, partway between Zion National Park and the North Rim of the Grand Canyon, the former Mormon ranch represented an oasis for would-be visitors. The twenty-three-acre site was viewed primarily as a resting place and re-fueling stop for travelers, rather than an attraction in its own right.

The monument's first general development plan, approved in February 1934, prescribed a campground, comfort station, a parking area and road, two residences, an equipment shed, and a garage. The historic structures, including two cabins and a "fort" used as shelter from Indian attacks, did not make the list in spite of their poor condition. The water at Pipe Spring was important to area cattlemen and Paiute Indians, particularly on the heels of a ten-year drought that had started in 1922. Use of that water would prove to be a point of friction between the monument custodian, Leonard Heaton, and the CCC through much of the program's four-year residence there. Throughout that time, only a small number of the boys in Company 2557 worked on monument projects, while most spent their work days outside Pipe Spring.

The relationship started out poorly, when the establishment of the CCC camp forced Heaton to move his family from the monument to the nearby town of Moccasin. It must have felt like an invasion to the man whose family had owned the isolated ranch from 1906 to 1923. Initially, twenty-five boys went to work building a boundary fence, a diversion ditch, and flagstone walks, as well as planting and irrigating trees in the campground area. Over the next few enrollment periods, work crept along on the parking area, curbing, landscaping, and campground. With limited Division of Grazing funds available for monument projects, though, only eight CCCers were assigned to them. Heaton became frustrated, complaining that the camp's adverse impact on the small monument outweighed any good they were doing.

The most pressing needs—water and sewage systems, and construction of a custodian's residence and comfort station—were neglected. Heaton had the boys plant trees and shrubbery, only to watch some of the plants die. When he had them work on weed control, he was upset to see they cut off some of the rose bushes he had planted. When some boys locked a coyote in one of the cabins, the frantic animal broke through a window. Heaton found bullet holes in rock walls, windows, and a door. During the harsh winter of 1936-37, some of the boys cut down cedar trees rather than dig through the snow for coal to heat their barracks.

Heaton was especially troubled when the CCCers fished in the monument pond and caught birds, reptiles, and small mammals to keep as pets or send home to their families. By 1937 the custodian was doing his own grass and tree planting, complaining about how the CCC wasted precious water, and wishing they would just leave.

Nonetheless, some progress was made the second year on landscaping, picnic tables, and a pioneer style watering trough at the fort. CCCers lined irrigation ditches with clay, graveled a road, and worked on installing a drinking fountain, forming the base out of local rock to give it a rustic appearance. By the end of 1937, the monument finally had a usable campground. Visitation, however, remained low—only 667 visitors in all of 1937. Finally, in 1938, work started on the water system, and later, the sewage system. Neither was completed before the CCC camp was moved to Ajo, Arizona, in October 1939. Boys from another Division of Grazing camp took up temporary residence in the monument the next year, and helped restore the old fort. But the days of a full-time camp there were over. CCCers from the National Park Service's Mount Elden Camp came to dismantle the buildings and haul them off for their own camp. Heaton was able to keep the infirmary, which he converted to a residence for his family in 1941. They lived there for the next twenty years.

Bureau of Reclamation camps in western Colorado improved water storage and irrigation canals. As with so many other projects, the work entailed breaking and moving rock. Morris Grodsky recalled using sledgehammers and chisels "with great precision" to split shale into flat slabs near Grand Junction. "Then we'd raise these over the head, march down the mountain and load them on

APPROACHING WINSOR
CASTLE, PIPE SPRING
NATIONAL MONUMENT,
ARIZONA —MICHAEL PLYLER
PHOTO

the trucks. Shirtless, exposed to the sun and to the elements, we took on the color of dark leather, and our body fat content dropped to the lower limits of whatever it is supposed to be." The slabs were used by another crew to line canals that irrigated nearby peach orchards.

Later that spring, Grodsky's entire company was moved to southwest Colorado, where their job was to clear timber from a valley that soon would be filled with Vallecito Reservoir. "We abandoned our sledge hammers and chisels and took up

CCC-BUILT INFRASTRUCTURE IS STILL EVIDENT AT PIPE SPRING NATIONAL MONUMENT, ARIZONA.
—MICHAEL PLYLER PHOTOS

our new tools, double-bitted axes and double-handled tree saws. Each day we got on the trucks and drove down precarious improvised roads to our work sites." The men would trim branches from the felled trees, cut them into twelve-foot logs, then haul them in two-man teams to a growing pile for transport to a lumber mill. "This was backbreaking labor, and it was our daily fare," Grodsky recalled. "On rare occasions we would take a break from our timber work and go to help put down some forest fire in the region nearby."

On July 23, 1935, Company 2803 was assigned to a Bureau of Reclamation camp two miles east of Grand Junction on the highway leading to Glenwood Springs. A cadre of twelve men was transferred from Company 825 at Colorado National Monument to help establish the new camp and make it ready for occupancy. The new company consisted of 189 men from Tulsa, Oklahoma, and sixteen LEMs, which put the total size at 205.

Their main assignment was maintenance and repair of the Grand Valley Canal, a federal irrigation project built during World War I to supply irrigation water to Palisade and Grand Junction. It conveyed water from the Colorado River through wooden flumes to laterals and farm turn-outs. The CCCers cemented two miles of canal to prevent seepage and replaced wooden head-gates and spillways with metal and concrete. They lined the canal with rock in places to prevent bank cutting, and poisoned prairie dogs. They also dug up poisonous and noxious weeds.

The men of Company 3841 near Montrose worked primarily on the Uncompahgre Federal Irrigation Project of Montrose and Delta counties. The twenty-five-year-old irrigation system, with 600 miles of canals and ditches, was in serious need of rehabilitation. A six-mile irrigation tunnel carried water from the Gunnison River to the Uncompahgre River ten miles south of Montrose and the river then carried the water to seven canals that distributed it to laterals throughout the project. CCCers replaced wooden structures with concrete or rock. They lined canal banks with riprap and built, rebuilt, or repaired bank roads, replaced wooden drops with rock and concrete ones, and installed rock at spillways to control erosion and protect irrigation structures.

A twenty-five-man side camp was established in the Black Canyon of the Gunnison River near the intake of the Gunnison Tunnel. Their job was to reconstruct the road from the top of the hill to the river, reducing the grade from about 25 percent to less than 15 percent so that equipment might be taken to the east portal when repairs became necessary. The citizens and water users of the valley were highly appreciative of the work these CCC boys did, especially when they learned that an explosion had severely injured one enrollee when he drilled into a blast site that had not detonated.

A Bureau of Reclamation camp first organized at Fort Sill, Oklahoma, on May 23, 1933, as a forest service camp was sent to Steamboat Springs, Colorado, to build trails and roads and thin timber. In the fall it moved to Oklahoma to work on state parks until January 1936, when it returned to Palisade, Colorado, and was designated BR-59-C. The camp was located on the banks of the Colorado River south of town. This company, 868, was joined by a contingent from Camp F-16-C to bring it up to strength. During the settling-in period the men cleaned up the campsite that had previously been occupied by a company from the Fifth Corps area recently transferred to California. They put walks and roads through the camp area and laid gravel.

The company was split into three divisions for its reclamation work assignments: the canyon division, the Orchard Mesa division, and the Main Canal Palisade division. The canyon division cleared canal banks and installed rock and brush riprap. Substantial rock riprap was used to counteract heavy erosion. Using steel and wire they back-filled with tons of rock, most of which had to be broken up from larger rocks. Where the bank erosion was less severe, they drove boiler flues into the bank close together, lined it, then poured and tamped brush behind it.

The Orchard Mesa division did clean-up work around the power plant and pump station. Weeds, sagebrush, rocks, old lumber, pipes, castings, and miscellaneous junk were loaded and hauled away. Then gravel was brought in for roads and trails around the plant. They constructed one mile of new road on the power canal bank. The men of this division also assisted in repairing canal pumps, did excavation, and made concrete supports to replace old wooden bulkheads.

The Main Canal division cleared willows, trees, and brush from a twenty-foot swath along four miles of both canal banks. After years of settling, the banks required a large amount of fill to bring them and canal floors to grade. The boys placed reinforcing steel on slopes and poured cement in midwinter to avoid interrupting the summer irrigation season. That timing required some creativity to prevent the green concrete from freezing. First, warm water was used for mixing and the gravel was heated as well. They made lumber frames to fit the sections of the ditch and covered them with sheeting under which oil heaters were placed to help assure the cement was frost-proof. In the spring when water flowed in the canal, the boys of the Main Canal Palisade division secured and hauled rocks for the next winter's work. They broke the rock and dumped it at convenient locations to speed their work the next fall.

To CCC boys stationed in more isolated camps, the recreational activities of this camp would have seemed unusually attractive. They took more recreational trips than any other western Colorado camp. The technical service staff felt the trips were necessary to keep the boys satisfied with camp life. The goal was to have enrollees fulfill the camp motto of giving full value for value received and living more productive lives.

NATIONAL PARKS AND MONUMENTS

In the premier western national parks and some monuments, much of the early tourism infrastructure had been developed, or at least advocated, by railroads. Lesser known places like Navajo and Capitol Reef national monuments remained isolated and little known. During the 1920s, however, automobiles became an increasing part of American transportation, shifting the focus from rails to roads. People could go more places, individually as well as in groups, and explore seldom-visited public lands. It was fortuitous timing in an otherwise bleak period. While the Depression slowed or ended private development in national parks and monuments, improved access and a large labor force brought attention to previously neglected parks and monuments. While the CCC continued with improvements to the best-known parks, the program's contributions to previously neglected parks and monuments also broadened the number of choices for tourists visiting the Colorado Plateau.

GRAND CANYON NATIONAL PARK, ARIZONA

Grand Canyon is the most visited park on the Colorado Plateau, the most photographed, and arguably the most majestic of them all. Set aside first as a forest reserve in 1893, it was shifted to national monument status in 1908, then became a national park in 1919. At that time, about 44,000 people came to the canyon annually. Park staff created a blueprint for Grand Canyon Village in 1924, and in 1930 embarked on an ambitious six-year development plan that included roads and trails, general layout of all tourist amenities, parking and administration areas, utility plans, and relocation and rearrangement of buildings.

Despite the early years of the Depression and the loss of the North Rim's Grand Canyon Lodge to fire in 1931, substantial progress was made in carrying out the park's development plan. A new administration building was completed in 1929, and the park's first hospital in 1931. An industrial-residential area was built at Bright Angel Point on the North Rim in 1930-31. The advent of the Civilian Conservation Corps allowed for a continuation of the plans already under way.

On May 29, 1933, the first company, 819, settled into their camp, NP-2-A, on the South Rim; the next day, Company 818 arrived at Camp NP-1-A on the North Rim. In all, seven companies served at the Grand Canyon between 1933 and 1942. Three were based at South Rim Village; three were based on the North Rim, one of which moved to Phantom Ranch during winter months; and one was assigned to Desert View, on the east end of the park. Most enrollees were from Arizona with significant numbers also from Texas and Oklahoma.

The South Rim boys of Company 819 barely had time to catch their breath in the first enrollment period. Like the canyon where they lived and worked, the CCCers' accomplishments were awe-inspiring. The diversity of their projects and breadth of their contributions set a high standard for the CCCers who would follow them at the Grand Canyon. Over the course of six months, they installed telephone wire and poles, surveyed the park boundary, put in a fence at Pasture Wash, and maintained the south entrance road. They constructed a stone wall and water tank at Yavapai Point, and another stone wall at Bright Angel Hotel. They demolished a barn and storage shed, began construction on a residence at Tusayan Ruins, completed a ranger dormitory, and built service roads, footpaths, sewer and water-line extensions, the Little Colorado River Spur Road, the Hermits Rest Rim Road, and an athletic field. At Desert View, they repaired the road, built the entrance station, and made improvements to the campground.

Although they would only stay four months on the North Rim, the enrollees in Company 818 got right to work. They spent their first month in what they dubbed "icebox canyon," a very rudimentary camp, with burlap-screened shower and trench latrine. Nonetheless, they built a residence at the entrance and a service road to the Utah Parks Company dormitory and dining hall; put in pit fireplaces, water, and electrical lines at the campground; and removed a fire tower from Bright Angel Point.

On October 7, forty-five of the enrollees were trucked to the South Rim, and from there hiked down to the floor of the canyon. Their winter camp, NP-3-A, was located near the mouth of Bright Angel Creek, on a delta shared by park service buildings and Fred Harvey's Phantom Ranch. Others hiked fourteen miles from the North Rim down the trans-canyon Kaibab Trail, to the two-hundred-man camp, which finally reached capacity in November. During the first

THE SWIMMING POOL AT PHANTOM RANCH IN GRAND CANYON NATIONAL PARK WAS BACKFILLED IN THE 1960s.
—COURTESY NATIONAL PARK SERVICE

winter Company 818 repaired stone work on the caretaker's cabin at Indian Garden, remodeled the bunkhouse, completed a cabin on Bright Angel Creek, and began work on a swimming pool at Phantom Ranch. They also did some erosion control along Bright Angel Creek and installed fireplaces, tables, and toilets at the campground.

Throughout the nine and a half years that the program lasted at the Grand Canyon, CCC projects addressed a wide range of needs. The boys wielded paint brushes and trowels as well as jackhammers and saws. Existing buildings and roads were improved and new ones constructed. In addition to creating the Colorado River Trail, the boys maintained seven miles of the North Kaibab Trail from its trailhead to about five miles above Phantom Ranch. At the ranch they built a stone mule shelter in the shape of a half moon with a harness room, storage room, and covered shelter. An attached corral made of stone pillars and cedar rails completed the circle. Fire destroyed the new barn on May 14, 1936, but the boys rebuilt it in the winter of 1937. They also built a new two-mile spur trail connecting the North Kaibab Trail to Ribbon Falls and two small suspension bridges across Bright Angel Creek. At a point opposite Phantom Ranch they changed the channel of Bright Angel Creek to protect the bank and constructed a masonry trailside shelter at the junction of Bright Angel Trail and the Colorado River at Pipe Creek. On the North Rim, they improved trails and viewpoints as well, both with resurfacing and installation of guard rails.

On the South Rim, CCCers built a rock retaining wall along the Rim Trail at Grand Canyon Village and resurfaced the trail between Yavapai Museum and Yaki Point. Four resthouses along the Bright Angel Trail are the lasting result of CCC work.

Existing trails had to be maintained, particularly after periodic rock slides. The boys repaired such damage, built retaining walls, dug drainage ditches, and installed culverts. The wear and tear of routine use had to be addressed as well, so the CCCers did whatever was necessary to keep the park trails safe and passable. With visitors on the trail while they worked, it was especially important that they take every precaution with rock and equipment. No explosives were allowed for breaking up rock slides, and salvaged rock had to be reused for retaining walls or to shore up dangerous sections of the trails.

Camping facilities got attention from CCCers as well. In the canyon, they leveled the campground near Phantom Ranch, planted cottonwood trees and dug small ditches to carry water to the trees and grass. In later years, they built tables and benches there. At the South Rim campground, the boys built roads, parking areas, foot paths, and a new area for trailers, as well as housekeeping cabins and temporary winter housing for employees.

In Grand Canyon Village, they built steps and handrails at Kolb Studio as well as paths, sidewalks, and parking areas. They painted existing buildings and razed old ones. At the railroad depot, they built an unloading platform. They added public toilets at the administration building, where they also excavated and built an electrical vault. They constructed a community building at the village, as well as equipment sheds, a fire equipment building, a paint shop, garages, and a shop building. The boys made rustic wood signs to replace old metal ones throughout the park.

At the North Rim, they built a tennis court, cabins, footpaths in the residential area, and a reservoir for livestock and wildlife. They also remodeled the mess hall, and built a powder house to store explosives and a fire lookout/weather station, as well as log benches at Cape Royal.

Park service employees benefited from CCC construction of new roads and footpaths in residential areas. The boys maintained existing roads, obliterated old ones, and built new ones, including a road to the dump at Desert View. Where needed along the Desert View Road, they added log posts and rails, as they also did on East Rim Drive at Grapevine Canyon. Parking at viewpoints also was improved.

Some CCC work was less visible, but nonetheless essential to the park's infrastructure. CCC boys installed water lines and new sewer systems, ran telephone and power lines, erected boundary fences, and installed culverts. Some also worked on road and land survey crews, and others strung telephone and electric lines to Desert View. They maintained four mule barns in the park, making roof and structure repairs, staining exterior walls, rodent-proofing, cleaning, and hauling debris from the sheds. The barns at the South Rim Village and at the head of the Kaibab Trail required the most attention.

The natural landscape of the park received substantial CCC attention as well. Grand Canyon suffered from the insect infestations that plagued the entire plateau and forced the cutting of many trees. Where insect eradication left the forest especially sparse, the boys planted trees. On occasion, they were called upon to fight large fires

on the Kaibab National Forest, sometimes traveling up to 165 miles in the back of a truck, part of it over primitive roads. Small fires also occurred within the park, most often in June and July. One year they fought two fires at the remote Grand Canyon National Monument, which had been created in 1932 adjacent to the northwest boundary of the national park. In July 1941 there were six fires, three on the North Rim, which required forty-two enrollees, and three on the South Rim that required only eight enrollees.

Bo Moorhead was enthusiastic about fighting fires initially, until he realized it wasn't the same as fighting fires in West Texas. "I thought we'd just go out there and take a bunch of tow sacks and put that fire out, see. But, no way. For forty-eight hours I didn't lay down. The next time they gave a call for fire fighters, I hid."

For years, trees had been cut within the national park for use in construction and maintenance. However, the sustained health of the forest was threatened by the loss of so many trees to insect damage, making additional cutting unacceptable. By January 1937, the park service chief forester's office prohibited any further harvesting of trees in the park, with the exception that logs from insect control projects could be used. Otherwise, any needed forest products would have to come from adjacent national forest lands or other sources. At that point, the park also stopped providing "ripe and mature timber" to the park concessionaire, the Fred Harvey Company, for its use in the park.

Deep snows and summer washouts led to some complicated budget and planning maneuvering between the park service, the concessionaire, the CCC, and other outside interests.

The Utah Parks Company operated at the North Rim for a short season, but with the distance from supply sources, the general cost of operation was high.

In 1936 the concessionaire had an unusually bad run of luck when a flood took out 2,100 feet of pipeline at Roaring Springs and caused other damage that made operations atypically costly. On September 8, 1936, fire destroyed the temporary dining facility, which was to serve as a lodge when the park reopened in late May 1937 if construction of the lodge was not finished.

The Utah Parks Company asked for a CCC crew to keep the road open during the winter from the north checking station to the lodge and preferably from Jacob Lake to the lodge. This would allow the company and contractors to continue construction of the lodge through the winter and have it ready for guests by May 1937. Although the park service was responsible for maintaining roads, including removing snow, the North Rim was closed in winter. Under the circumstances, though, it was agreed the park service should do everything possible to facilitate construction on the lodge.

The more remote Pasture Wash area west of the South Rim Village received CCC attention as well, with extension of telephone lines and construction of fences and water tanks. In 1936 a truck trail from Grand Canyon Village to the Pasture Wash ranger station was built entirely within the park, a distance of more than twenty miles. Park service personnel and mail carriers used the road, as did the Havasupai Indians who travelled from their reservation through the park to buy food at Grand Canyon Village. Where the road left the park and continued to the Havasupai Reservation it was in very poor condition. The park service assigned men and equipment to clear snow from the road in winter, but otherwise did not maintain it.

In the brutal winter of 1936-37, heavy snows closed the road, isolating the Havasupai. When an epidemic broke out among them, one woman died because the Indian Service physician could not reach them. It took park service personnel three weeks to clear snow and reopen the road, prompting discussion about alternative routes.

Roland Brents accompanied rescuers taking food to Supai Village. "The snow was about six foot [deep] on the level. . . . We was gone from the third day of January until the ninth day of February getting out there and back."

In 1937 another twenty-mile truck trail was approved, running from Grand Canyon Village west to the Abyss and on to Pasture Wash ranger station and Signal Hill fire tower. CCCers from Camp NP-2-A completed the work in January 1939. The twelve-foot-wide trail paralleled the telephone line to the ranger station and the Signal Hill fire tower, but the road beyond the park was not to be maintained by the park service or the CCC.

In September 1939, after an especially dry summer, nine days of continuous rain brought more than eight inches of precipitation. Heavy washouts occurred, especially on the ungraded Pasture Wash Road, making much of it impassable, with gullies four to six feet deep. In addition, heavy slides destroyed many miles of trail used mainly by Indians and other visitors to the village, who preferred the route to other options. There was considerable consternation about keeping truck trails open through the park for the convenience of those who lived

GRAND CANYON NATIONAL PARK'S COMMUNITY BUILDING, BUILT AND LANDSCAPED BY THE CCC, IS STILL BEING USED TODAY FOR EDUCATION AND COMMUNITY EVENTS.
—COURTESY NATIONAL PARK SERVICE

outside the boundary, but the park service had a no-win situation. So the park service sought approval for a twenty-man CCC side camp at the upper end of the destroyed road to use a plow and bulldozer to carve out a passable road, keeping it out of the stream bed as far as possible. The unimproved truck road was graded, primarily as a service.

Other suggested CCC projects occasionally met resistance as well. A. E. Borell, associate wildlife technician, strongly objected to the proposal for a hikers' shelter at Clear Creek. He reasoned that a shelter was unnecessary because the site was remote and received few visitors. Another wildlife technician, W. B. McDougall, also objected because the construction would require a side camp, which he believed would substantially damage wildlife habitat.

The strong-willed park superintendent, M. R. Tillotson, objected to their comments, writing that postal regulations prohibited his sending through the mail his true estimate of Borell's "utterly ridiculous comments and unfounded criticisms." He asserted that the issues were unrelated to wildlife problems and added that McDougall's comments were contrary to fact. Although the National Park Service director approved the design—perhaps in response to favorable comments from the Branch of Plans and Designs—the regional office chastised Tillotson for his language and attitude.

Conrad L. Wirth, who recently had been put in charge of National Park Service CCC projects, suggested Tillotson's strongly worded criticism violated the policy requiring field technicians to submit honest reports. Borell's comments were intelligent and sincere, he noted, particularly in light of the fact that the project had been turned down twice before. Tillotson's harsh criticism would foster fear among field technicians, effectively brow-beating them, he warned, adding that as a result, the system would not work and the director, who had final approval of projects, would be left exposed.

In the waning months of the CCC at the Grand Canyon, enrollees continued to dig, build, and clear. They extended water and sewer lines, put additions on buildings, and extended the Yavapai Point parking area. As always, they did a great deal of cleaning, painting, and building maintenance. During nine years of CCC activity at Grand Canyon, the men of the corps had worked in all parts of the park, completing as many as 250 projects.

PETRIFIED FOREST NATIONAL MONUMENT, ARIZONA

Petrified Forest was established as a national monument in 1906, reduced to about half its original size in 1911, then expanded in 1932 to incorporate the Painted Desert. Within its desert environment are extensive depositions of trees turned to colorful stone, as well as prehistoric habitations and pictographs, distinct landforms, and scenic vistas.

On July 3, 1934, Company 831 with 165 men, most of them from Colorado, was moved to a campsite located on the Rio Puerco. They had sixteen approved projects, four of them considered high priority.

As soon as possible, the CCC boys were to begin work on two reservoirs to provide water for antelope on the monument. They also began putting in sixteen miles of metallic circuit telephone lines, three miles of minor roads leading to

the Pictograph Rocks and the Blue Forest (now known as Blue Mesa), ten miles of foot trails leading to points of interest in the monument, and two miles of fencing. To protect the forest from intruders intent on taking the petrified wood, it proved necessary to place guards on duty 6 a.m. to 8 p.m. and to install woven and barbed wire fences.

Challenging conditions affected the CCCers' ability to work. The tent camp at Rio Puerco was established to save time and truck transportation costs when working far from headquarters, but the site had its limitations. They had to purchase about 500 gallons of water per day from the Santa Fe Railroad at a cost of 50¢ per 100 gallons, and haul it sixteen miles from Adamana. There also was no suitable place to hold education classes. Supplies were kept in sheds with dirt floors, wooden walls, and metal roofs. Severe dust storms blowing up the river bed filled tents and supplies with sand, and caused much discomfort to the men. Barracks were needed both for cleanliness and comfort. Progress on many of the work projects was reported as unsatisfactory, so the men were moved to a newly built barrack camp near the headquarters, close to where many of the projects were located.

The new camp included a fine facility for education classes and was better for both efficiency and morale. The highest priority was now placed on developing springs and wells. In addition, they were directed to extend the Blue Forest Scenic Drive as a loop road, extending the road and trail to enhance scenic possibilities. Building new antelope tanks and creating and surfacing parking areas along the monument road also made the project list. They were to start only a limited number of projects, hoping for better truck usage, fewer foremen, and greater efficiency.

BARRACKS AT PETRIFIED FOREST NATIONAL PARK, ARIZONA.
—Courtesy National Park Service

Despite such handicaps as a three-month snowstorm from December 1936 to March 1937, which virtually halted all work, they accomplished a great deal. They became especially adept at quarrying and building with stone, erecting several dwellings of native sandstone at the headquarters area and at Painted Desert. They even used sandstone for such utilitarian structures as a dynamite storage area, a coal storage shed, and a power house for electrical generators at Painted Desert. They combined sandstone and stucco in the Painted Desert contact station. Next to the Painted Desert Inn, the most complex project was the combined park operators facility and government office. The structure included a museum and comfort stations, kitchen, heating equipment, showers, display tables, log and pole ceilings, ornamental paintings, and wood carvings.

In 1941 a quarry with colored stone was opened to give variety to the main quarry's predominantly gray stone. In addition to the many structures the boys built, they improved the grounds around the inn and utility area at Painted Desert by grading, curbing, cleaning up, painting, and planting. They installed paved gutters adjacent to the road at the headquarters area, stone curbs along service roads, a pole fence from the equipment building to the gas station, and stone walls with connecting walks in the residential area. By January 1941, camp enrollment had shrunk to forty men. Despite the lack of manpower, the camp remained fully equipped with tools, including such heavy equipment as a compressor, six jackhammers, a Caterpillar, fifteen 1.5-ton stake and dump trucks, and two half-ton pickup trucks. The few in camp kept busy with stone and concrete construction, planting and landscaping, and water, road, and fence development.

Other CCC achievements at Petrified Forest include twenty-two miles of monument boundary fence, guard rails, a sewage system, telephone lines, a water system with a pump house, pumping equipment, pipe lines, a concrete storage reservoir, and drinking fountains; diversion ditches to protect the trans-monument highway; riprap lining of waterways where washes crossed the highway; wire-basket rock stream protectors; six acres of leveled and surfaced parking area; and obliteration of old roads and borrow pits. They made concrete highway and boundary signs; quarried stone, then hauled and stockpiled it for projects; and built stone and masonry walls at headquarters. They built truck trails, walking trails, and flagstone paths; and did planting and landscaping, including seeding and sodding around parking areas and old road scars. They cleared two acres of campground, then put in a shelter and tables; removed stone structure ruins at Painted Desert; and salvaged lumber from buildings at abandoned Camp NM-1-A; hauled firewood; and conducted a general survey of areas in the south part of the monument containing petrified wood.

Up until the summer of 1938, the Flagstaff, Arizona, area had only seasonal CCC camps. That changed with the August arrival of 195 men from Pennsylvania. Their destination was the first permanent CCC camp, at Mount Elden, four miles east of town. The mission of Company 3345 was to make improvements to three national monuments: Sunset Crater, Walnut Canyon, and Wupatki.

Theirs was a large, well-appointed camp, with seventeen buildings—four barracks, a bath house, garages, a kitchen and mess hall, a dispensary, a blacksmith shop, and a recreation hall said to be the best around. From that base, men would be sent to work on projects around the three monuments, often staying in small spike camps. Things got off to a shaky start. Between poor meals and no trucks to take them into town on weekends, morale was low and dishonorable discharges high. A year later, conditions had improved and morale followed suit.

Wupatki

Among the dry eastern flanks of the San Francisco Peaks, early farmers now known as Sinagua (Spanish for without water) settled around A.D. 500. They lived in simple pit houses for centuries, until a series of volcanic eruptions about 1064 drove them away. Within decades, they returned, lured by increased rainfall and the happy discovery that volcanic ash helped the soil retain moisture. Others came into the area from both north and south, as evidenced by the architecture that developed by the 1200s and trade goods found there centuries later.

In an echo of what happened throughout the Colorado Plateau, they moved away around 1300, leaving behind more than 2,000 ruins both simple and complex. In 1924, the area was set aside for protection as a national monument.

WUPATKI RUIN, WUPATKI
NATIONAL MONUMENT, ARIZONA

Wupatki was one and a half hours from the Mount Elden Camp, so twenty-two enrollees were selected to live at Heiser Spring during the week and return to the main camp on weekends. The break from routine made it a desirable assignment. Their first project was building a water system for the ranger's residence and administration building, including a 3,000-gallon reservoir and 1,000-gallon sump. That finished, they built a home for the park ranger, a one-story dwelling of the same red Moenkopi sandstone used by the Sinagua. With its flat roof and native stone, it blended well into the environment. The house was completed in 1941 and is still in use today.

They also built a two-car garage and workshop and a stone pump house. They excavated solid rock for an administration building foundation, and put in a sewage disposal system and pipeline. Not all their work was in rock, however. They cleaned and trenched the Wupatki Spring, planted shrubs around residential and administrative buildings, did other landscaping, and developed a visitors' parking area with walls and walks. The boys also put in ten miles of truck trails and improved minor roads, particularly a road connecting Wupatki to Sunset Crater over fourteen miles of loose cinders. Since Wupatki National Monument, like its sister monument at Walnut Canyon, centers around prehistoric Indian

ruins, the CCC men also did archaeological reconnaissance, and excavated and stabilized ruins. Roofs had collapsed and walls tumbled, so much stabilization was needed to forestall further deterioration. The walls today stand in their original location but have been rebuilt and supported in many cases. The CCCers put in drains to keep water from pooling in rooms and even reconstructed one room to serve as a CCC office. The park service later used it as an office and museum, and park rangers lived in one of the reconstructed Sinagua dwellings from the late 1930s until well into the 1940s. Two enrollees also served as guides for tourists at Wupatki.

Walnut Canyon

In the sheltering walls of Walnut Canyon, the Sinagua people built cliff dwellings eight centuries ago. Like their contemporaries in the region, they were

THE CCC BUILT A STAIRWAY TO GIVE VISITORS ACCESS TO THE DWELLINGS AT WALNUT CANYON NATIONAL MONUMENT, ARIZONA. —Courtesy National Park Service

farmers, but they enjoyed a more favorable environment than most, with adequate water, plants, and animal life. Nonetheless, they moved on, leaving behind their homes and storage rooms, a network of mesa top paths, and examples of their distinctive pottery.

Unfortunately, sightseeing and pothunting inflicted heavy damage on the prehistoric structures before they came under government protection as a national monument in 1915. The last two standing walls fell in 1934, four years before the Civilian Conservation Corps arrived at the monument. The CCC had much to do, both protecting and restoring what remained of the Sinagua settlements and creating monument infrastructure.

The CCC established a side camp at Walnut Canyon National Monument just off Highway 66 southeast of Flagstaff. It was located in an attractive area, and designed to be one of the army's show camps. The work performed was described as "exceptionally good," and those in charge also were commended for their whole-hearted cooperation and conscientious direction of the camp.

Some of the boys stabilized four Sinagua cliff dwellings in the canyon. Others produced high quality stone construction in a custodian's residence, a ranger's residence, a comfort station, and an administration building that included an exhibit room, storage and dark rooms, and lobby. They quarried additional stone, dressed it, and stored it for later use. Once the buildings were finished, CCCers landscaped around them and in the residential area. They erected a wood rail fence on the monument boundary, installed a sewage and waste disposal system as well as a water system, built five directional signs and markers and sets of rustic log tables and benches for the picnic area. They improved the entrance road by cutting and filling, developed parking areas, and constructed a headquarters road to re-route the through traffic and simplify administrative control, as well as building foot trails to the ruins in the canyon.

The CCC provided protection by policing the canyon and fighting fires in cooperation with the forest service on the Coconino National Forest. Boys from Walnut Canyon razed the abandoned CCC buildings at Pipe Spring National Monument, salvaged the materials, and cleaned up the site. They even captured and transplanted twelve antelope to Tucson Mountain Recreational Area.

In August 1941 the boys began constructing a landing strip but were not able to finish it. In late February 1942, they were ordered to consolidate the ongoing landscape jobs so that they would have a consistent appearance. With the war threatening CCC funding and manpower, the camp was closed shortly thereafter, leaving some already approved jobs to await a future work crew.

Sunset Crater

The 1,000-foot-wide cinder cone that is Sunset Crater was formed in 1064, along with lava flows, lava tubes, and fumaroles. When a movie company asked to blow up part of the crater in 1930, officials opted to protect the four-and-a-half-square-mile area instead. Although its major features are volcanic, the monument also has evidence of early Sinagua pithouses near the entrance.

CCCers did not do as much at Sunset Crater as they had at Wupatki or Walnut Canyon. Cinders from the monument were used to surface roads in the area, including the Sunset Crater entrance road. They did put considerable effort

into improving the entrance road, surfacing it with cinders. There also was some fire suppression work near Sunset Crater.

In late October 1940 the Coconino County sheriff requested a contingent of fifty enrollees from the Mount Elden Camp to assist in searching for a seven-year-old boy, Bruce Crozier. He was lost near the Promontory Lookout on the Sitgreaves National Forest, about 105 miles to the south. The day after those men left, a request came for another thirty. The search continued from November 1 until about 4 p.m. on November 4, when the boy who had spent six nights and seven days in the hills without food or shelter, walked into a hunter's camp. He had covered the equivalent of about thirty-two air miles in his wanderings.

ZION NATIONAL PARK, UTAH

Zion National Park is the embodiment of Colorado Plateau geology, visible in its sheer cliffs and slot canyons. In contrast to its neighbor to the south, the Grand Canyon, visitors to Zion must look—and hike—up to read the stories in stone from 200 million years of inland seas, vast sand dunes, rain-swollen rivers, and hot, dry winds. Its stunning vistas and enchanting microcosms were set aside as Mukuntuweap National Monument in 1909. Through the 1920s, development—both government and private—focused on linking Zion with other national parks and monuments in the region as part of a circle tour. Key to that plan was construction of the Zion–Mount Carmel Highway, which was completed in 1930 and featured two tunnels blasted through solid rock, one of them more than a mile long. The Union Pacific Railroad built a hotel, cabins, and a campground in Zion in anticipation of increased visitation.

Visitors did come, from a total of 16,817 in 1925 to more than 55,000 in 1930. But the Union Pacific had not counted on the power of independence offered by the automobile. Between 1929 and 1930, the number of visitors who came to Zion by car doubled, while railroad visitation

FLOOD CONTROL, ZION NATIONAL PARK, UTAH
—COURTESY NATIONAL PARK SERVICE

declined by 20 percent. Independence getting to the park meant independence once there. Zion would need to expand its infrastructure to meet this new demand.

The first Zion CCC camp was established May 29, 1933, with one army officer, six enlisted men, and twenty-two enrollees at the south entrance area. By June 3, there were fifty enrollees, and by July 15 the camp was at full strength. At first, a small crew placed irrigation intakes while another prepared a tent camp at Blue Springs to the north, on the Kolob Terrace. Most of the men were sent to the Blue Springs tent camp while a permanent camp (Bridge Mountain) was being constructed in Zion, near the headquarters. The Blue Springs Camp residents put in more than 1,100 check dams and road fills and constructed seven miles of a planned twenty-two mile Virgin-Blue Springs Road intended for truck traffic. The men from the Blue Springs Camp moved to their permanent camp in Zion when cold weather set in.

Other smaller parks and monuments in the area were served by Zion's enrollees who moved about to seasonal camps, the duration of their stays largely determined by weather and workload. In many instances a group might be left behind while the majority of CCCers returned to their base camp in late summer or early fall. Because many national parks were located at elevations where it was difficult to live and work in winter months, the National Park Service operated more camps in summer than in winter. In 1934, a second seasonal camp was established at Zion, from which men would move to Bryce Canyon to work in the summer. Also in 1934, a drought relief camp was established next to the Bridge Mountain Camp, housing Company 1966. It was disbanded in 1936, but during its brief history, 962 men served in the company. The number of authorized camps fluctuated with each enrollment period, but because Zion offered a good climate for year-round camps, it was able to host additional camps in winter months.

As park service holdings grew in Utah with the proclamation of additional monuments, Zion superintendent Preston P. Patraw oversaw a virtual fiefdom consisting of Zion, Bryce Canyon, Cedar Breaks, Capitol Reef, Timpanogos Cave north of Provo in the Wasatch Mountains, and Pipe Spring in northern Arizona. At one time or another, most of these had at least one spike camp for which Patraw was responsible. In 1935 when the seasonal Bryce Canyon company was reduced to eighty men, they were divided between two side camps. One group went to Henrieville to establish a Division of Grazing camp and the other to Pipe Spring to set up the Division of Grazing camp there. From 1933 to 1938, eighty-one projects were initiated at Zion, with fifty-six of them completed and twenty-five in progress.

The natural environment in and around Zion received considerable attention from CCC crews. Perhaps no river on the plateau had more man hours

PATHWAY MADE WITH LOCAL STONE, ZION NATIONAL PARK, UTAH. —COURTESY NATIONAL PARK SERVICE

expended and more riprap installed along its banks than the Virgin River. Thousands of man hours each year went into various measures to help control the tempestuous river—much of it to no avail. In 1940, floods washed out and damaged bridges and basket revetments. These had to be replaced, and bridge relocations forced the construction of new trail connections. The boys also installed a 50,000-gallon reservoir in Oak Creek Canyon and built basket dams and cribbing.

Crews built several miles of fire trails and, when called on, fought fires. For example, on October 29, 1937, twenty-six men were sent to fight a major

fire on the Dixie National Forest. Then twenty-five more were sent following a call for additional help. The fire was contained over the next three days. Some men also were detailed to work on tamarisk eradication, and some worked on spraying tent caterpillars, which spun extensive webs in cottonwood trees and, if left unattended, could kill them. They also transplanted trees, cleaned and eradicated weeds in the south campground, and cut posts on East Zion.

Their wildlife research resulted in a project to capture sickly deer and remove them to other locations, including Bryce Canyon. Some bucks trapped during hunting season were released immediately, because park deer did not know the ways of the wild and would surely be easy prey for hunters. From October 18, 1938, to February 1939, 114 deer were trapped and shipped out. Three captured deer died in transport and one buck had to be destroyed after it broke a leg. Deer removal continued through 1941.

Most significantly, skilled stone masons constructed several buildings using dressed stone they cut from a local quarry. Zion was often cited as the example of what rockwork in the National Park Service should look like. It was exemplary and the men took pride in their stonework skills.

Even decades later, J. L. Crawford could point out with pride what he had done. "I helped build that stone pylon at the south entrance to the park," he recalled. "I learned stone dressing. I was the one who designed the window sills in the warehouse. I can still pick out many of the rocks that I dressed, including that west window sill in the warehouse."

One crew also cut steps into a cliff for use in the annual Easter Pageant. CCCers constructed an outdoor amphitheater, which was dedicated with the showing of a movie. Unfortunately, rainfall disrupted the film, and the dedication. In good weather, especially in the spring and fall, church services were held at this south amphitheater. The boys undertook construction of the employee dormitory in 1941 and had it 85 percent complete by year's end. It was completed in 1942, but before the planned landscaping could be finished the CCC camps were terminated.

Road and trail maintenance and improvement were done virtually every year. CCCers built the Canyon Overlook Trail and parking areas at the Great White Throne, Weeping Rock, and the Court of the Patriarchs, as well as doing grading, planting, curbing, and trailhead work. They installed campground roads, built the twelve-mile East Rim truck trail from the east checking station

AMPHITHEATER, ZION NATIONAL PARK, UTAH
—COURTESY NATIONAL PARK SERVICE

to an observation point on Cable Mountain as well as new roads at the Grotto and the Utah Parks Company Lodge.

In 1938 the CCCers undertook a big project to landscape and fine-grade the Nevada switchbacks on the Zion–Mt. Carmel Highway. Their work helped control the rolling rocks that had plagued this section of the Zion road to the tunnel since its completion in 1930.

In the spring of 1941 there were two spectacular landslides. The first, on May 14, covered the roadway with 100,000 cubic yards of soil, and dammed the river, which subsequently washed out 300 feet of road. The second took out another 200 feet of road. The whole lower canyon from the utility area to the Virgin River bridge required a great deal of work to remove the landslide debris, landscape the slide area, and construct not only retaining walls but also a diversion dam and basket dams. Two CCC crews worked on the slide in eight-hour shifts.

Despite the men's good work, the safety and project trainer, C. R. Byram, struggled at times to enforce safety provisions. Inspectors found numerous violations by simply watching the men ride to work. Some were transported in pickups without seats or guard rails. Often seats were not anchored in the stake body trucks. The project superintendent's only excuse was that he wanted to get work done.

Nevertheless they completed much construction at Zion. Many young men who were stationed there, either year-round or seasonally, found lifetime careers as a result of their work and training at Zion CCC camps.

BRYCE CANYON NATIONAL PARK, UTAH

In this land of plateaus and captivating rock formations, Bryce Canyon stands apart. Not a canyon at all, but rather a series of amphitheaters carved into the edge of the Paunsaugunt Plateau, Bryce and its colorful hoodoos became a national monument in 1923. Five years later, it was elevated to national park status, but remained under the administrative wing of Zion National Park until 1956. For many years it was open only in the warmer months of May to October. In 1933, when the CCC was established, Bryce Canyon had one full-time park ranger, a seasonal ranger-naturalist, and two seasonal rangers.

The beginning of long-term development of Bryce Canyon National Park had come in 1930 which included proposals for a rim road running from the park's northern boundary to Rainbow Point, with spurs to scenic vistas. By March 1933, Bryce had a six-year development program, and the following year most of the proposed road construction was completed. A Public Works Administration (PWA) grant was received July 21, 1933, to build two employee cabins, extend the office building, and construct a comfort station and an equipment shed. These were wood frame buildings with shingle roofs, exterior wood siding, interior plasterboard, and wood floors, and represented the only PWA expenditures at Bryce. Fortunately for the park, the Civilian Conservation Corps filled the void.

In the spring of 1934, Camp NP-3-U was opened to improve a three-acre public campground and construct roads and parking spurs. An advance party of Company 962 arrived from Zion in late April to prepare a camp about three miles south of the headquarters area. Water came from a spring developed by the Utah Parks Company years before, but they had to reconstruct the badly neglected pipeline. The camp consisted of a few wooden buildings, including a mess hall, a recreational building, a latrine, and tents to quarter the enrollees. CCCers worked at Bryce Canyon in the warm months, then returned to Zion for the winter. The size of their workforce varied from year to year—200 the first year, but only 80 the second, and 113 the third. In 1937, 165 men, most of them new enrollees who were young and small, and 8 LEMs were assigned to Bryce Canyon. They adjusted well to work and camp life. The group was slightly larger the following year but by 1940–42, only a small stub camp was assigned to Bryce. Despite their fluctuating numbers and seasonal schedule, the CCCers who lived and worked at Bryce Canyon made many lasting contributions to the park.

Of particular note is the boys' trail work. They built an 18.8-mile horse trail from Bryce Point to Rainbow Point, with a stub trail to the rim road. Working from side camps along the trail, crews greatly improved and reconstructed the Fairyland Canyon Trail from Campbell's Canyon to the head of Fairyland Canyon. They also built the Under-the-Rim Trail and, in 1937, began work on three other trails, the longest from the administrative area to Bryce Point. A shorter trail ran from the campground to the rim, and another from the museum to the rim. In 1939, they built footpaths at Rainbow Point.

From boundary fences to drinking fountains, the CCCers improved the park's infrastructure. They expanded the campground, built fireplaces and a campfire circle, helped install a power line, put in road signs and an entrance marker, and landscaped the grounds around buildings. Their road work focused on sloping banks, cleaning up downed timber, building parking areas, and plowing snow when they first arrived for the season. They also built numerous erosion control check dams.

In 1934, the boys built the first CCC structures in the park, an employee's cabin, a checking station, and a comfort station at Sunset Point. In 1939, they began work on the museum/overlook at Rainbow Point.

LOG RESTROOM STILL IN
SERVICE AT BRYCE CANYON
NATIONAL PARK, UTAH
—Michael Plyler Photo

The one consistent job, year after year, was combating insects in the forest. In 1934 alone, they cut and burned more than 1,600 Douglas-fir and about 900 ponderosa pines. It wasn't enough. Three years later, the entire company was put to work on insect control, and it remained the predominant job through the remaining CCC years.

The WPA worked at Bryce Canyon as well, initially helping with the battle against insects in 1938. Between 1938 and 1941, WPA workers constructed a garbage pit, excavated sewage filtration trenches, worked on trail improvement, constructed campground tables, made signs, built museum equipment, and remodeled the mess hall. They also constructed a rangers' dormitory with lumber salvaged from the old dormitory, constructed five miles of boundary fence, obliterated old roads, and did tree planting and miscellaneous landscaping jobs. An average of about thirty-two WPA employees per month worked from May through October. The final WPA project came in February 1941, to improve the "Tropic sector" of the park highway.

In retrospect, the major accomplishments of the CCC and WPA at Bryce were of long-term benefit to the park and its patrons. They managed to keep pace with the steady increase in visitation through the CCC years, from just under 33,000 in the first year to more than 124,000 in 1941. As occurred throughout the country, visitation plummeted the following year with the beginning of World War II, but would spike again after it ended. When it did, the park was ready for them, thanks to the CCC and WPA.

Cedar Breaks National Monument is a spectacular amphitheater filled with vividly colored, wondrous rock formations. Dense forests top the Markagunt Plateau, giving no hint of the carved bands of red, orange, and cream limestone along its western and eastern edges. Visitors who venture to the rim behold the handiwork of wind and water—falling, flowing, and frozen—which the region's earliest inhabitants deemed the Circle of Painted Cliffs.

ALPINE POND, CEDAR BREAKS NATIONAL MONUMENT, UTAH
—MICHAEL PLYLER PHOTO

Like Bryce Canyon, its geologic sibling to the
east, Cedar Breaks' high elevation meant that it was
accessible only seasonally. Much development work
was needed after its 1933 declaration as a national
monument. It never had its own permanent CCC
camp. Rather, a twenty-five-man stub camp from
Bryce Canyon was assigned to the national monument
in June 1934. Their camp was set up at the site of a
former forest service campground by the Cedar Breaks
Rim Road, a mile and a quarter from a lodge which
would survive into the 1970s. By August, the camp
population doubled with the addition of men from
Camp NP-2, at Zion.

Their stay at Cedar Breaks was short, however. By October all the men were moved to winter
camps elsewhere. It was a pattern that would endure
through 1938, with small groups of CCCers assigned
to Cedar Breaks for varying periods of time between
May and October. One year Zion superintendent
Patraw directed that a small contingent remain
behind at Cedar Breaks to finish up several projects.
Another year, the work force was divided to work on
both monument and forest service projects.

Weather, especially heavy summer rains, ham-
pered progress most years, as did a shortage of trucks
and trained foremen to oversee projects. Despite such

challenges, the boys helped prepare the monument for its dedication on July 4, 1934, and enhanced the roads, trails, and other amenities.

In the course of their four years of seasonal work at Cedar Breaks, CCCers cleared and laid gravel on more than six miles of truck trails, removed downed timber from four miles of roadside, and built log guard rails at scenic points along the rim. They built more than six miles of foot paths, including one from behind the lodge to Point Perfection and beyond, to a point near the southeast corner of the monument. They built the four-foot-wide Rim Trail and installed seats along it so that visitors could pause to enjoy the view. They also built a trail to the top of Brianhead Peak on the national forest outside the monument.

Using cedar posts from Bryce Canyon and Zion, CCCers built an eight-mile boundary fence to keep cattle from grazing within the monument. Others surveyed boundaries or worked on building a variety of structures, including a combined museum/administration building, a cabin, three latrines, and toilets. They also graded and graveled parking areas and finished installation of a sewer line and cesspool sewage disposal system.

Monument visitors especially came to enjoy the two-acre campground developed by the CCCers. The boys installed a water line to the area, built twelve picnic tables and twelve fireplaces, and made parking areas and log barriers to keep people from setting up camp in undeveloped areas. CCCers were responsible for an arched log sign at the monument entrance, and also worked with Utah State Agriculture College at Logan to lay out a snow measurement course with stations at Cedar Breaks, Duck Creek, and Harris Flat. Park service employees then made wintertime measurements at the stations.

The last period of CCC work in the monument came in May and June 1938, when twenty men were directed to tear down old camp buildings so they

could be moved to Capitol Reef National Monument. The Cedar Breaks Camp was officially abandoned July 15 and reestablished at Capitol Reef on July 18.

CAPITOL REEF
NATIONAL PARK, UTAH

Sixty-five million years ago, movements in the earth's crust a thousand miles away set in motion the process that formed today's landscape in southern Utah. As one massive plate of the crust slid under another, the earth buckled and folded. Layers of sedimentary rock that had formed under inland seas, alongside waterways, and in swaths of sand dunes corrugated and broke. Wind, water, and ice ate into the newly exposed surfaces. Even volcanic activity played a part, spewing ash and lava in places and pushing up against the crust in others.

In southern Utah, the surface thrust up in a hundred-mile-long crease now known as the Waterpocket Fold which forms the central geologic feature of Capitol Reef National Park, a landscape of cliffs, pinnacles, arches, and natural bridges. The resultant pockets and creases gather and hold water, which in turn has attracted not only wildlife, but also human beings. Archaic hunters, hunter-gatherers, the region's earliest farmers, and eventually Pueblo builders all left signs of their presence. Finally, Mormon pioneers settled in the area, planted orchards, and founded the town of Fruita.

At the urging of Zion superintendent Preston P. Patraw, Capitol Reef was made a national monument in 1937. Despite its scenic beauty, the area was so isolated and minimally developed that the county lacked any oil-surfaced roads.

Patraw recommended establishing a CCC camp, with a budget of $21,000 to begin work the next winter on campgrounds, water and sanitation systems, and trails. However, a freeze order on new camps delayed the improvements. The monument opened with twenty miles of unimproved dirt roads, no bridges or culverts, and only a single-wire telephone line from Torrey through Fruita to Capitol Gorge—a line that usually was out of service.

The first development funds came early in 1938 with a $3,425 Emergency Relief Administration grant for road improvements. The WPA began work in May, installing an erosion control basket dam and rip-rap along a stretch of the road above Sulphur Creek.

Meanwhile, approval was given to move the side camp from Cedar Breaks to Capitol Reef. In July 1938 foreman Marion Willis arrived with a crew of seventeen enrollees to set up a camp 1,000 feet west of Chimney Rock on the north side of the entrance road. At first the camp consisted of tents and one small frame building that housed a radio for communication with Zion and Bryce. Water from a spring about a quarter mile northwest of the camp was stored in a 2,300-gallon corrugated iron tank. A portable generator supplied electricity. Eventually frame buildings were constructed with material salvaged from razing the abandoned camp at Cedar Breaks.

Once the camp was established and the full complement of men arrived, the first work was on the road above Sulphur Creek and at a quarry, where CCCers cut sandstone for construction of a building. In August a flash flood inundated part of the camp and washed out the bridge over the Fremont River. It wiped out some of the first road work, too, further setting back such improvements. On October 8, 1938, the camp closed for the year, as the CCC boys returned first to Bryce to help close the camp there, then to Zion for the winter.

Each spring the camp at Capitol Reef reopened, and the work continued on a seasonal basis through April 1942, when the side camp closed permanently.

In their four years of seasonal work at the national monument, CCCers focused substantial energy on improving roads and erosion control features, sometimes in cooperation with the WPA. They worked on a four-mile road from the Mulford property at Fruita to the Slick Rock Divide, which was finished by the WPA. They flattened slopes on another road between Fruita and Capitol Gorge to improve sight distance on curves and widened it from eleven to eighteen feet. They built rock check dams in roadside ditches and rock culverts, widened the road from Chimney Rock to Sulphur Creek, and made improvements on another southeast of the Fremont River Bridge in Fruita. While the CCC boys were accomplishing their tasks, WPA workers put in a wooden bridge over Sulphur Creek and began work on the Danish Hill portion of a road south of Fruita.

The CCCers also improved a rough horse trail from the Fremont River to the 230-foot Hickman Bridge, making a permanent trail that led about one mile north from the river to the natural bridge. They built a dry-laid rock retaining wall to support the trail up a short stretch of steep cliff overlooking the river, and new trail switchbacks to the rim. In 1951, the park service rebuilt some of the rock walls and switchbacks that had been washed out in a flood.

CCCers cut sandstone blocks from a local quarry, and a forty-man crew used them to build a structure on the western edge of Fruita. Built in what was termed "early Mormon-type architecture," the structure was deemed the "ranger station" until its precise use—it could be a residence, a museum, or a checking station—was determined. It would be the only permanent park service residence in the monument until the 1960s. The boys also built a small explosives and equipment shack near the park storage yard.

Once the CCC was disbanded, development virtually stopped at Capitol Reef for about twenty years. With the onset of World War II, the park service once again directed its limited resources toward major, long-established parks. Newly established units were left with a minimal park service presence. Remnants of the CCC camp near Chimney Rock were set afire by vandals in April 1947. Nonetheless, the work of the CCC was critical to the initial development of the monument, which was upgraded to a national park in December 1971.

DINOSAUR NATIONAL MONUMENT, UTAH-COLORADO

Dinosaur National Monument straddles Utah and Colorado on the far northern edge of the Colorado Plateau. Its reason for existence is distinct among national parks and monuments on the plateau. Contained within a layer of rock that was once a river bed are the fossilized bones of ten kinds of dinosaurs that roamed the area 150 million years ago. In 1909, paleontologist Earl Douglass came west in search of dinosaur skeletons for the Carnegie Museum in Pittsburgh, Pennsylvania. Here, in this remote place, he found a site so rich in the quantity and variety of dinosaur fossils that excavations continued from 1909 to 1924. Meanwhile, President Woodrow Wilson declared the quarry a national monument in 1915.

Despite the declaration, little was done to develop the monument for decades. The CWA and WPA both did repair and clean-up work at the quarry as well as removing overlying earth to expose the fossil layer. Although a CCC camp was proposed for the third enrollment period to complete their work, it did not materialize, and no CCC work was done there.

A visitor center finally was built around the quarry and dedicated in 1958, offering people a close-up view of scientists excavating fossils still embedded in the rock face.

Of the many landforms on the Colorado Plateau, perhaps none captivates visitors more than free-standing sandstone arches. In seeming defiance of gravity, they span as much as 300 feet from one pillar to another. None is better known than Delicate Arch in southeastern Utah. More than 2,000 stone arches—including Delicate Arch—are found in Arches National Park, which was set aside as a national monument in 1929 and upgraded to a national park in 1971.

The region was home to early Native American inhabitants whose rock inscriptions remind visitors of their presence long ago. In the decade following declaration as a national monument, limited budgets, isolation, and rugged terrain kept park service presence to a minimum, with only a caretaker resident. In September 1939, Henry G. Schmidt arrived as custodian.

What followed demonstrates how communities and federal programs worked together to enhance public lands. Into the late 1930s, access to the monument was limited to an unimproved dirt road through Willow Springs Wash. Planners contemplated building a road from the head of Moab Canyon to a proposed headquarters site, then up Courthouse Towers to Devil's Garden. In July 1938, Jerry S. Farmer, of the Moab Soil Conservation camp, offered to provide fifty CCC enrollees from the SCS camp during the winter months to begin construction if the National Park Service could offer proper supervision. Although the plan proved untenable, it prompted the park service to consider requesting a CCC camp for Arches.

An application for Camp NP-7 to develop Arches was approved by the park service director for the fall of 1939. Then, in August, it was announced that the anticipated camp would be sent to Texas in the Eighth Corps area, a disappointing reversal for the park service and the people of Moab. In October they learned that a camp would be located at Arches the following year to build the highway into the monument and do other development work. Almost immediately, the Division of Grazing CCC camp from Dalton Wells, supervised by C. M. Conway, drilled a well. The drillers hit water at sixty-five feet and brought in a well that supplied more than twenty gallons of water per minute.

Camp construction soon got under way at the mouth of Moab Canyon, about one-half mile west of the Colorado River. The county road department graded and surfaced a road to the campsite. Despite the announcement in 1940 that President Roosevelt had ordered the closing of 273 camps beginning March 31, CCC director James McEntee, announced that the Arches Camp would go forward as approved. By May 1, 1940, a crew of forty enrollees from Dalton Wells Camp began construction of the Arches Camp on ten acres of level land. Under command of Lieutenant Coffin, they set up tents to house the crew, installed a pump on the well, erected a storage tank, and installed a pipeline. The camp eventually had twenty-four buildings, including five barracks, a bath house, a mess hall, recreation building, infirmary, equipment house and warehouses, and a generator house for the camp's power plant.

The 198 men of Company 6428 from the Fourth Corps area arrived July 9, 1940, from Winsboro, South Carolina. Except for a small number from Georgia and Florida, all the men were South Carolinians.

Unfortunately, the cooperation which spawned the camp did not develop within it. Morale and productivity were low, organization poor, and dissension problematic. As a result, far less was accomplished than had been hoped for. Problems plagued both the army as it ran the camp and the park service as it oversaw work projects.

The CCCers' first task was to finish the partially completed camp buildings, which took about thirty days. Their first development work included constructing a storehouse and a custodian residence, the latter built in "old Mormon style" using native stone from a nearby quarry. A small crew also was assigned to maintain the old road into Arches. They started building an arch bridge across Moab Canyon Wash and extended a road from Highway 450 to the monument headquarters. Building a road to ascend the cliffs on the north side of Moab Canyon required much heavy construction, including drilling, blasting, and removal of material. Progress was slow, in part because the equipment was old and in only fair or good condition, but primarily because the project was poorly organized. As a result, officials gave the rate of construction unsatisfactory marks.

A large number of boys left at the end of each enrollment period. By August 1941 fewer than fifty men remained, and reports indicate considerable laxity in camp records, reports, and command. Camp problems reached a climax on Wednesday, December 18, 1940, when an enrollee identified only as Griner instigated a strike with the assistance of a few others. The boys complained about working in bad weather, as they had to do on December 16. Blowing snow shut down any project work the following day, but when Wednesday dawned cloudy but much warmer, officials decided to put the boys back to work. They refused, instead staying in the barracks.

When asked to explain their actions, leaders and assistant leaders replied they had decided the weather was too bad and they would not work. All striking leaders and assistant leaders were demoted—a significant financial blow to them. They also lost their exemption from KP duty and the privilege of riding to and from work inside the truck cabs. Only one boy, an enrollee with the last name Alexander, declared his intention to work. In retaliation, several strikers beat him so seriously that he had to spend the next day and a half in the infirmary. Lieutenant Coffin took no disciplinary action, and reported only that the men remained in camp due to inclement weather. The park custodian believed he was afraid of the men and therefore would not challenge the strike leaders.

STONE BRIDGE UNDER CONSTRUCTION, ARCHES NATIONAL PARK, UTAH
—Courtesy National Park Service

At the same time, a vandal wearing CCC winter overshoes cut phone lines at various places, then dragged them away from the poles and left them on the ground. Some believed the vandalism— which occurred the night of December 19, a day after the boys refused to go to work—was an act of revenge against the project personnel. Repairing the damage was more costly and complex than if the culprit had simply cut the line. Superintendent Miller felt the army, whose jurisdiction the men were under at the time of the vandalism, should lead the investigation. Again, Lieutenant Coffin showed little interest, made no effort to

help identify the guilty party, and even refused to assist local law enforcement.

Arches's unusual administrative structure may have complicated the difficulties. While the monument was in the Ninth Corps area, it was supervised by the park service from Arizona, in the Eighth Corps area. The army camp commander was supposed to report discipline issues to headquarters immediately, but he did not.

Lt. L. R. Litman of the Dalton Wells Camp later found an army car just off the state highway about a mile south of the Dalton Wells Camp. Inside, he found Lieutenant Coffin's body with a bullet hole through his head and powder burns about his face. He appeared to have been dead about twelve hours. A coroner's inquest ruled death was by a self-inflicted gunshot wound from a Colt .45 automatic.

As if such tragedy were not enough, further construction delays came on May 18, 1941, when high wind and a severe sand storm heavily damaged camp buildings and equipment. Almost immediately, the men began a planting program to mitigate future wind storm damage. By the time of the June inspection, in the middle of an enrollment period, all jobs except the culvert project were shut down due to lack of enrollees.

The productivity of the camp remained disappointing, although by the spring of 1942, the crews had completed the custodian residence, worked on the road, excavated a reservoir, put in a water system and pipeline, maintained roads, done some fire prevention work, put in a sewage disposal system, and built a channel diversion on the Moab Wash. As camps began closing in 1942, the Arches Camp was chosen, along with the Chaco Canyon Camp in New Mexico, to be the first closed in the Eighth and Ninth Corps areas, based largely on negative inspection reports. A general clean-up of the campsite was ordered and the men began moving out May 30, 1942. All work was closed out as of May 31, 1942.

In 1939 when a CCC camp was requested for Arches, the top priority had been to construct the entrance road for a distance of at least three miles from headquarters to the top of Courthouse Towers. Admittedly, it was a difficult section because of steep grades and curved switchbacks, but locals were nonetheless disappointed when the CCC camp closed in 1942. Only one mile of the entrance road had been blasted and graded. The closing of the camp indefinitely deferred construction of a permanent road.

Nonetheless, the CCC had made other road-related contributions at Arches. For example, they completed a unique culvert across the Moab Canyon Wash, built to harmonize with the natural surroundings, and finished a graded route from there to the monument headquarters. The masonry headwalls of the culvert were constructed of locally quarried sandstone to complement and blend in with the reds, whites, and browns of the desert country. CCCers installed stone riprap upstream along one side of the wash to stabilize the banks and protect the culvert. Downstream they piled stone rubble to safeguard the abutment of the culvert. The headwalls remain today much as they were when originally constructed. The Moab Canyon Wash culvert, the headquarters area with buildings and a parking lot for twenty cars, and maintenance buildings were the completed testimonials to the accomplishments of the Arches CCC camp.

MESA VERDE NATIONAL PARK, COLORADO
In the midst of parks and monuments set aside for their distinctive landforms, Mesa Verde's geology played a different role in assuring its protection as a national park. For reasons that remain tantalizingly beyond knowing, ancient inhabitants saw deep alcoves in the region's sheer sandstone cliffs as ideal home sites. At first, they dug simple, shallow pit houses under the sheltering rock.

CLIFF PALACE, MESA VERDE NATIONAL PARK, COLORADO

Then, after centuries of living on the mesa tops, they returned to the alcoves. This time, they built multi-story structures of interconnected rooms, towers, and subterranean kivas. A century later, they simply left.

After decades of private plundering, the cliff dwellings of Mesa Verde—actually cliff structures, since some were meant for storage or ceremonial use, not habitation—finally came under federal protection in 1906. By then the damage from centuries of weathering, coupled with aggressive pot hunting and curious exploration had taken their toll. It would require decades of work to clean up and stabilize the structures, and control the flow of tourists to the sites.

Through the 1920s, development focused on the Chapin Mesa area—close to several major cliff dwellings—and on road access into the park. Superintendent Jesse Nusbaum (1921–31, 1936–39, 1942–46) spearheaded a comprehensive plan for the headquarters area including staff housing, administrative facilities, and a museum, all in the distinctive Modern Pueblo Revival style. He also set standards for an entrance road that would take advantage of views along the way and a mesa top road guiding visitors to various surface and cliff sites. Nusbaum was gone when the CCC came to Mesa Verde, but his vision for the park guided their work until his return in 1936.

The first CCC camp, NP-2, was set up in May 1933, midway between the northern entrance and Chapin Mesa, in Prater Canyon. Weeks of thunderstorms made living conditions miserable, so tents quickly gave way to two wood-frame barracks. Despite an auxiliary heating plant and solar-water-heating system for showers, the cold air that settled into the canyon at night made everyone miserable. The boys of Company 825 worked on conservation, insect control, and camp projects during their stay, and five months after their arrival, were transferred to Colorado National Monument.

Impressed with the CCCers' work, Nusbaum's successor as superintendent requested two permanent camps for the park. Both companies, 861 and 1843, briefly occupied the Prater Canyon Camp in 1934, but moved to permanent camps on Chapin Mesa by late fall. They worked separately for the most part, but enjoyed a friendly rivalry during their years of coexistence in the park, and morale remained high throughout their time at Mesa Verde. Company 1843 was initially designated as a drought relief unit (one of six for the state), but subsequently became a park service unit.

On July 9, 1933, fire broke out. Before it was contained two weeks later, it had spread across 4,400 acres. A fire crew of fifty boys from Company 861 helped fight the blaze on Wild Horse and Wickiup mesas, joined by early arrivals from Company 1843 a week and a half later. After the wildfire was under control, CCCers spent weeks cutting fire roads and cleaning up debris. In 1937, with enrollment declining, 1843 was disbanded, and its continuing enrollees transferred to 861.

Evidence of CCC projects abounds at Mesa Verde, from headquarters area buildings to roads and trails. Many of the boys became skilled stone cutters or masons during their stay in the park, while others learned the intricacies of Ancestral Puebloan pottery designs, or the persistent nature of tent caterpillars and porcupines.

CCCers built two of the staff homes in the headquarters area, using sandstone quarried in the park, and made renovations on those that had been built in the 1920s. One in particular had started out as a stone water tower. The boys remodeled it into a staff residence which was featured in a mystery set in the park many years later, *Ill Wind*, by Nevada Barr, who had worked in the park herself. They also built some of the stone hogans, traditional Navajo structures provided for park employees on the stabilization crew. The most evident example of their construction work, though, is the Chapin Mesa Archeological Museum. They added significantly to the original 1920s structure, including an entrance lobby, auditorium, exhibit halls, display cases, chairs and benches, and the dioramas.

Across the road from the museum, they built what is called the "round lot," a parking area ringed by dressed stone walls with built-in benches. More subtly, the stone curbing throughout the area is the handiwork of CCCers, as are countless stone-lined drainage features throughout the park. They built a new campground, complete with dressed stone fireplaces, tables, benches, and comfort stations. Some of the fireplaces remain in what is now a picnic area. In the park utility area, they erected several maintenance buildings and moved others to the area. Nearby,

TOWER HOUSE, MESA VERDE NATIONAL PARK, COLORADO, SERVES AS A RESIDENCE TODAY.
—Courtesy National Park Service

they built a total of nineteen housekeeping cabins for park staff, complete with stone foundations and chimneys and rough wood siding.

West of the headquarters area, overlooking Spruce Canyon, they built a stone amphitheater large enough to accommodate 250 people. Blocks in the upper tiers are four feet long and eighteen inches high. At the highest point in the park, they constructed a fire lookout tower which survives today, in spite of being threatened by the Bircher Fire in 2000. At the entrance to the park, they built and erected directional signs, added rooms to the staff residence, and built a parking area and checking stations.

The CCC boys did much to improve the efficiency, safety, and natural appearance of roads by

sloping banks, installing guard rails, and creating pull-outs and parking areas. They naturalized areas and controlled erosion by transplanting trees and shrubs, and adding other plants as needed. Catch basins, sandstone culvert headwalls, drop inlets, and retaining walls also attest to their skills and hard work. Along the Ruins Road first developed by Nusbaum, they created parking areas, pathways, and stone drainage structures.

Roads and trails received considerable attention from CCCers, who widened and graveled the headquarters loop road and Ruins Road. They built truck trails in Morefield Canyon and elsewhere for quick access in case of fire. Once the Knife Edge Road was closed, they helped obliterate it and plant new vegetation there. They built four miles of new trails, and did extensive work on paths and walks throughout the headquarters area.

The plantscape of the park was the focus of two eradication programs. In 1934 alone, CCCers removed 45,168 tent caterpillars from trees, doused them with kerosene, and burned them. Other boys went on the prowl for porcupines at night, and were authorized to kill them—contrary to park service policy—because of the damage they were inflicting on trees.

Far less visible, but equally important to the park, was the CCCers' work on water and sewer systems, underground electrical lines, water outlets, and drinking fountains. They repaired the impound reservoir, installed an automatic pump, and laid cast iron water mains to connect all buildings and fire hydrants.

Some CCCers even guided visitors through archaeological sites, while others focused on museum work. In 1934, boys used a weak hydrochloric acid solution to clean 3,786 pot sherds. Others restored broken pottery, retouched Ancestral Puebloan painting on pots, and made color or black and white sketches of pottery.

COLORADO NATIONAL MONUMENT, COLORADO

Building Rim Rock Drive was the highest priority at Colorado National Monument, and the primary focus for both permanent CCC camps in the monument. As Company 824 was moving to its permanent camp, the second company arrived from Mesa Verde National Park. The boys of

SIMPLE TOOLS AND MANPOWER LITERALLY MOVED MOUNTAINS.
—COURTESY NATIONAL PARK SERVICE

Company 825 had spent the summer battling insects and fire as well as working on roads in Southwest Colorado. They had come from a temporary camp in Mesa Verde, but still found conditions challenging in their new home.

The 227 men took up residence on Piñon Mesa, overlooking the town of Grand Junction, and almost immediately were quarantined by an outbreak of diphtheria. With only two oil lanterns to light their sleeping quarters, the boys would hurry through supper so they would have time to write a letter or get to bed while they had light enough to see. Roll call was at 6:20 a.m. by lantern light. It was difficult to find their own beds, let alone arrange them properly to pass inspection later in broad daylight.

PARK CUSTODIAN'S
RESIDENCE, CONSTRUCTED
OF NATIVE STONE, COLORADO
NATIONAL MONUMENT
—COURTESY NATIONAL PARK SERVICE

The boys built "ladders" for better access between work and what would become their permanent camp, NM-3-C, which was under construction at the mouth of Fruita Canyon. The series of wooden ladders climbed 400 feet from the canyon floor to the rim overhead. More than one enrollee experienced a considerable rush as he made the climb and recognized the potential danger from a long fall.

They finally moved to their permanent camp on June 2, 1934. Not only was it considered "the last word" in CCC camps, but the location at the mouth of Fruita Canyon gave them much easier access to Grand Junction. However, on August 5th a fire burned the company latrine, bathhouse, and electric light plant. A new latrine was hastily built and the light plant was replaced in a new, separate location, but for a time the boys were back to using lantern light.

Securing a reliable source of water was an issue at the camps from the outset. Water was piped a half mile up the mountainside from Fruita. An agreement between Fruita and the National Park Service granted 10 percent of the pipeline flow to the park service in return for replacing the original wooden water line with cast iron pipe. A $10 per year fee was dropped during the construction period. Drought in 1934 forced both camps to haul water from Grand Junction for cooking, washing, and drinking. Three trucks and nine drivers were assigned to haul water twenty-four hours a day. Needless to say, baths were at a premium. To present a further challenge, on July 13, 1934, floods from hard rains washed out two road fills and isolated Camp NP-3-C for several days, during which time supplies ran dangerously low. In April 1935, when Company 825 experienced a second quarantine for diphtheria, the boys must have wondered about their apparent string of bad luck.

Despite the challenges of their living arrangements the CCCers were quite productive. Each morning part of Company 825 was taken to work on the Fruita Canyon end of the Rim Rock Drive and the others were driven to Cold Shivers Point to work on the road from that end. At the west end, the road traversed a 5 percent grade up the side of Fruita Canyon. The route then closely followed the rim of the cliffs to Cold Shivers Point. They cut through two enormous cliffs of solid rock, creating two tunnels of 520 feet in combined length. There also were large fills along the way, with the largest containing about 73,000 cubic yards of material.

Another group of twenty enrollees worked on a nine-mile-long, eight-foot-high steel wire fence with three strands of barbed wire on top. A five-foot-wide trail was constructed on each side of the fence. It ran around the boundary of the monument on the Colorado River side (north) to keep wild buffalo in and stray livestock out. After the fence was completed, it was no longer necessary to feed wildlife on the monument, which partly proved the park service's contention that encroachment by domestic livestock had wiped out much of the native vegetation. In 1981, the buffalo were removed from the monument, but the fence remains today.

In addition to Rim Rock Drive, CCCers built a one-mile road around headquarters, a utility area, and a nine-foot woven wire fence with steel gates to protect government equipment and structures. They replaced old, temporary frame buildings with permanent stone structures, including an equipment storage garage and a fireproof oil storage area.

They built a custodian's residence and the monument's first public campground, including twenty-seven individual campsites equipped with fireplaces, tables, and benches, piped water, a modern comfort station, stone firewood bins, and garbage receptacles. For their own enjoyment, they built a baseball field, which required adding ten feet of fill to make it level.

With the onset of war, work came to a halt, and Rim Rock Drive remained incomplete. Even the custodian and rangers at the monument were called to active duty. In 1946 the remaining CCC buildings were removed and the areas of the camps were restored to their natural condition. Rim Rock Drive was finally finished in 1950, at which point Serpent's Trail was converted to a hiking trail.

The remote, harsh environment of Chaco Canyon was, more than 1,000 years ago, the epicenter of a far-reaching culture. In its heyday, Chaco sprouted numerous multi-storied village complexes. The best known, Pueblo Bonito (Beautiful Village), is a semi-circle of more than 600 rooms arranged around a large central plaza. In the three-acre masonry structure, which has three great kivas and thirty smaller ones, archaeologists have found evidence of trade with Central America and coastal communities. The builders of these "apartment buildings" had to travel to distant forests for the logs used in construction. In Chetro Ketl alone, more than 5,000 trees were used for roof and wall support, the largest a twenty-six-inch beam that was hand-hewed to a rectangular shape. Only slightly smaller than Pueblo Bonito, Chetro Ketl contains 500 rooms. Roads radiate from the area in every direction, suggesting its central role over the span of more than two centuries. An ancient stairway in the cliff behind Chetro Ketl, for example, reaches roadways leading to other complexes and outlying areas.

Like other Ancestral Puebloan sites in the Southwest, Chaco's structures suffered from centuries of exposure to the elements and a period of unregulated exploration and pilfering before they came under federal protection. The area was established as a national monument in 1907, then expanded and redesignated as a National Historical Park in 1980.

In the early years of New Deal programs, Chaco Canyon (as well as northwestern New Mexico's other national monument, Aztec Ruins) was served by the Civil Works Administration (CWA), Public Works Administration (PWA), and Works Progress Administration (WPA). Chetro Ketl received particular attention from these programs.

The short-lived CWA provided laborers for projects at Chaco Canyon and Aztec Ruins national monuments through the winter of 1933-1934. On November 24, 1933, 114 CWA employees began organizing research and doing archaeological reconnaissance, and miscellaneous drainage and erosion control work at Chaco Canyon. As part of archaeological reconnaissance, workers dug six test pits, each five feet out from the ruin walls at Chetro Ketl and six to eight feet long. They put in a surface drainage ditch north of the excavated rooms of Chetro Ketl, repaired the north wall, put in wall supports, and provided general protection from flood waters. At Pueblo Bonito, they did kiva repairs.

CWA workers also took the first step in building a much-needed fence to protect the monument from overgrazing by hauling a shipment of posts and wire sixty-five miles from the railroad line at Thoreau. In addition they did protection work on Kin Kletso and worked along the Chaco Arroyo. Their work at Chaco Canyon ended June 7, 1934.

Shortly thereafter, the Soil Conservation Service (SCS) began some erosion control work where the Chaco Wash was threatening important ruins and approach roads. Most of this work was done outside the monument itself. At the canyon the SCS installed a small amount of riprap and some small diversion dams, but could give only minimal assistance because of limited funding.

In the fall of 1935 the PWA, with an appropriation of $30,000, hired workers to construct a sheep-tight fence around the monument to eliminate grazing. In the meantime, the WPA was established in April 1935 to concentrate on such infrastructure improvements as roads, buildings, airports, dams, water projects, and sewage plants under federal grants to local and state governments as well as agencies and institutions such as universities.

Through its archaeology department, the University of New Mexico's field school at Chaco Canyon, the School of American Research, received a WPA grant for construction and repairs to hogans and other buildings used for archaeological research at Chetro Ketl. On September 21, 1935, nineteen WPA employees set up a work camp near the monument. Paul Reiter, an instructor of anthropology at the university, was appointed camp superintendent. The men, most of them from Albuquerque, began building six hogans to be used as student and staff dormitories. They also constructed a research facility, worked on restoration of Casa Rinconada, extended the walls of Chetro Ketl, and completed excavation of a small house.

Due to the remoteness of Chaco Canyon, telephone service did not reach the area until 1934. That made it difficult to recruit men with families for WPA work. They were reluctant to leave their homes to work at such an isolated location for 31¢ an hour. Because of the difficulty in hiring men willing to live in the WPA camp, six men from Blanco, who lived close enough to drive back and forth to work, were hired in 1938. That winter there were only five families camped at Chaco, although the camp was capable of furnishing quarters for more families if they would agree to bring their own stoves and stove pipes.

As early as 1934, National Park Service officials sought a summer CCC camp at Chaco Canyon for erosion control work, and construction of dams, fencing, and a road up the canyon to Wijiji. It would be three years before a CCC-Indian Division mobile camp would be established in the monument. Their work is discussed in Chapter Six.

In September 1938, the Southwest Monuments superintendent Frank Pinkley urgently requested that a regular 200-man CCC camp be assigned to the monument by the following April. Although the National Park Service director had approved a CCC camp for the twelfth enrollment period, it was subsequently cancelled for lack of funding. But in response to Pinkley's plea, several officials met on March 15, 1939, to determine a location for a CCC camp.

Construction of their camp near Fajada Butte was far from complete when, on August 29, 1939, after months of delays and setbacks, a 131-man crew from Virginia finally was put to work. Fifty men were assigned to erosion control work, four as guides and contact workers, four on a surveying crew, sixty-two on the approach road, six on overhead jobs, and the remainder on the boundary fence. Soon fifteen boys and a foreman were sent twenty-five miles east of Jemez Springs to cut 115 trees for telephone poles. Due to lack of machinery, the work on the approach road had to be done entirely by hand. Despite slow progress, the men eliminated the worst bumps from six miles of road.

Work on erosion control went well, even though the entire camp was handicapped by equipment that was either poor or non-existent. Most of the useful equipment was supplied by the Soil Conservation Service. Despite monthly reports saying morale was good, heavy turnover at the end of each enrollment period continued to plague the Chaco Camp.

Safety was a major concern from the time the camp received its first enrollees until it closed. Indeed, the Chaco Camp had a rather poor safety record and was encouraged from time to time to double its emphasis on safety. James Mulholland, a seventeen-year-old enrollee from Philadelphia, fell from a cliff and died. In September 1940 the camp had five accidents with a total of thirty-two man days lost—the worst report of any among the five camps and the mobile unit in their administrative area in twelve months. In fact, for the fiscal year July 1, 1939, to June 30, 1940, the other camps of the area together had five accidents with thirty-five man days lost, an amount equaled by the

Chaco Camp in September alone. On September 29, 1941, with diminishing enrollment and several camps at extremely low strength, officials decided to eliminate camps in Utah and New Mexico.

At Chaco, poor road conditions and distance had created problems, from inability to get equipment and supplies to safety hazards. After only twenty-seven often frustrating months of existence, the Chaco Canyon Camp was disbanded on November 17, 1941. Nonetheless, CCCers had constructed extensive earthen berms to slow or prevent erosion, planted 100,000 cottonwood, tamarisk, plum, and willow trees throughout the canyon, and improved many roads and trails. They had started building a road to the top of the cliff above Pueblo Bonito, but the project was abandoned after the camp closed.

AZTEC RUINS NATIONAL MONUMENT

On the bank of the Animas River in northwestern New Mexico lies a complex comparable to many at Chaco Canyon. The three-story structure, which had as many as 500 rooms, includes a great kiva that is more than forty feet across. The complex was excavated and the great kiva restored by Earl Morris, a leader in early southwestern archaeology who helped with federal acquisition of the ruins and establishment of the national monument in 1923.

The name Aztec stems from a misconception that builders of the structure were from the much later Central American civilization. The pueblo dates from approximately A.D. 1100, but was built over the span of about three decades. Located fifty-five miles north of Chaco Canyon, its architecture and artifacts suggest that its inhabitants blended Chacoan and Mesa Verdean cultures.

During the winter of 1933–34, local men from the Farmington area were hired through the CWA to work on an entrance road, a parking area, and general clean-up. In the same year a crew of local men was hired through the PWA to rebuild the Great Kiva under Morris's direction. Workers dismantled the walls and relaid the masonry, sometimes filling in with stones from excavated Ancestral Puebloan villages on the La Plata River north of Farmington. Most of the stone used in rebuilding the exterior of the walls, however, came from stockpiles stored during the original excavations of the structures. The rebuilt Great Kiva is now one of the main attractions of Aztec Ruins National Monument.

GRINDING STONES, AZTEC RUINS NATIONAL MONUMENT, NEW MEXICO

The proposal in 1934 for a CCC camp at Chaco Canyon included a side camp at Aztec for the purpose of planting trees. That was not approved, and Aztec did not receive its own CCC camp. However, starting in April 1935, fifteen to twenty boys and three supervisors travelled thirty-five miles each way from a state park camp in Durango, Colorado, to make improvements to the grounds around the ruins.

They graded, graveled, and landscaped a patio behind the administration building, built a foot bridge over a pond, installed a drinking fountain, and removed an old shed that leaned against the ruins as well as the garage Morris had set up in one room of the ruins. They also planted native trees and shrubs in the farm field, obliterated borrow pits, dumps, and exploration trenches, and hauled debris from these areas to fill arroyos. Additional work involved paving bottoms and banks of irrigation ditches, constructing a 175-foot-long adobe wall three to nine feet high around the residential area and installing cement seats for public use along the patio wall.

In November a crew from the Durango Camp returned to commence work on a second residence. When the adobe bricks the crew made froze and cracked, work on the residence ended. Instead, the men built a sewage tank and a cesspool with a connecting line. They also put in a cattle guard at the entrance gate and installed entrance, residential, and service gates.

Word came that the camp was to be terminated on January 1, 1936, and all the Aztec Ruins projects started by the Durango workers would have to be completed by then. The only alternative would be if Mesa Verde superintendent Paul Franke was willing to assign a spike camp from Mesa Verde, where half the men from the Durango Camp were to be transferred. Franke was instructed to request three trucks and a pickup from the Durango Camp for Aztec, so that Mesa Verde might simply inherit the trucks from the Durango Camp. The army had to concur with the plan for a side camp, and the park service pressed for approval. Although Major A. B. Helsley said he was "leaning over backwards to cooperate," he considered Aztec Ruins "too damn far from Mesa Verde for a side camp." As it turned out, the Durango State Park Camp continued until April 1936, and men continued to commute from there to Aztec.

By March 1936 all projects other than the ranger house were completed. The proposed residence would not be built until 1949. The pond over which the CCCers built the footbridge was filled and converted to lawn in 1961. The cattle guard also was removed, but the grove of trees they planted remains a popular picnic spot.

GUIDED TRIPS THROUGH RUINS ON THE HOUR FROM 8:00 AM TO 5:00 PM

25,000 ACRES OF MESA
& CANYON WILDERNESS,
40 MILES OF TRAILS
·
FREE CAMP GROUNDS
·
OVERNIGHT ACCOMODA-
TIONS . . AT THE NEW
FRIJOLES CANYON LODGE
48 MILES NORTHWEST
OF SANTA FE

BANDELIER
NATIONAL MONUMENT
U.S. DEPT. OF THE INTERIOR NATIONAL PARK SERVICE
A · NATIONAL · PARK · SERVICE · AREA
WPA·CCC

Chapter Six

With the granting of American citizenship to all American Indians in 1924, some federal officials resolved to move away from the government's paternalistic role in tribal affairs. Soon afterward, a survey report commissioned by the Department of the Interior issued a ringing indictment of federal policies related to Indians. It deemed health facilities "lacking," education "largely ineffective," boarding schools "grossly inadequate," and economic programs off the mark. In summary, the 1928 report said, Indian Service social and economic programs had weakened family life and activities by failing to "appreciate" the importance of family and communal life.

On the heels of such a critical report, and spurred by the federal push to increase local responsibility, Indian participation in the CCC took on a distinctly different character from the rest of the program.

Indians' economic plight had been characterized as "poor, even extremely poor" in the 1926–28 survey. Even so, cultural insensitivity and paternalism persisted through the 1930s, including in the CCC-Indian Division.

The Depression only deepened Native Americans' economic problems. At the same time, unemployment among Indians who had left the reservation caused many to return, further burdening reservation Indians who now had

221

to share their meager goods with returning relatives. By 1933 per capita Indian income in the Southwest dropped to $81 per year; Indians were on the brink of starvation, needing help and money.

Before creation of the Civilian Conservation Corps, the United States Congress had granted little funding to protect Indian forest- and rangelands. Native Americans lived under federal jurisdiction in twenty-three states, with the largest single population in Arizona. New Mexico was second, with 34,196 Indians tallied in the 1930 census, many of them Navajos who lived mainly on the Colorado Plateau in the northwestern corner of the state.

President Roosevelt approved an Indian CCC on April 27, 1933, and CCC director Robert Fechner announced it on April 30. The legislation authorized $5,875,000 for the first six-month period, to be used in establishing and running seventy-two Indian camps on thirty-three reservations, with the greatest number in the Southwest. New Mexico and Arizona would receive forty-three of the camps, twenty-five of which were assigned specifically to reservations. With the War Department resisting responsibility for operating camps on Indian reservations, the Bureau of Indian Affairs assumed responsibility for the program.

In the Southwest, district offices were located in Phoenix, Arizona, and Albuquerque, New Mexico, to provide technical advice to the reservations. Each office was headed by a production coordinator assisted by a staff of foresters and engineers to supply information on such issues as soil conservation and water development. An overall Indian CCC director, Jay B. Nash, was appointed to handle bureau administration while a general production supervisor, J. P. Kinney, checked on and approved projects.

One striking difference from the regular CCC was the paucity of record keeping. While most military and technical service administrators cranked out volumes of reports detailing every aspect of their work projects and camp life, there are few such records from the CCC-ID. There are even fewer oral histories from those who participated, in part because many were older at the time they served. By the time historians became interested in gathering information about their experiences it was too late; a greater proportion of CCC-ID participants had passed away or their memories had faded beyond retrieval.

Typically, CCC-ID camps were smaller than the normal 200-man limit of the regular CCC. When a new enrollment period began or a new camp was established, the reservation superintendent posted notice of openings and selected applicants who most needed jobs. Indian Service physicians administered medical exams and gave smallpox and typhoid vaccinations. Enrollees had to be free of communicable disease, but neither physical defect nor age automatically disqualified a prospective Indian enrollee. Because of this leniency, only 2 percent of applicants failed the medical exam. Handicapped people were accepted if they could do office work, help around the camp, or do other light chores. Most enrollees were under thirty years old, but some were in their sixties.

Day-to-day administration of the CCC-ID fell to the already overburdened white reservation superintendents who recruited, kept records, requisitioned supplies, and handled such issues as discipline, education, and recreation. A staff of specialists including teachers, doctors, nurses, home and agricultural extension experts, and foresters provided assistance in planning projects and developing educational and recreational programs. The bureau also relied heavily on expertise in the Department of Agriculture.

The CCC-ID admitted some white men who were reservation residents married to Indian women. Additionally, some outside whites were hired in supervisory positions initially because the reservations frequently had no one with the needed technical skill or experience as supervisors. Although many Indian enrollees were inexperienced and lacked the desired skills, Indian CCC workers received preference in the CCC-ID, and those who qualified were to be moved to higher-paying skilled jobs as soon as possible. Even so, white employees continued to dominate higher-paying foreman and project manager positions.

The Indian program had to meet most CCC regulations even though it was administered separately. For example, they had to consult the director for any expenditure on supplies exceeding $2,500. In cases of conflict, the rules of the parent CCC organization took precedence. Similar to the parent CCC, during the cold winter of 1936–37 many programs were reduced. In the Southwest, however, tribes continued to work on soil erosion projects through the winter months.

Three types of Indian Division camps developed. Boarding camps came closest to the regular CCC organization in that they housed single men at sites where work would last for at least a full summer. A minority of CCC-ID workers stayed in boarding camps. Temporary family camps were popular for short-duration projects or instances in which there were too few unmarried enrollees to justify a boarding camp for single men. A third arrangement allowed workers to live at home and commute to work.

CCC-ID enrollees in each type of living arrangement received $30 a month pay or $1.50 for a day's work for the twenty workdays per month allowed by the CCC. When weather conditions cancelled part or all of a day's work, workers made up the time on weekends or with longer workdays. Unlike in the regular CCC, Indian workers, received all of their paycheck, although there were attempts to withhold and deposit a portion of the pay into individual savings accounts. Enrollees' general objections to this practice brought it to an end.

Just as with regular CCC, assistant leaders, leaders, and skilled equipment operators were paid more and Indian CCC workers who lived in boarding camps received free quarters and food. Salaried supervisory employees paid their own room and board if they lived in a boarding camp. Married supervisors lived in separate quarters with their families. Those living in family camps or at home were paid a commuting allowance.

The bureau used its regular medical division for health services. Sick or injured enrollees reported to an agency doctor or a private doctor under contract to the bureau, while the seriously ill or injured were treated at Indian hospitals. Agency doctors also checked on camp sanitation and taught classes in first aid and safety. Quick treatment and detection, a balanced diet, outdoor work, and an emphasis on personal cleanliness contributed to enrollees' generally improved health.

As in the regular CCC, safety instruction played an important part in job training for the CCC-ID. At district training centers bilingual instructors taught first aid and safety as well as classes in fighting forest fires. The Indian CCC

averaged four to six accidents per month per thousand men, about the same as the regular CCC. The most common causes of accidents were improper use of hand tools, falls, falling trees, and truck collisions—the last two also responsible for most fatal accidents. At various times Indian CCC enrollees who were trained in first aid saved people from bleeding to death or assisted in incidents of snakebites and drowning.

CCC-ID CAMPS

Boarding camps housed the men in square army tents used for regular CCC spike camps. Enrollees installed wooden floors and boarded up the sides to about four feet in height, and sometimes built rough shacks made of readily available or surplus materials. Boarding camps had an office, a combination kitchen and dining hall, a meat storage area, shower house, outdoor toilet, and a warehouse for supplies and tools. There was also a designated place for parking and repairing trucks and motorized equipment.

In a few cases where projects lasted beyond a single summer, permanent bunkhouses were built. At these facilities, enrollees built separate recreation facilities that offered books, magazines, a radio, and tables for playing cards or other games. Boarding camps also provided a canteen run by enrollees where the men could purchase candy and other personal items. As at regular CCC camps, the small profits were used to buy recreational or educational equipment.

Most often the first purchase was a projector for weekly movies that were highly popular with Indian enrollees and their families, who paid a small admission.

In New Mexico many Navajos had exhausted their credit at the trading posts where they purchased food and necessities. Consequently, many suffered from malnutrition and showed signs of scurvy and rickets. Some enrollees in 1933 collapsed when put to work, so director Nash ordered camp managers to provide them with a special diet of brown rice, whole wheat bread, tomatoes, and dried fruit. For many Navajos, the CCC experience came to mean the difference between starvation rations and a more comfortable existence.

Food service in the dining hall was cafeteria style. Supplies came from the regular agency warehouses or wholesalers, including purchases from Indian farmers and ranchers. Navajo camps served locally purchased goat meat two or three times a day in response to enrollees' preference. Food costs ran about 16.5¢ per meal, which allowed for only simple fare that usually included meat, vegetables, fruit, and milk. This simple food and the vigorous outdoor labor, however, put weight on most Indian enrollees.

A camp manager, later called a camp assistant, was in charge of the men from the time they returned to the camp from work until they boarded trucks for the next day's work. He was also the camp record keeper, with major responsibilities but little authority. The camp assistant might coax enrollees, or even yell at them, but he could not use harsh discipline. The best results usually came from keeping men constantly occupied with recreation, education, or camp improvement projects. Off-duty classes were the responsibility of camp assistants, while foremen and production officials often taught the classes.

The camp routine was essentially the same as in regular CCC camps. Men made their own beds, swept and mopped the barracks, built fires, and took care of their personal belongings. The day began with reveille at 6 a.m., with the first half hour devoted to cleaning quarters and washing up before breakfast. After breakfast, enrollees policed the camp area for trash and at 7 a.m. began loading tools on the truck and then left for the day's work. At noon the kitchen force brought a hot lunch and the work crew broke for an hour to eat and relax. By 5 p.m. the men reported back to camp and showered before eating supper at 6 p.m. Enrollees were then on their own to participate in sports, read, write letters, or play games. Lights went out at 9:30 or 10 p.m.

Men were allowed to leave camp during off-duty time and failure to report back before lights-out usually caused no problem so long as the enrollee reported for work the next morning. Since most CCC-ID boarding camps were remote, leaving camp during the week usually was impossible. On weekends most enrollees went home or visited nearby towns, with camp trucks often providing the transportation.

The most common discipline problems usually involved refusal to work, bringing liquor to camp, drinking, stealing, and interpersonal disputes. Camp assistants were authorized to deal with the problems but often they turned to tribal judges or allowed enrollees to organize camp courts. Louis Schroeder, who helped organize all units in New Mexico in 1933, reported that most discipline problems stemmed from weekend drinking when the men were away from camp. Strict discipline was difficult because the absence of contracts or definite periods of enlistment in the Indian CCC meant that a disgruntled enrollee could draw his pay and leave.

CCC-ID director Nash concentrated his efforts on camp organization in New Mexico and Arizona. A party of social workers, teachers, and students travelled with Nash to perform cooking and sewing demonstrations, make clothing for workers' children, and organize recreation programs. Over time, the Navajos became amused and perplexed by the eastern experts. Navajos had joined the CCC for the work and wages, not to sit and listen to incomprehensible discourses on camp sanitation. They had survived all their lives without special attention to sanitation or organized recreation and they saw no reason to learn about unseen germs and tent ventilation. When CCC officials promised baseball equipment, a common response was, "We can't eat baseball bats. When we finish work we are tired and do not want to play. The Indian knows how to play his own games when he wishes to play them." Over time the camps came to more generally fit tribal culture and local conditions.

The camps contributed to enrollees' character, work skills, recreational activities, and economic progress. Boarding camp enrollees received better care and supervision than Indian CCCers who lived at home or were part of mobile units. Camp life had more potential to provide them with such self-improvement skills as working on a schedule, taking orders, and earning wages. Enrollees who were at first awed by bulldozers, cranes, jackhammers, and other machinery learned to operate them skillfully. Some became proficient in telephone work, welding, and other skills useful for off-reservation work.

CCC-ID EDUCATION

The 1937 Civilian Conservation Corps legislation marked a turning point for the CCC-ID, placing education on a more systematic and mandatory basis. With its mandate for ten hours of training per week per enrollee, educational activities gained more emphasis. Besides education, welfare programs sought out needy enrollees and provided more recreational opportunities. Bureau vocational school projects also related to CCC work, showing enrollees how particular projects would benefit their tribe.

Robert M. Patterson was the first CCC-ID education director. Enrollee education remained flexible and fitted to tribal customs and economic needs, with the majority of training aimed at younger and more capable enrollees. Superintendents were expected to establish a budget for education, but many had no idea what to do with education funds. Some wanted to buy movie projectors but the Washington office declined their requests. Others treated the education money as a slush fund for incidental camp expenses. Many superintendents offered excuses for weak educational programs. The use of so many fly camps, for example, seemed a major obstacle to Indian education. They cited the scattered nature of the work, the generally small work crews, absence of permanent boarding camps, poor educational backgrounds of the enrollees, and high turnover among workers.

Claude C. Cornwall, who had graduated from the University of Utah's department of engineering, took over the education program and made it mandatory for every reservation with CCC-ID projects. Still the workers spent, on average, less than four hours per week in classes, although some enrollees did begin to take correspondence courses. Many of the subjects taught concentrated on such practical things as tractor operation, blasting techniques, telephone and radio communications, first aid, and life saving. Ten Native Americans were sent to foremanship courses in Washington, D. C., then returned to offer weekend seminars for enrollees in the field.

Increased training provided an avenue for younger and more ambitious Indians to advance. Youths with a particular aptitude for mechanics were placed in CCC shops for training and many qualified for jobs with the BIA or in the private sector. By 1941 Navajo enrollees were receiving nearly nine hours of training per week, double the overall average of CCC-ID.

CCC-ID MOBILE CAMPS AND AT-HOME PROGRAMS

Married enrollees often lived in mobile camps as they worked on water development, soil erosion, and other projects, frequently residing near the work site in shacks or tents with their families. Responsibility for enrollees in married mobile camps usually extended only to the work day. When a mobile-force work project was finished, the force generally broke up or moved to a new project at a new location.

In addition to their pay, workers residing in family or mobile camps or living at home received a $12-per-month commuting allowance, which was raised to $15 in 1935, which was less than half the cost of boarding and feeding an enrollee in a boarding camp.

Due to a surplus of eager, destitute Navajo applicants, the CCC-ID sometimes staggered employment among the enrollees who lived at home, with separate crews alternating in two-week intervals. While the arrangement offered CCC wages to more enrollees, each man received only half the usual pay. The scheme did benefit enrollees who used their two weeks off each month to care for a farm or livestock.

When enrollees, whether married or unmarried, lived at home the workers would gather each morning at pick-up points and ride to their work on Indian CCC trucks. Even so, they received the same commuting allowance as mobile camp enrollees to cover the cost of their getting from home to the pick-up point each day. Living at home was common in the Indian CCC. It was difficult to develop off-duty programs for the live-at-home enrollees. They had no devotion to the Indian CCC and generally believed their responsibilities extended only to the work day itself.

Having more money, particularly since none of their pay was saved or sent to family, caused social problems for some CCC-ID enrollees. Open gambling such as craps, blackjack, and poker were common in towns adjoining the reservation, as was drinking. The Bureau of Indian Affairs (BIA) hired ten special-deputy officers to assist in enforcement of liquor laws, but there was still a rapid increase in alcohol consumption both on and off the reservation. Special officers worked at night to find and arrest enrollees who were drunk, then try to learn from them where they obtained the liquor, but attempts to dry up the sources generally failed. In Gallup, bootleggers who sold to Indians were generally protected, even by the local police. The BIA never was able to solve these problems.

PROJECTS

A wide variety of projects were undertaken, most of them related to conservation of water, soil, and forests. Altogether there were 126 different types of activities, including, for example, archaeological stabilization at Chaco Canyon and other southwestern monuments.

Each proposed new activity was judged by CCC director Fechner, who often had a difference of opinion with CCC-ID officials about what constituted valid projects. Fechner's approval never came easily for any innovation. According to his critics, he seemed to reject every new proposal out of hand and then think of reasons to justify his rejection. Typically officials waited a year, then resubmitted the same proposals in new ways. Despite his reluctance, Fechner approved several new activities for CCC-ID that he had strongly rejected just a year earlier. A more lenient policy on water development, for example, led to well drilling and the installation of windmills, pumps, and storage tanks.

In the summer of 1933, with the entire CCC program gearing up at the same time, confusion surrounded efforts to begin local conservation projects. There was no guiding precedent and channels to Washington were in chaos because of urgent requests for help and information. The Bureau of Indian Affairs, for example, had trouble securing even harnesses, horse-drawn scrapers, and small hand tools, not to mention heavy machinery. Programs had to be revised because of delays caused by waiting for equipment. Nevertheless, by September 1933 the bureau had enrolled 13,000 of its national quota of 14,400 enrollees.

CCC ENROLLEES GATHERING ADOBE FOR RESURFACING THE PLAZA AT PUEBLO BONITO, CHACO CANYON NATIONAL MONUMENT, NOW CALLED CHACO CULTURE NATIONAL HISTORICAL PARK, NEW MEXICO —COURTESY WESTERN ARCHAEOLOGICAL AND CONSERVATION CENTER

Initially, some of the work was of poor quality. Many early truck trails had to be rebuilt because of slides or inadequate culverts and drainage. Dams lacked storage capacity and spillways were often too small to handle overflows. As a result, some of the first dams the Indian CCC built failed. Over time, much of the hand and horse labor was supplanted by the use of heavy equipment. The CCC-ID bought and rented new equipment and also obtained used equipment from the army and the regular CCC. Whenever a camp was closed, Fechner made the equipment of the defunct unit available to nearby CCC camps, provided officials were willing to pay for moving it.

CCC-ID officials established four leader camps for 222 enrollees in New Mexico and at Cameron, Arizona. Instruction covered a wide variety of subjects, including erosion control, range improvement, telephone line construction, surveying, water development, reforestation, and camp management. Camp training lasted ten weeks with actual production work taking up to 75 percent of the time and classroom studies 25 percent.

Because local superintendents selected the participants, there was a sizable disparity in age, educational background, ability, and interest among the men selected. Older men had trouble comprehending and remembering instruction. Some participants came believing they could obtain a college degree in ten weeks and others thought they would be allowed to specialize in one area of study. Ten weeks also proved insufficient for effectively training leaders, particularly in an egalitarian culture like that of the Navajo. Leader training proved somewhat impractical because, as with the regular CCC, there was a tendency for the more capable to become self-employed, take jobs in other relief programs that paid more, or enter private industry.

Separate agreements between the Bureau of Indian Affairs and both the forest service and the park service provided for joint firefighting and CCC-ID enrollees helped fight fires on both national forests and national parks. During fire season the camp assistant had the authority to keep some of the men in camp over weekends for detecting and fighting fires.

Drought conditions helped focus Indian CCC attention on water development and range improvement. Enrollees built reservoirs and located wet ground as an indicator of potential springs, then dug down to release water to be piped into stock tanks. While spring development remained an important component of Indian CCC work, early projects also created charcos, or ponds, for holding water from summer rains. These were located in shallow washes where enrollees sometimes dug ditches above the dams to divert more water into the ponds. In larger washes, dirt embankments could not hold heavier flood waters. Even in shallow washes many dams were washed out by summer cloudbursts. Indian CCC workers also built masonry dams in mountainous areas, anchoring them to solid-rock sides and floors of narrow canyons. Pipes ran through the embankment to stock tanks below.

Enrollees also cut willow branches and stuck them in moist soil along arroyos in the spring so that they would take root and slow water flow. Cholla cactus was planted in shallow arroyos for the same reason. Shrubs, cactus, and small check dams made of earth and brush were used to divert water from washes onto more level areas, spreading it out and thus giving it more opportunity to soak into the soil and restore vegetation.

CCC funds also paid for drilling and improving wells. In New Mexico the CCC sometimes hired private contractors to drill the wells, but at other times crews did the drilling with rigs purchased with CCC funds. Wells reached down

500 to 1,500 feet, too deep for hand pumping; windmills or electric motors installed by CCCers were used to pump water into large steel tanks for storage. CCC crews also improved many existing wells by cleaning them and putting in new casings.

On the Kaibab Paiute Indian Reservation in northwestern Arizona, the CCC provided $2,000 to replace a pipeline. The original, installed in 1926, was "wasteful" and had "served its period of usefulness," according to the project proposal. The new water line would not only supply homes, but also provide enough water for "a few acres of subsistence gardens." Indian Division CCCers worked on the pipeline from late 1940 into 1941.

UINTAH–OURAY RESERVATION, UTAH

In 1933, Utah's Indian enrollment quota was two hundred. Despite how difficult the Depression was for them, Utah seldom filled its Indian enrollment quota, in part because some candidates did not meet all three criteria: need, physical strength to do the work, and freedom from contagious disease. The CCC provided employment for an average of about one hundred Indian men each year, almost all of whom were Utes on the Uintah–Ouray Reservation, the only reservation in Utah that lay entirely within the state. In 1939 approximately one-fourth of Utah's Ute Indians were enrolled in the corps. By 1942, 746 Utah Indians had served in the CCC-Indian Division on reservation conservation projects.

Utah had two authorized CCC-ID camps, both on the Uintah–Ouray Reservation. The Ute Tribal Council helped select the projects, many of which focused on erosion control in the reservation's arid regions. Other activities included building catch-dams for watering livestock, constructing roads and fire trails, and stringing telephone lines. Fence construction proved most difficult.

Of the thirty miles of fence line built, only four miles could be reached by truck. For twenty-six miles the wire, posts, staples, and other supplies had to be packed in by horseback. Posthole diggers proved worthless in the rocky soil, so the men had to dig holes by hand. Another CCC-ID project in Utah involved raising hay for reservation livestock.

Additionally, Indians in southern Utah, working under direction of subagent Parwin E. Church, endeavored to improve grazing conditions on the Kaibab Paiute Indian Reservation in northern Arizona. They built fences, troughs, springs, and reservoirs, and surveyed for a proposed road across the reservation. A North Dakota company composed mostly of Indians also occupied a regular CCC camp in southern Utah. Typically, Utah Indian enrollees lived at home and worked on CCC projects part time or travelled with their families to work on projects on their own reservation.

NAVAJO RESERVATION, FOUR CORNERS REGION

No Indians were more favorably inclined to join the CCC than the destitute Navajos. Their numerous willing enrollees prompted the CCC-ID to establish its first boarding camp for young single men from the Navajo Reservation. They came in droves to join or hear the program explained. While Navajos filled their quotas, some other tribes did not meet half their allotted positions. In those instances, the Bureau of Indian Affairs would transfer funds to other agencies or bring in additional members of needy and willing tribes.

The Navajo Reservation covered thirteen million acres in northeast Arizona, northwest New Mexico, and a narrow strip of southeast Utah. Rather than having a central headquarters, Navajos had six autonomous agencies: one each at Fort Defiance, Tuba City, Leupp, and Keams Canyon in Arizona; and at Shiprock and Crownpoint in New Mexico. The Keams Canyon agency also served Hopis, whose tribal lands were surrounded by the Navajo Reservation. Each agency had its own independent, non-Indian superintendent. By the mid-1930s, the Bureau of Indian Affairs consolidated Navajo government into one central unit.

Federal officials hoped that they could use the CCC to improve range management on the reservation, but controversial administrative decisions inextricably linked the CCC-ID with efforts to move the Navajos away from their traditionally pastoral economy. Six months after creation of the CCC-ID, John Collier took over as commissioner of Indian Affairs, intent on reducing the number of sheep, goats, and horses on the reservation. In exchange for giving up 150,000 head of sheep and goats, Collier promised, the Navajos would gain additional reservation land in New Mexico, where individual allotments had created a checkerboard reservation. However, Anglo ranchers and sheepherders resisted the loss of their grazing land and Collier was unable to keep his end of the deal. The consequences of that broken promise and the Navajos' loss of their animals would foster deep resentment.

The root cause of land management problems on their reservation extended back to the 1864–68 confinement of Navajos at Bosque Redondo in southern New Mexico. Following the failed attempt at converting them to concentrated agriculture in an inhospitable environment, they were allowed to return to their native lands. Before their captivity at Bosque Redondo, Navajos had grown corn, fruit, and other crops on the Colorado Plateau, while also hunting and raising livestock as crucial hedges against crop failure in the harsh environment. However, they returned to a diminished territory that proved far more confining than their traditional lands had been. The Navajos would have to change their ways—give up raiding neighboring tribes and settlements for horses and livestock, of course—and concentrate on growing what crops and livestock they could on their own land. But as their population increased, so did their herds.

By the 1930s, sheep, goats, and horses had grown so plentiful that overgrazing had stripped the land of vegetation. With no grasses to hold the soil, powerful summer cloudbursts eroded deep gullies across the landscape, stripping away the soil and with it, both the wild game they'd once hunted and the ability to grow crops. By all accounts, their situation was desperate. The animals could not survive on the landscape, and the Navajos believed they could not survive without them.

In 1933, a 47,000-acre tract north of Gallup known as Mexican Springs was chosen as a demonstration area because of the many examples of erosion it contained. CCCers fenced the land and removed all the animals. Enrollees spent a month at the demonstration area learning about conservation practices, then returned to their homes as "range conservation missionaries." Some remained longer to be trained as "conservation directors" for their communities. The initial goal was to reduce reservation sheep herds by 100,000 head, in the belief that improved management of the remaining herds would offset loss of income from the reduction.

Things didn't go as planned. Indians sold only their culls. When the biggest herders refused to sell a larger portion of their sheep, the bureau backed off, conceding that everyone would take only a 10 percent reduction. However, the policy

COPY   PART I

                                            Sanders,
                                            Arizona

Mr. E. R. Fryer
    Window Rock, Arizona.

Dear sir:
    We had a excess of sheep when we had a permit of Grazing 10 sheep units of livestock on Navajo Reservation. But now I want to know some reasons about.
    We can't make a living of only 5 or ten sheep, because I had four children and my wife. Thats a large family for only few sheep.
    That will do no good. We all want more sheep than ten.
    Honestly dear.

                    PART II

    Please, we are pleasing you very much.
    We might be hungry to death this winter, cause we kill sheep for mutton in every week. So that only 10 sheep won't last long to winter. We want to 100 sheeps.
    Please I used to work at Fort Wingate job but the roofs fall on me and hurt me badly so I can't work again. Now please let us have 100 hundred sheep on our Grazing Permit. The notice of Trespass was given to us by DeGraftenried. We don't want to be relief by governer. Cause we are shame of that kind.
    I can't stop pleasing 'til you give me a permit of 100 sheep.

                    PART III

    If you write to me again back I and my family will go over there and please you or hug you to give us 100 hundred sheep.
    If you do what we told you to do we would appreciate it and welcome for it.
    We were scarce when we got on 10 sheep unit.
    We think only those people who don't have children can have only 10 sheep. But I had lots of children.
    Dearest my agent Please aid me about this.
    Don't delay to do this friend. Dearest esteem my friend
    Don't you hesitate this
    Reply this letter Friend.
    My dear.

                    PART IV

Dear sir: I write for my dad
                What he said.
    I wish the same too and all my sister and brother. Please my agent. We can't make a living like white peoples 'cause we cant afford it.
                            Write by Isabella Lewis
            Talking message - from Tom Lewis

My grazing permit No. 7298
                            Reply to Isabella Lewis, Sanders, Arizona

THE LIVESTOCK REDUCTION PROGRAM WAS A HARDSHIP FOR INDIAN FAMILIES.
—COURTESY CENTER OF SOUTHWEST STUDIES, FORT LEWIS COLLEGE

WATER CONSERVATION WAS A MAJOR FOCUS OF CCC WORK ON INDIAN RESERVATIONS. —COURTESY CENTER OF SOUTHWEST STUDIES, FORT LEWIS COLLEGE

change imposed a greater hardship on families with small, subsistence herds. As a result, the reduction program was largely unsuccessful and antagonized many Navajos. It was becoming impossible to keep CCC operations separate from the strong influence of the Soil Erosion Service, which oversaw range improvement programs on the reservation and had put 500 enrollees to work under their supervisors. Their projects focused on erosion control, reseeding, and water conservation.

In 1934, when the Soil Erosion Service was transferred from the Department of Interior to Agriculture and renamed the Soil Conservation Service, an official of the SCS was placed in charge of land management at Window Rock. He controlled all soil erosion work, water development, irrigation, and range management, as well as road work. SCS findings were used to divide the entire Navajo Reservation into eighteen grazing districts and Navajo Services conducted an intensive study of each area to determine grazing capacity and conservation needs. Many Navajos felt the agency's experts were arrogant and had no understanding of Indians. They feared further forced sales of livestock and accused the SCS men of caring more for the land than for the welfare of the Navajos.

In March 1936, Collier appointed E. Reeseman Fryer as the general Navajo superintendent. Fryer had worked as a foreman on the Mexican Springs project, overseeing construction of erosion control structures. Although he introduced alternative industries to the reservation, including a meat canning operation, a flour mill, a sawmill, an arts and crafts guild, and irrigation works, his association with livestock reduction overshadowed his contributions. Fryer asked for lump sum funding and began revising CCC projects, sometimes not awaiting approval from the Washington office. As CCC crews completed work in one district, Fryer moved them to another area of the reservation. He established base camps in districts under development to serve as administrative headquarters. Most of the enrollees now lived in small temporary installations or fly camps near the project and cooked their own meals, which they preferred to boarding arrangements.

The 1937 act extending the CCC prohibited future hiring of whites in the CCC-Indian Division. Meanwhile, a delegation of Navajos appeared before a Senate subcommittee on Indian Affairs in June to lodge bitter complaints against Collier and Fryer. Their main grievance was with grazing regulations and herd reductions, but they also accused Fryer of hiring only Indians who favored the bureau and giving too many jobs to whites. Collier said whites—all of them former traders—held only 10 percent of the positions in Navajo Services, which had assumed control of all conservation and range management programs in 1936.

Between 1936 and 1940, CCC-ID enrollees were given the task of rounding up half-wild horses from the open range. Navajos were reluctant to part with the horses even though they trampled grass, drank water, broke up salt blocks, and chased other livestock away from water. For people who measured their standing among peers by the number of horses they owned—no matter how starved they were—these round-ups were a devastating blow. C. E. Faris, John Collier's personal representative to the Navajo, assigned CCC crews to round up the horses and drive them to sales pens. To secure support for the herd reduction program, Indians were allowed to add five sheep to their grazing load for every horse captured and sold. By 1940 Indian CCC crews had removed 10,000 horses from the reservation. Overall, from 1933 to 1941, livestock numbers were reduced from a high of 1.35 million to 830,000.

CANYON DE CHELLY NATIONAL MONUMENT

There was one noteworthy exception to the grazing rights turmoil that afflicted Navajo CCC projects. Within the windswept desert of northeastern Arizona lies a sheer-walled canyon oasis known as Canyon de Chelly. It is one of a few National Park Service units that lie wholly within Navajo tribal lands. Several Navajo families live in the canyon during the growing season, raising a variety of crops and fruit trees. In the winter, the canyon is devoid of residents, but still dotted with the structures and rock art that reflect many centuries of occupation dating back to Ancestral Puebloan times.

The monument, managed by the National Park Service in partnership with the Navajo Nation, was established April 1, 1931, and enlarged to 83,840 acres in 1933. When Canyon de Chelly became a national monument, discussion focused on scientific development, opportunities for educational and scientific exhibits, and the need for repairs and minimal restoration of structures in the canyon. From the beginning it was agreed that Navajos would continue to occupy the canyon, and access

OVERGRAZING TOOK ITS TOLL ON LIVESTOCK AND THE LAND. —COURTESY CENTER OF SOUTHWEST STUDIES, FORT LEWIS COLLEGE

would be limited to avoid overrunning it. A museum and quarters for a custodian were needed near the entrance in order to control traffic.

In 1932, archaeologist Earl A. Morris did some necessary stabilization at Mummy Cave. The Carnegie Institute supplied transportation and the park service furnished $400 to cover materials, supplies, and salaries for workers. They stabilized the tower wall, built and bonded corners of the tower, and made ceiling repairs. Ironically, Morris's crew did not include any Navajos, even though they were becoming skilled in stabilization work elsewhere on the plateau.

In August 1934, with the appointment of Robert Budlong as the first custodian at Canyon de Chelly, the park service was ready to begin other development and protection work. Federal officials wanted rim roads and proper trails to various ruins. Since the BIA was responsible for the CCC program within Indian reservations, it was agreed that Navajo CCC workers would be employed on all road and trail construction. In July 1934 thirty-three Navajos from the CCC-ID began construction of a canyon rim drive opposite White House Ruin, supervised by a white foreman. The road was to include a lookout point as well as a trail from the rim to the canyon floor.

The National Park Service was eager to maintain Canyon de Chelly in unaltered condition while also providing safe and attractive accommodations for the visiting public. With $6,000 from an erosion control project, Indian

CCC laborers began work on the 4,085-foot-long White House Trail, supervised by a park service engineer. Each year Indian CCC enrollees did further work on roads leading to Canyon de Chelly as well as roads and trails within the monument. Visitation remained low at the monument, partly because of "bad roads." So during 1940 and 1941 CCCers worked on a roadway from Twin Trails to Mummy Cave, as well as other rim roads, the White House Trail, and others.

Cozy McSparon, who owned the Thunderbird Ranch, held an exclusive park service permit to operate a hotel, a camp, and transportation services to take visitors into Canyon de Chelly. He asked the park service to build new concessionaire structures for him. His request was denied because the monument had no regular Civilian Conservation Corps camp, nor did the park service and CCC contemplate establishing one.

All CCC work at Canyon de Chelly continued to be done by Civilian Conservation Corps–Indian Division employees. In addition to road and trail work and erosion protection, they made repairs at Antelope and White House and built a guard wall at the first lookout on the south rim. Navajos agreed to relinquish grazing rights in the canyon for three years as a means of restoring vegetation on the valley floor.

The park service also allowed the CCC-ID to undertake projects that went against park service regulations, such as poisoning rodents and grasshoppers, and Navajos were allowed to continue introducing non-native trees and plants within the monument. Park officials did not want to interfere with Indian life in the canyon, and they took the position that the agency was there only to protect the ruins and guide visitors. The Indians were to continue handling their own farm and stock operations, making decisions without park service interference.

In a similar vein of cooperation, the park service and the Bureau of Indian Affairs worked out an agreement to assist each other on fire prevention and suppression. Park service employees would assist with fire look-out and suppression on Indian lands and the men of the Indian Civilian Conservation Corps would assist the National Park Service with fires on national park service lands.

NAVAJO NATIONAL MONUMENT, ARIZONA

One of the most remote national monuments on the plateau, Navajo National Monument was, for nearly four decades, the neglected step-child of the National Park Service. Even the first custodian, John Wetherill, lived miles from the three small units that comprised the monument.

Navajo National Monument was set aside in 1909, sight unseen, by bureaucrats in Washington, D. C., to protect three Ancestral Puebloan cliff structures: Betatakin, Keet Seel, and Inscription House. Surrounded by the Navajo Reservation, and separated from one another by as much as forty miles, the three units were virtually impossible to protect, despite the provisions of the 1906 Antiquities Act. And with no usable roads leading to them, visitation was limited to rival archaeologists, pothunters, and a few others.

Even with the appointment of Frank "Boss" Pinkley—a strong proponent of protecting the region's antiquities—as superintendent of southwestern monuments in 1924, Navajo National Monument received scant attention. His headquarters at Casa Grande National Monument in southern Arizona were simply too far away.

Discussion of the need to expand the Navajo Reservation raised hope among some National Park Service officials that perhaps their agency's role could be expanded in the region. They could create a Navajo National Park that both

NATURAL RESOURCES CONSERVATION SERVICE

(formerly Soil Conservation Service)

Motto:
Helping People Help the Land

protected ancient structures and offered a living cultural park. Such a park, they argued, could assure the preservation of the Navajos' traditional way of life.

It was a dream that evaporated in the desert winds. However, Navajo National Monument did, finally, get noticed. A Civil Works Administration crew stabilized rooms at Keet Seel in 1933–34. With the demise of the program, the monument again fell to the bottom of the list. Not until a permanent park ranger, James W. Brewer, Jr., was assigned in 1938 did it capture enough attention to receive help. The following year, a CCC-ID crew was assigned to build a home for Brewer and his wife on a promontory known as Tsegi Point. The cozy, two-room stone and wood structure became both office and residence for the couple. Sallie Brewer pronounced it "beautiful," despite their isolation.

CHACO CULTURE NATIONAL HISTORICAL PARK, NEW MEXICO

In July 1937, the National Park Service appointed an engineer, Robert Harris, to establish an Indian CCC mobile unit to work on stabilizing ruins at Chaco Canyon. Three months later, Harris left to attend school, and R. Gordon Vivian assumed responsibility for supervising the unit. Focusing first on Pueblo Bonito, where there was immediate danger of walls collapsing, they removed earthen fill to dry out wet spots in walls and floors. They drained the plaza and sealed the floor with an impervious layer above the original plaza floor level.

Stabilization also was necessary at Wijiji ruins, where the high walls were in danger of falling. The SCS, in cooperation with the National Park Service, employed rodent-control measures to counteract damage to erosion control dikes and structures that had been installed years earlier. The work of the mobile unit at Chaco went well, although a shortage of funds for materials necessitated use of the Chaco Antiquities account, a fund normally used for surveying and preserving antiquities, not materials.

Hoping to complete the plaza drainage project before winter set in, Vivian asked the BIA to increase production and efficiency by doubling the size of the work crew. The important work of wall support, he contended, could only go forward with extra workers. No sooner had an additional detail of twenty-five enrollees arrived from Bandelier National Monument than they went on strike against the hard work, unsatisfactory food, and isolation of the mobile camp. They were charged with going AWOL and denied a meal, after which they returned to work but accomplished very little. After the strike was reported, district headquarters ordered them to return to Bandelier. Nonetheless, the work of the CCC-ID mobile stabilization unit laid the groundwork for a National Park Service mobile stabilization crew staffed by Navajos in later years.

AZTEC RUINS NATIONAL MONUMENT, NEW MEXICO

AZTEC RUINS NATIONAL MONUMENT, NEW MEXICO

In 1937 Aztec National Monument superintendent Thomas C. Miller received $100 to mend unstable walls, reroute drainage around Kiva E, and waterproof roofs. At this time the park service began approaching repair of ruins more systematically. Stabilization involved strengthening architectural remnants as inconspicuously as possible rather than reconstructing them. An agreement for use of Indian CCCers stipulated that the park service would provide materials, equipment, and supervision. In return, the BIA would furnish the Navajo crew of twenty-five enrollees based at Chaco Canyon.

The mobile unit became an efficient group of stonemasons. In an amazing eight days at Aztec Ruins in 1938, this group cleared three rooms in the West Ruin to facilitate visitor access. Today's interpretative trail passes through these rooms. From 1938 to 1942 they did extensive stabilization work at Aztec Ruins, redoing walls of fourteen rooms in the west wing, covering six ceilings with a two-inch waterproof layer, re-roofing Kiva E, and removing old lumber-and-tarpaper roofs and the concrete covering it. They raised the masonry of the outer wall above the roof level and removed unsuitable wooden railings leading to the ladder in the kiva. The crew repaired Rooms 249, 202, and 193, and painted the Great Kiva roof with hot tar and rolled it with sand. The men also worked on the continuing drainage problem and undertook various stabilization efforts including repairs to Kiva K and Kiva L. They also installed sunken tile drains in several rooms to gather or direct surface water away from the ruins and rolled the plaza surface and former ruin floors to compact them and reduce erosion.

After Threatening Rock crashed down on Pueblo Bonito at Chaco Canyon in January 1941, cleaning up the damage to thirty rooms of the structure and doing repairs kept the CCC mobile unit busy until September. They then returned to Aztec Ruins to work on twenty-nine rooms and three kivas. The men continued on this project through the winter of 1941–42.

In April 1942, with participation in the mobile unit declining, it was disbanded. However, in 1946, the group was revived as a division of the National Park Service, and

remained under Vivian's leadership for more than a decade. Working from their base at Chaco, the men stabilized and repaired sites throughout the Southwest. In the course of their work, they developed substantial skills and specialized knowledge. The materials and methods they employed set the standard for both arresting deterioration of ancient structures and repairing them enough to assure their survival. The park service Regional Stabilization Unit that grew out of the CCC-ID program existed until 1978—a history of more than fifty years—when individual parks and monuments established their own stabilization programs.

CUTBACKS AND ENDING THE INDIAN CCC

In 1938 CCC–Indian Division funding was cut by $600,000, forcing a reduction in supervisory personnel, enrollees, equipment purchases, and projects. Such expensive projects as well drilling and installation of large stock tanks were curtailed. Half-completed projects which required machinery were abandoned and cheaper materials were purchased. On the Navajo Reservation, the CCC concentrated on work that required more hand labor. There would be no more requests to the Washington office for additional funds; field officials could spend only what was sent to them.

Cooperative agreements with other divisions of the bureau became more popular. For example, CCC-ID workers hand-cleared rights-of-way for truck trails, while the road division took over grading and surfacing road beds. For water projects, CCC-ID furnished labor, supervisors, and machinery, but the Public Works Administration provided gasoline and materials. CCC regulations were stretched to their fullest to permit such cooperative work. Officials pared spending to a minimum, and they were reluctant to retain personnel who were contributing little to programs. Money was used for the most essential activities.

With the approach of World War II, the CCC-ID became more involved with national defense preparations. Indians were eligible for benefits of the National Defense Vocation Training Act of 1941, operated by the United States Office of Education in conjunction with state departments of education.

District camp supervisors and camp managers quickly made agreements with states to start classes for CCC-ID enrollees. States appointed the instructors and supplied the equipment and texts. Enrollees studied radio operations and repair, welding, auto mechanics, sheet metal work, carpentry, and other skills related to national defense. Classes ran twelve to fifteen hours per week for about two months. At first, CCC members in defense training received five hours off per week, with pay, to attend classes.

Proficiency tests were administered at the end of each course and many who passed obtained immediate job placement in industry. Enrollees could leave $1.50-per-day CCC work for jobs paying $10 per day or higher. Indians found work in shipyards, airplane plants, machine shops, ordnance factories, and other types of war industry where they served as welders, stonemasons, sheet metal workers, mechanics, machinery operators, and truck drivers. Hundreds of Navajos, along with other southwestern Indians, helped build an $11 million army ordnance depot at Fort Wingate, New Mexico, in 1941 and 1942. Other Navajo and Indian laborers were employed in constructing the Navajo Ordnance Depot at Bellemont, Arizona, west of Flagstaff.

Meanwhile, CCC-ID officials struggled to meet rising prices with reduced funds. Retrenchment meant more than merely halting nonessential spending. It became difficult to keep CCC-ID programs operating at all. Camp managers could not feed the men properly with dwindling food budgets. The draft and activation of reserve officers removed key supervisory leaders at all levels.

Boarding units were asked to reduce the number of camp personnel to a bare minimum. All enrollees were required to attend national defense training classes during off-duty hours. Meanwhile, production was restored to a full forty-hour week and travel to and from work no longer counted as duty time.

Remaining enrollees planted victory gardens at their camps, attended national defense classes, and purchased war bonds and stamps. Most Indians, however, left the CCC to enter war production or the military. By the end of 1942, of 11,000 Indians in the armed services, 6,400 were former CCCers and another 8,000 former enrollees were employed in war production.

In July 1942, CCC production was stopped and all enrollees were laid off, except a few retained to safeguard and administer transfer of property to other agencies. From 1933 to 1942 the CCC-ID had produced impressive results. Eighty-five thousand enrollees participated in the CCC-ID nationwide, doing work that ranged from menial to highly technical. Approximately $72 million was spent on the nation's reservations.

By 1939 it was becoming commonplace for agencies to have Indians in supervisory positions except for project managers and trail locators. The CCC-ID had fenced tribal lands to keep cattle from trespassing. They had developed new sources of water and restored rangelands. Indian CCC crews built hundreds of miles of truck trails, foot and horse trails, built bridges and lookout towers, and installed telephone lines. They undertook considerable fire protection work, reseeded, thinned and removed unproductive growth, and in the course of their work improved their education and skills. CCC service gave many a Native American an opportunity to mature, to learn new skills, and to prepare for a lifetime occupation.

A FREE GOVERNMENT SERVICE
GRAND CANYON
NATIONAL PARK
U.S. DEPARTMENT
OF THE INTERIOR

NATIONAL PARK
SERVICE

Chapter Seven

BENEFITS OF THE CCC

The Civilian Conservation Corps' contributions to the nation remain impressive, even seventy-five years later. Between April 5, 1933, and June 30, 1942, nearly 3.5 million CCCers lived and worked in a total of 4,500 different camps across the United States, plus Alaska, Hawaii, Puerto Rico, and the Virgin Islands. Another 264,000 people were employed operating the program. The government spent $3 billion on the program, including about $1,000 per enrollee per year for food, clothing, overhead, and allotments to dependents—which alone accounted for nearly $700 million.

If they accomplished nothing else in nine and one-half years, it could be said the federal government spent about $1 per tree planted. But CCCers did far more than plant trees, much of it described in preceding chapters. Nonetheless, the sheer numbers lend further weight to their accomplishments. Nationwide, CCC enrollees:

- Built 63,256 buildings and 3,116 lookout towers, and restored 3,980 historic structures
- Erected 405,037 signs, markers, and monuments
- Developed 800 state parks
- Arrested soil erosion on 20 million acres of public and private land, improved 40 million acres of farmland, and restored vegetation on 814,000 acres

253

—COURTESY DOUG LEEN, RANGER DOUG ENTERPRISES

- Planted more than 4 billion trees and spent more than 8 million man-days fighting fires
- Built 125,000 miles of roads, 46,854 bridges, and 28,087 miles of trails
- Strung 89,000 miles of telephone line
- Developed 52,000 acres of public campgrounds
- Stocked nearly 1 billion fish
- Protected 154 million square yards of stream and lake banks
- Controlled mosquitoes on 248,000 acres
- Installed 5,000 miles of water lines
- Improved 3,462 beaches

PUBLIC LANDS BENEFITS

Public lands agencies received an unparalleled boost from the CCC, not only in their infrastructure but also in employee recruitment and public support. The National Park Service, for example, had hired many additional employees using

254

CCC funds. It would be a long time before the agency would again, if ever, have the money and manpower to forge ahead at top speed with development in so many areas at once.

The CCC helped the park service accelerate the development of a bureau capable of executing large-scale programs. It provided the funding and manpower to enable the park service to broaden its mission and brought the agency an invaluable transfusion of professional talent unmatched in its history. In many ways, the same could be said for the forest service.

Future employees like Meredith Guillet, Kenny Ross, J. L. Crawford, Hobart Feltner, and countless others came from within the ranks of CCC enrollees. Even those CCCers who went on to other kinds of work often retained a profound connection to the parks, monuments, and forests where they had worked. In essence, the program created a generation of public lands advocates, people whose intimate experience of them dramatically increased use in the boom years after World War II. After the CCC years, the nation's parks, monuments, and forests truly became the public's lands.

COMMUNITY BENEFITS

Perhaps no community could claim greater benefit from the Civilian Conservation Corps' presence than Blanding, Utah. But countless other communities benefited from the program as well, despite early misgivings about job stealing and negative social influences.

Bo Montella offered a list of CCC contributions to Blanding, Utah, where he worked in the CCC, married, and remained. From simple services like laundry and ironing, to purchases in local stores, the boys spent money in the small town. The CCC camp doctor not only delivered babies at no charge, but also opened the camp infirmary to Blanding residents who were ill. Needy families received food from the camp, which also hosted the entire community at Thanksgiving and Christmas dinners. What's more, Montella concluded, the economic benefits have continued. Many descendants of the 1,600 men who served in the Blanding camp have visited the area as tourists.

It is likely a list that could be reiterated for countless communities across the plateau. The CCC gave jobs to local men with some work experience, purchased some of their supplies in neighboring communities, offered special assistance to these communities in times of distress or crisis, and filled their restaurants, churches, movie theaters, and other businesses on the weekends with young men who had a bit of spare change in their pockets. They enhanced nearby tourist attractions, guaranteeing that when times improved, tourists would come and stay awhile. In the meantime, they had new hiking trails, fishing holes, stock ponds for their cattle, roads to previously unseen places, and ever so much more. It wasn't only their coffers that were enriched. The quality of their environment was enriched as well.

WORKERS' BENEFITS

The Civilian Conservation Corps took men from the depths of economic despair and gave them hope. It helped them support their families, fed and sheltered them, and taught them skills that many would employ for decades afterward. They went on to become surveyors, engineers, heavy equipment operators, business owners, educators, and countless other professions. They learned to be responsible, to follow orders as well as give them, to build a better life through education. In a time when defeat lurked around every corner, they learned to believe in themselves. Those lessons stayed with them throughout their lives, prompting many to agree with Cecil Arnold, who said the CCC was, quite simply, "the best thing that ever happened to me."

Arnold was a nineteen-year-old Texan with few options when he reported to the CCC camp at Grand Canyon's South Rim. He learned to operate a radio, work on telephone lines, and install electrical wiring. But most of all, he learned to follow orders. "I learned from the CCCs that the best thing that can happen to a person first in life is to become a good follower. . . . And I do think that in later life, I became a good leader because I knew how to follow."

One veteran of Grand Canyon Company 819 not only found "a place of security" in the corps, but also embraced "the opportunity to act responsibly, build confidence, learn to be a good follower and in turn to be a leader." Albert Spudy, who was assigned to the Mount Elden camp in Arizona, echoed their sentiments, adding he'd volunteer again. "You had discipline, the food was good, you didn't run all night, because you had to be in bed at bed-check. . . . I would go tomorrow to be a leader or something . . . because it was that great. I loved it."

R. L. Welch, who had waited all night at a train station in Texas because he couldn't afford lodging, spent only one enrollment period in the CCC. They had been "all just kids, half scared to death" when they arrived at their camp, but quickly realized how different life in the corps would be. "Every job that I had, I was responsible to my superior, and I was responsible to myself, and I was responsible to the government . . . for the privilege of having a job. I never had thought about those sorts of things before in my life. . . . This was the beginning of responsibility right here, and I could never be more grateful for it."

His time in the CCC fostered a newfound ambition. Despite having quit the eighth grade to help support his family, he realized he could aspire to something more than picking cotton. He went on to a successful career, and retired "comfortably" at age fifty-nine. "I give this CCC camp a lot of credit for my insight on certain priorities and certain goals to set and certain standards to keep, and remember my obligation to the community, to my children, to the schools, to the PTA, all those things."

Buck Brewer's achievement was simpler, but no less profound. The Oklahoman could not even sign his name on a payroll slip when he arrived at his Division of Grazing camp near Durango, Colorado. By the end of his enrollment, in April 1936, he was able to write an intelligent, legible letter to friends still in camp.

Louis Purvis, who had doubted his ability to operate a jackhammer or blast rock for a trail in the Grand Canyon, said those skills were not his most meaningful lessons. "I learned to be resourceful. I learned to respect people." Dempsey Malaney, who worked at Holbrook, Arizona, and Perryton, Texas, "grew up a lot" during his time in the CCC, including developing social skills. "I'd never been around a lot of people, and I learned how to get along with people." For the school dropout, having a second chance at an education was especially valuable. "I got back into school and started night classes and took all the advantages I could to learn more about the country. It was just a real learning experience for me to be in the three C camps."

William Ivy Byrd had grown up "very poor" in Alabama, but still dreamed of being a lawyer. In CCC camps at Eureka and Green River, Utah, the company clerk trained him to "handle correspondence, type orders, payroll, filing and the usual paperwork." In the evenings, he helped teach less educated enrollees to read and write. "The CCC served a purpose to feed, clothe, house, and train poor boys as well as to reclaim natural resources," he recalled, adding, "It certainly served my purpose which was to save some money to enroll in college to pursue my dream of being a lawyer, which I did."

Byrd realized his dream, and enjoyed a fifty-year career as a lawyer and circuit judge. He remained "truly thankful" for his CCC experiences, which he said inspired him "to help others obtain an education by awarding scholarships on my own and serving on committees for that purpose."

Max Castillo had wanted to operate a jackhammer, and persevered despite being told he was too small. From that experience, he learned it was up to him to better himself. During the time he was in the CCC, he did "more maturing and more growing up than any eight-month period in my life. I done it right here in this camp. I learned what responsibility was. I learned what truth and honesty was. You know the old saying, 'the truth will set you free.' I learned that stuff right here in this camp."

Like Castillo, Paul Brown was an orphan. Thanks to the CCC, he was able to get his sister into college and "later help her in many ways." He joined the Navy after leaving the CCC, and was able to continue supporting her. "I don't think I would have made it without the CCCs," he recalled.

BUILDING THE COLORADO RIVER TRAIL, GRAND CANYON NATIONAL PARK —Courtesy National Park Service

MILITARY BENEFITS

President Roosevelt could not have known of the long-term benefit when he insisted, in 1933, that the military run CCC camps. It was an arrangement that contributed substantially to the nation's preparedness after the Japanese attacked Pearl Harbor on December 7, 1941.

Through their work in the CCC, active duty and reserve army officers received training in organizing and handling men. As a result, many moved from CCC positions into major positions in the war. In turn, the military style camps taught CCCers how to live and work together. They came out with many skills that were helpful to the national defense effort. Toward the end of the program, some enrollees were drafted directly from camps into the military. Further, when camps closed, the army had first claim on the trucks, equipment, surplus buildings, and supplies that remained. The technical service agencies got what was left over.

"We didn't know it at the time," recalled educational advisor Robert Ashe, "but actually the CCC was really the beginning of the backbone . . . of the military services in World War II. If it hadn't been for the CCCs, we would have been two years—at least a year, maybe two years—behind where we were in getting ready for World War II."

Cecil Arnold was one of the men who was called to military duty from the CCC. He had, in fact, joined the National Guard "for the one dollar that you got for attending National Guard meetings on Monday night." While still working at Grand Canyon, he received a letter from the commanding officer of the Guard unit, offering him a promotion if he would mobilize. "I think that the armed forces were handed a ready-made cadre in 1940 when the National Guard was called into service and then with subsequent events."

Arnold served in three infantry divisions and was sent to officer training on the recommendation of General George Patton. He reached the rank of captain and served as a company commander. "The very fact that we learned discipline in the CCCs was half the battle. We went into the military service, it made it relatively easy for us."

Even the CCC camps themselves proved useful during the war. Some were used to house conscientious objectors, while others held Japanese American internees and Austrian prisoners of war. With so many young men gone to fight in the war, western Colorado's peach growers faced a labor shortage at harvest time. German prisoners of war who had been captured in North Africa and were housed at Camp Carson, south of Colorado Springs, were brought to Mesa County to pick peaches. They were housed in two former CCC camps, one in Palisade and the second, Colorado National Monument's Fruita Canyon camp, NM-3-C. POWs who worked in the canning factories, beet fields, and orchards were paid 80¢ a day in canteen coupons. By 1946, all the prisoners were gone, returned to Germany.

Joseph Cmar was far less fortunate during his military service. Nonetheless, his CCC training at Mount Elden Camp in northern Arizona proved especially valuable. Cmar was captured by the Japanese and held prisoner for three and one-half years. "While working in the CCC camps, my physical well-being reached its peak. This I believe to be one of the factors which helped me to survive the gross inhumanities inflicted upon me while in the hands of the barbarous Japanese."

Whether serving in the military, surviving internment as a prisoner of war, or pursuing civilian jobs, the boys of the CCC were prepared, because they had learned what they were capable of achieving. Bo Moorhead perhaps summed it up best for them all: "I hadn't been away from home at all and it really set me for life. The companionship and meeting other young men. It just taught me what was out in this old world and how to get along with people."

Notes on Appendices

The following listings are provided courtesy of the National Association of CCC Alumni Web site (www.cccalumni.org).

The information contained in these listings was taken from Strength Reports showing company location and date. The NACCCA headquarters now has reports of one day each year as follows: 30 September 1933; 30 June 1934; 30 June 1935; 30 June 1936; 30 June 1937; 30 June 1938; 11 December 1939; 30 June 1940; 31 October 1941; 31 January 1942; and 31 July 1942.

KEY TO ABBREVIATIONS

A	Agriculture (Bureau of Animal Industry)
Army	Army Military Reservations
BF	Federal Game Refuge
BR	Federal Reclamation Project
BS	Biological Survey
C of E	State Land (Corps of Engineers)
CP	County Parks
D	Private Land (Soil Conservation Service)
DF	Department of Forestry
DG	Public Domain (Bureau of Grazing)
DPE	Drainage Private Land Erosion
DSP	Department of State Parks
F	National Forest
FWS	Fish and Wildlife Service
G	Department of Grazing
GF	Oregon and California Land Grant (Grazing)
GLO	Grazing Service/Land Grant
GNP	Grazing Service/National Park
MA	Municipal Area
MC	Private Land (Mosquito Control)
MP	Military Park
NA	National Arboretum (Bureau of Plant Industry)
Navy	Naval Military Reservation
NM	National Monument
NP	Department of National Parks
PF	Private Forest
PE	Private Land Erosion
S	State Forest
SCS	Soil Conservation
SP	State Park
TVA	Tennessee Valley Authority
TVA-P	Tennessee Valley Authority

COLUMN HEADINGS

Project: The number given by the state to the project and camp

Co. #: The number given by the federal government to each company. Some company numbers have a letter following the number: "C" stands for colored, meaning the company was made up of African Americans; "V" stands for veterans, meaning the company was made up of veterans of World War I; "X" or "Mix" stands for integrated camp.

Date: The date that company occupied that particular camp

Railroad: The closest railroad stop to the camp

Post Office: The closest post office to the camp

Location: Distance from the railroad stop; additional notes

Appendix A

PROJECT	CO. #	DATE	RAILROAD	POST OFFICE	LOCATION
F-32	311	10/20/39	Clarkdale	Clarkdale	Sedona 24 mi. NE
F-80	311	4/30/40	Flagstaff	Flagstaff	3.5 mi. N
G-133	340	6/5/39	Kingman	Kingman	4 mi. SW
SCS-25	368	10/6/39	Safford	Safford	Solomon 9 mi. E
F-16	804	5/23/33	Globe	Globe	
F-14	805	5/28/33	Safford	Safford	Columbine 45 mi. SW
F-16	806	5/23/33	Globe	Globe	
F-23	807	5/24/33	Globe	Payson	Indian Gardens 123 mi. N
F-34	807	10/8/37	Phoenix	Cave Creek	Ashdale 52 mi. N
F-77	807	5/18/40	Flagstaff	Kohl's Ranch	East Verda 85 mi. SE
F-16	807	11/7/41	Globe	Globe	Pinal Mountain 6 mi. S
NP-1	818	5/30/33	Flagstaff	Kanab, UT	
NP-1	818	5/15/34	Grand Canyon	Grand Canyon	North Rim 224 mi. N
SP-3	818	10/17/36	Phoenix	Phoenix	South Mountain Park 8 mi. S
NP-2	819	5/29/33	Grand Canyon	Grand Canyon	South Rim .5 mi. SE
F-18	820	5/27/33	Prescott	Prescott	Groon Creek 7 mi. SE
F-5	821	5/25/33	Flagstaff	Flagstaff	5 mi. N
F-20	822	5/29/33	Prescott	Prescott	Thumb Butte 4.5 mi. W
F-33	822	11/3/36	Mayer	Mayer	.5 mi. S
F-19	822	5/22/37	Prescott	Prescott	Fairgrounds 1.5 mi. NW
F-80	822	6/24/41	Flagstaff	Flagstaff	3.5 mi. N
F-32	822	1/4/42	Clarkdale	Clarkdale	Sedona 24 mi. NE
F-21	823	5/29/33	Winslow	Winslow	
F-22	823	5/3/34	McNary	McNary	Los Burros 3.5 mi. N
F-10	825	6/1/33	Rodeo, NM	Borlal, Arizona	
NM-2	828	5/7/34	Williams	Willcox	Bonite Canyon 67 mi. N
SP-8	830	6/10/34	Kingman	Kingman	
NM-1	831	7/3/34	Adamana	Holbrook	Petrified Forest 19 mi. SE
F-11	832	6/1/33	Ft. Huachuca	Sonoita	
F-19	835	5/5/36	Prescott	Prescott	Fairgrounds 1 mi. NW
F-9	840	6/5/33	Flagstaff	Flagstaff	

PROJECT	CO. #	DATE	RAILROAD	POST OFFICE	LOCATION
F-13	841	6/5/33	Ft. Huachuca	Ft. Huachuca	
F-3	842	6/11/33	Silver City, NM	Blue	
F-54	842	5/5/34	Silver City, NM	Springerville	Buffalo Crossing 154 mi. NW
F-3	842	10/21/39	Phoenix	Springerville	
F-54	842	5/19/40	Holbrook	Springerville	Holbrook 129 mi. SE
F-4	847	5/27/33	Silver City, NM	Springerville	
NP-4	847	10/18/34	Grand Canyon	Grand Canyon	South Rim #2 .5 mi. SE
G-109	847	10/7/38	Buckeye	Arlington	16 mi. W
G-170	847	8/10/40	Phoenix	Fredonia	Phoenix 399 mi. NW
F-28	848	5/26/33	Williams	Williams	
SCS-3	848	10/8/34	Safford	Safford	Artesia 11 mi. S
F-27	851	5/26/33	Bellemont	Bellemont	
SCS-2	852	10/7/34	Pima	Pima	
SP-10	858	5/5/34	Vail	Vail	
F-62	860	5/1/34	Prescott	Prescott	11 mi. SE
F-55	862	5/22/35	Silver City, NM	Springerville	Three Forks 142 mi. NW
F-22	862	5/8/36	McNary	McNary	Los Burros
F-4	863	5/1/34	Flagstaff	Flagstaff	Fred S. Breen 30 mi. S
F-6	863	6/1/36	Flagstaff	Flagstaff	Double Springs 29 mi. SE
F-75	863	5/29/37	Flagstaff	Pine	Pivot Rock 75 mi. S
F-35	863	10/28/39	Duncan	Duncan	C.A. Ranch 19 mi. N
F-24	864	6/13/33	Globe	Young	
SP-9	874	7/5/34	Kingman	Kingman	
F-22	898	6/5/33	McNary	McNary	
G-136	1814	10/4/39	Duncan	Duncan	C.A. Ranch 19 mi.N
G-173	1814	8/10/40	Phoenix	Fredonia	Bull Rush
G-138	1820	11/14/39	Ajo	Ajo	7 mi. N
G-135	1820	4/16/40	Phoenix	Short Creek	Phoenix 436 mi. NW
F-19	1823 -V	7/12/33	Prescott	Prescott	
F-29	1823 -V	4/30/34	Williams	Williams	
F-30	1826 -V	5/21/35	Tucson	Tucson	Madora Canyon 36 mi. SE
SP-6	1826 -V	5/16/37	Tucson	Tucson	Manville Wells 25 mi. NE
SP-3	1826 -V	6/30/38	Phoenix	Phoenix	South Mountain Park 8 mi. S
F-15	1830 -V	7/13/33	Pima	Pima	
F-55	1830 -V	5/10/34	Silver City, NM	Springerville	
F-12	1834 -V	7/11/33	Douglas	Douglas	
SP-6	1837	8/1/34	Tucson	Tucson	Manville Wells 34 mi. NE
SP-8	1837	7/1/35	Kingman	Kingman	Hualpai 20 mi. SE

PROJECT	CO. #	DATE	RAILROAD	POST OFFICE	LOCATION
NP-8	1837	6/22/41	Holbrook	Adamana	Petrified Forest 35 mi. E
DF-42	1838	7/13/34	Tucson	Tucson	
F-38	1838	5/16/35	Williams	Williams	J.D. Dam 9 mi. S
DF-74	1839	7/30/34	Safford	Safford	
SCS-1	1840	7/11/34	Duncan	Duncan	Camp 1 mi. N
DF-13	1841	7/19/34	Ft. Huachuca	Ft. Huachuca	Sunnyside 34 mi. SW
DG-8	1849	1/13/34	Hillside	Hillside	Yaua 7 mi. NE
DG-44	2557	10/20/35	Maryvale, UT	Fredonia	Pipe Springs 160 mi. S
DG-45	2558	10/27/35	Cedar City, UT	St. George, UT	St. George 55 mi. SW
F-28	2833	4/30/36	Williams	Williams	St. George 55 mi. SW
NP-1	2833	6/18/37	Grand Canyon	Kaibab Forest	North Rim 224 mi. N
F-64	2847	12/7/35	Nogales	Nogales	Pana Blanca 21 mi. NE
F-18	2847	5/17/37	Prescott	Prescott	Groom Creek 7 mi. SE
SCS-7	2848	8/6/35	Bowie	Bowie	Orange Butte 12 mi. NE
F-76	2848	5/28/38	McNary	Springerville	Greer 30 mi. E
BR-19	2849	1/12/36	Phoenix	Phoenix	Tempe 8 mi. NE
DG-50	2850	8/20/35	Duncan	Duncan	Slick Rock Canyon 21 mi. SW
SP-10	2851	8/20/35	Vail	Vail	Colossal Cave 6 mi. N
SCS-15	2852	8/5/35	Tucson	Tucson	Rillito 7 mi. NW
DG-41	2854	11/4/36	Pima	Pima	Teague Springs 16 mi. NW
G-137	2854	10/27/39	Safford	Safford	Solomonsville 10 mi. E
F-62	2855	5/16/36	Prescott	Prescott	Lynx Creek 12 mi. SE
F-16	2855	6/5/37	Globe	Globe	Pinal Mountain 6 mi. S
F-74	2855	5/22/38	Safford	Safford	Columbine 41 mi. SW
SCS-10	2856	7/22/35	Ft. Thomas	Ft. Thomas	Black Rock 10 mi. SW
F-48	2857	8/20/35	Clifton	Clifton	Eagle Creek 39 mi. N
SCS-21	2858	6/14/36	Tucson	Tucson	Randolph Park 3 mi. E
DG-48	2859	8/20/35	Winkleman	Winkleman	.5 mi.
SP-4	2860	1/11/36	Phoenix	Phoenix	South Mountain Park 8 mi. S
SCS-9	2861	7/22/35	Pima	Pima	Teague Springs 16 mi. NW
F-62	2861	5/16/37	Prescott	Prescott	Lynx Creek 12 mi. SE
SP-11	2862	7/20/35	Tucson	Tucson	Tanque Verde 18 mi. E
SCS-5	2863	7/22/35	Duncan	Duncan	C.A. Ranch 21 mi. N
SCS-22	2863	10/28/36	Rodeo, NM	Portal	Cave Creek 12 mi. NW
SCS-34	2863	10/6/38	Douglas	Douglas	Rucker Canyon 40 mi. NE
SCS-27	2863	5/17/41	Prescott	Prescott	Long Meadow 22 mi. NW
SCS 20	2864	8/5/35	Mesa	Mesa	Superstition Wash 20 mi. E
DG-46	2865	8/21/35	Kingman	Kingman	Bound Valley 26 mi. SE

PROJECT	CO. #	DATE	RAILROAD	POST OFFICE	LOCATION
SCS-11	2867	7/12/35	Safford	Safford	Sanchez 12 mi. S
F-18	2870	5/16/36	Prescott	Prescott	Groom Creek 7 mi. SE
F-12	2870	5/15/37	Douglas	Douglas	Rucker Canyon 38 mi. NE
SCS-14	2881	8/20/35	San Simon	San Simon	9 mi. S
SCS-13	2894	8/20/35	Bowie	Bowie	Apache Pass 12 mi. S
BR-13	2935	10/11/39	Yuma	Yuma	4 mi. SE
F-41	2948	10/11/39	Safford	Safford	Moon Creek 15 mi. E
MA-1	3318	10/23/39	Tucson	Tucson	Randolph Park 4 mi. E
F-33	3320	11/11/39	Mayer	Mayer	.5 mi. S
F-79	3320	06/29/40	Prescott	Prescott	43.6 miles NW—Walnut Creek
NP-8	3342	8/2/38	Holbrook	Adamana	Petrified Forest 35 mi. E
NP-12	3345	8/2/38	Flagstaff	Flagstaff	Mount Elden 4 mi. E
F-78	3346	6/27/39	Winslow	Winslow	Chevalon Canyon 35 mi. S
F-64	3348	10/21/39	Nogales	Nogales	Pena Blanca 21 mi. NW
F-28	3348	5/5/40	Williams	Williams	J.D. Dam 9 mi. S
F-78	3804	4/30/41	Winslow	Winslow	Chevalon Canon 35 mi. S
BR-74	3832	10/18/39	Yuma	Yuma	Yuma Airport 5 mi. SE
NP-12	3838	5/10/41	Flagstaff	Flagstaff	Mt. Elden 4 mi. E
SCS-18	3839	8/24/35	Naco	Naco	At Railhead
SCS-19	3840	8/23/35	Benson	Benson	St. David 8 mi. S
SCS-26	3840	10/1/39	Nogales	Patagonia	Flux Canyon 17 mi. NE
FWS-1	3840	9/14/41	Parker	Parker	Parker Dam 19 mi. N
G-133	4812	6/25/41	Kingman	Kingman	

Appendix B

PROJECTS AND CAMPS COMPLETED IN COLORADO

PROJECT	CO. #	DATE	RAILROAD	POST OFFICE	LOCATION
F-26	801	5/10/33	Florence	Florence	
SP-4	801	5/15/34	Pueblo	Beulah	27 mi SW
F-12	802	5/10/33	Divide	Lake George	
F-4	802	5/31/34	Granby	Granby	
SP-2	802	6/20/35	Boulder	Boulder	
NP-1	802	5/8/36	Lyons	Estes Park	Camp Horseshoe Park 33 mi NW
F-23	803	5/19/34	Larqunts	Larqunts	
F-34	803	10/3/34	Buena Vista	Buena Vista	Trout Creek 12 mi E
F-16	803	6/20/37	Delta	Grand Mesa	Trickle Park 35 mi SW
F-24	805	5/6/33	Buena Vista	Buena Vista	
F-52	805	6/5/36	Lyons	Estes Park	Horseshoe Park 33 mi
DG-2	806	5/22/35	Grand Junction	Grand Junction	Lincoln Park 1.5 mi NE
NP-12	808	4/30/40	Granby	Grand Lake	12 mi N
NP-1	809	6/13/33	Estes Park	Estes Park	
SP-2	809	5/14/34	Boulder	Boulder	
NP-7	809	6/30/35	Granby	Grand Lake	26 mi N
SCS-8	809	10/15/35	Ft. Collins	Wellington	25 mi NE Buckeye
F-49	811	5/16/35	South Fork	South Fork	4 mi SW
F-27	812	6/11/34	Delta	Delta	32 mi SW
F-55	812	11/15/35	Pueblo	Beulah	27 mi SW Pueblo Mountain
F-59	812	4/26/37	Pueblo	San Isabel	San Isabel 45 mi W Or Rye
NM-1	824	5/21/33	Grand Junction	Glade Park	26 mi NW
NP-13	824	10/5/41	Mancos	Mancos	
NP-2	825	5/27/33	Mancos	Mancos	
NM-3	825	11/1/33	Grand Junction	Fruita	17 mi SE
SP-7	825	5/15/34	Rifle	Rifle	
F-2	826	1/15/33	Ft. Collins	Eggers	
SP-10	826	10/5/34	Glenwood Springs	Glenwood Springs	Roaring Fork 2 mi E

PROJECT	CO. #	DATE	RAILROAD	POST OFFICE	LOCATION
F-28	827	6/2/33	Dolores	Dolores	
F-6	828	6/3/33	Rifle	Marvine	
F-60	828	6/26/40	Monument	Monument	2 mi SW
F-11	829	5/3/33	Idaho Springs	Idaho Springs	
F-1	829	6/3/34	Lyons	Peaceful Valley	
F-58	829	5/19/35	Ft. Logan	Golden	21 mi SW Bear Creek
P-304	829	5/19/35	Ft. Logan	Golden	21 mi SW Bear Creek
F-63	829	6/8/38	Denver	Idaho Springs	37 mi W
F-20	830	6/2/33	Gunnison	Pitkia	52 mi SW
F-15	831	6/1/33	Minturn	Minturn	21 mi E of Denver
F-51	831	5/6/34	(unknown)	Meredith	
F-55	835	5/7/37	Pueblo	Beulah	27 mi SW
NP-4	836	6/15/34	Estes Park	Estes Park	
SCS-12	843	4/20/40	Monte Vista	La Jara	19 mi S Capulin
F-29	846	5/18/35	Pagosa Springs	Pagosa Springs	27 mi S
NP-7	847	5/6/38	Granby	Grand Lake	26 mi N
F-20	848	5/15/34	Gunnison	Pitkin	
F-38	851	5/16/34	Yampa	Yampa	
F-55	851	7/26/34	Mancos	Mesa Verde	
F-51	851	5/17/35	Emma	Meredith	22 mi SE
F-7	859	5/31/33	Dillon	Dillon	
F-8	859	6/1/34	Taberna	Taberna	
NP-6	861	10/10/34	Mancos	Mesa Verde	29 mi SW
NP-1	864	5/10/35	Lyons	Estes Park	33 mi NW
NP-1	865	4/30/34	Estes Park	Estes Park	
F-19	867	5/31/33	Doyis	Hot Springs	
F-5	868	5/30/33	Steamboat	Steamboat	
BR-59	868	1/11/36	Palisade	Palisade	1 mi SE
F-8	870	6/1/33	Tabernash	Tabernash	
F-1	894	6/2/33	Lyons	Peaceful Valley	
SP-14	894	4/16/38	Denver	Golden	
F-28	896	5/10/35	Delores	Delores	19 mi NE
F-29	898	5/1/34	Pagosa	Pagosa	
F-53	898	11/22/35	Delores	Delores	Lone Dome 7 mi NW
F-27	1801	5/25/33	Dolton	Dolton	

PROJECT	CO. #	DATE	RAILROAD	POST OFFICE	LOCATION
NP-3	1809	6/25/33	Granby	Grand Lake	
SP-11	1809	10/27/34	Trinidad	Trinidad	Stonewall 35 mi W
F-16	1812	6/15/33	Palisade	Mena	
NP-3	1812	6/14/34	Granby	Grand Lake	
NP-4	1812	10/14/34	Lyons	Estes Park	29 mi NW Mill Creek
SP-2	1813	6/29/33	Boulder	Boulder	
F-10	1814	6/6/33	Bailey	Bailey	
F-4	1816	6/23/33	Granby	Golden	
F-14	1819	6/26/33	Woodland Park	Woodland Park	
SP-8	1819	7/1/34	Trinidad	Trinidad	
F-33	1819	9/15/34	Colorado Springs	Manitou	4 mi W
F-64	1819	6/11/38	Colorado Springs	Woodland Park	27 mi NW
F-40	1820	5/15/34	Alamosa	Alamosa	
F-23	1821 -V	7/12/33	Sargenta	Sargenta	
F-27	1822 -V	7/13/33	Grand Junction	White Water	
F-16	1822 -V	5/15/34	Delta	Cedaredge	
SP-9	1822 -V	10/6/34	Loveland	Loveland	8 mi W
F-30	1830	6/25/33	Alamosa	Alamosa	
SP-5	1831	8/14/33	Ft. Logan	Nederland	
SP-4	1832	8/22/33	Ft. Logan	Parker	
DG-1	1839	5/18/35	Craig	Elk Springs	6 mi W
F-48	1842	7/27/34	Placerville	Norwood	18 mi SW
F-27	1842	6/19/36	Delta	Delta	Divide 32 mi SW
F-51	1842	6/5/38	Glenwood	Meredith	45 mi SE
F-65	1842	10/28/39	Glenwood Springs	Glenwood Springs	1.5 mi S
F-68	1842	6/15/40	Eagle	Eagle	Yoeman Park 17 mi S
NP-2	1843	7/27/34	Mancos	Mancos	
NP-5	1843	10/10/34	Mancos	Mesa Verde	26 mi SW
SP-46	1844	7/26/34	Culsenburg	Gardner	
F-52	1844	5/27/35	Granby	Walden	Canadian 5 mi S
DP-3	1845	7/25/34	Castle Rock	Castle Rock	Frankstown 4 mi NE
F-24	1846	7/22/34	Buena Vista	Buena Vista	
SCS-6	1846	10/3/34	Colorado Springs	Colorado Springs	Templeton Gap 4 mi NE
SCS-18	1846	1/15/41	Walsenburg	Gardner	31 mi NW
DSP-5	1847	7/25/34	Ft. Logan	Ft. Logan	

PROJECT	CO. #	DATE	RAILROAD	POST OFFICE	LOCATION
SP-12	1847	9/17/34	Colorado Springs	Colorado Springs	Palmer Pk 5 mi E
DSP-2	1848	7/25/34	Durango	Durango	
SP-13	1848	6/30/35	Ft. Logan	Morrison	Red Rocks 20 mi N
DG-55	1849	5/4/37	Craig	Skull Creek	73 mi SW (Massadona)
G-81	1849	10/29/41	Craig	Sunbeam	49 mi W Two Bar Ranch
DSP-1	1860 -V	7/26/34	Greeley	Greeley	1.5 mi NW Island Grove
SP-13	1860 -V	5/15/37	Denver	Mt. Morrison	15 mi W Red Rock
BR-23	1860 -V	7/8/41	Montrose	Montrose	1 mi N
SCS-7	2116	7/20/38	Castle Rock	Castle Rock	4 mi NE
SCS-9	2117	7/20/38	Castle Rock	Elbert	30 mi SE
F-53	2118	7/10/38	Dolores	Dolores	7 mi NW Lone Cone
G-125	2119	11/7/38	Placerville	Paradox	66 mi NW
BR-59	2120	7/12/38	Palisades	Palisades	1 mi SW
G-139	2121	10/28/39	Monte Vista	Sagoache	
G-107	2122	7/15/38	Rifle	Meeker	52 mi White River NW
NP-8	2123	10/15/39	Grand Junction	Grand Junction	
F-60	2124	7/23/38	Monument	Monument	2 mi SW
SCS-2	2125	7/23/38	Pueblo	Beulah	18 mi SW Burnt Mill
DG-81	2127	7/19/38	Craig	Sunbeam	Two Bar Ranch 49 mi W
F-46	2134	7/8/38	Walsonburg	Gardner	31 mi NW
F-49	2135	7/8/38	South Fork	South Fork	3.5 mi SW
NP-11	2138	11/4/39	Lyons	Estes Park	Mill Creek 29 mi NW
G-140	2139	10/18/39	Craig	Briggs, Wyoming	
SCS-9	2547	10/23/35	Elbert	Elbert	5.5 mi N
NP-4	2552	10/25/35	Lyons	Estes Park	Mill Creek 29 mi NE
F-16	2802	6/26/35	Delta	Cedaredge	Trickle Pk 37 mi E
BR-22	2803	7/25/35	Grand Junction	Grand Junction	1.5 mi NE
SCS-2	2804	7/22/35	Pueblo	Beulah	Burn Mill 18 mi SW
F-50	2805	7/19/35	Ft. Collins	Red Feather	Red Feather Lake 46 mi NW
SCS-1	2818	1/11/36	Trinidad	Trinidad	1 mi E
SCS-17	2818	10/21/39	Sterling	Sterling	1.7 mi N
NP-11	2822	6/30/40	Lyons	Estes Park	27 mi NW
DG-1	2854	5/6/36	Craig	Elk Spring	62 mi W
F-51	2864	6/4/37	Glenwood	Meredith	
SCS-11	2894	4/9/38	Grand Junction	Grand Junction	19 mi SW

PROJECT	CO. #	DATE	RAILROAD	POST OFFICE	LOCATION
F-62	3810	5/5/37	Monument	Monument	
SCS-3	3825	7/25/35	Hugo	Hugo	.25 mi E
SCS-15	3825	10/15/40	Simla	Kutch	26 mi S
SCS-4	3826	7/25/35	Cheyenne Wells	Cheyenne Wells	1 mi
SCS-5	3827	7/26/35	Lamar	Springfield	50 mi S
SCS-14	3837	8/22/39	Mancos	Cortez	18 mi W
BR-23	3841	7/27/35	Montrose	Montrose	.5 mi E
DG-9	3842	7/26/35	Durango	Durango	Red Moon 30 mi SE
DG-10	3843	7/27/35	Montrose	Montrose	.5 mi E
BR-93	3843	10/24/41	Mancos	Mancos	4.5 mi N
DG-11	3844	7/28/35	Placerville	Redvale	52 mi SW
G-125	3844	10/29/41	Placerville	Paradox	66 mi NW
F-29	3845	5/3/36	Duloe, NM	Pagosa Springs	Blanco 23 mi NE
SCS-10	3845	10/17/36	Durango	Durango	Reservoir Hill 1.25 mi
SCS-10	3845	6/17/40	Durango	Durango	Reservoir Hill 1.5 mi NE
NP-4	3884	10/23/36	Lyons	Estes Park	Mill Creek 29 mi
SCS-9	3885	10/23/36	Castle Rock	Elbert	30 mi E
F-1	3888	6/6/38	Lyons	Peaceful Valley	25 mi SW
F-66	3888	6/20/40	Ft. Collins	Ft. Collins	Chambers Lake 69 mi W
G-139	3888	10/16/40	Monte Vista	Sagache	
G-107	3890	1/6/40	Rifle	Meeker	White River 52 mi NW
G-2	3890	11/3/41	Grand Junction	Grand Junction	1.5 mi
G-125	3891	1/4/40	Placerville	Paradox	64 mi NW
G-181	3891	9/25/41	Parkdale	Parkdale	1 mi W
NP-8	3892	1/4/49	Grand Junction	Grand Junction	Glade Pk 19 mi SW
BR-61	3893	4/24/40	Ignacio	Vallecito	Pine River 24 mi W
BR-94	3893	10/29/41	Mancos	Mancos	4.5 mi N
F-67	3894	6/29/40	Palisade	Mesa	26 mi NE
SCS-2	3895	1/6/40	Pueblo	Beulah	Burnt Mill 18 mi SW
SCS-9	3896	1/6/40	Castle Rock	Elbert	30 mi E
F-49	3897	1/6/40	South Fork	South Fork	3.5 mi SW
F-53	3898	1/6/40	Dolores	Dolores	Lone Dome 7 mi NW
G-79	3899	4/29/40	Gunnison	Gunnison	2 mi E
G-80	4804	6/26/41	Walden	Walden	North Park 4.3 mi W

Appendix C

PROJECTS AND CAMPS IN NEW MEXICO

PROJECT	CO. #	DATE	RAILROAD	POST OFFICE	LOCATION
BR-82	320	7/12/38	Carlsbad	Carlsbad	3 mi NW
SP-5	804	6/13/34	Clovis	Portales	Camp Roosevelt 11 mi SW
DG-3	805	10/11/34	Engel	Elephant Butte	12 mi NW
F-33	811	11/03/33	Dozingo	Pena Blanca	
F-5	811	5/24/33	Taos Junction	El Rito	
F-25	813	10/15/34	Silver City	Glenwood	67 mi NW
F-12	813	5/10/33	Silver City	Pinoa Altos	
F-51	814	11/15/39	Engel	Monticello	38 mi NW
F-57	814	11/15/41	Socorro	Magdalena	Augustine 27 mi SW
F-35	814	5/1/34	Mountain Air	Mountain Air	
F-8	814	5/10/33	Albuquerque	Sandia Peak	
F-8	814	5/11/40	Albuquerque	Sandia Peak	24 mi NE
F-8	814	6/4/35	Albuquerque	Sandia Peak	Sandia Peak 25 mi NW
NM-1	815	11/06/33	Santa Fe	Santa Fe	Bandolier 46 mi NW
NP-4	815	10/06/39	Santa Fe	Santa Fe	#3 28 mi NW
F-29	815	5/16/33	Santa Fe	Santa Fe	
SCS-28	815	6/29/41	Las Vegas	La Guava	26 mi NE
F-24	816	10/01/33	Alamogordo	High Rolls	1 mi W
F-16	816	6/3/33	Capitan	Capitan	
NP-3	831	12/02/33	Roswell	Roswell	Bottomless Lakes 10 mi N
NP-1	831	6/30/38	Carlsbad	Carlsbad	Rattle Snake Springs 28 mi SW
SP-1	833	11/03/33	Santa Fe	Santa Fe	1 mi W
SP-8	833	6/22/41	Tucumcari	Conchas Dam	59 mi NW
SP-1	835	11/02/35	Santa Fe	Santa Fe	1 mi W
F-34	835	5/1/34	Silver City	Silver City	
SCS-17	836	11/17/35	Santa Fe	Santa Fe	1.5 mi NW
SCS-6	836	1/12/36	Capitan	Ft. Stanton	7 mi NW
F-23	836	5/30/33	Santa Fe	Santa Fe	

PROJECT	CO. #	DATE	RAILROAD	POST OFFICE	LOCATION
SCS-17	837	10/11/37	Santa Fe	Santa Fe	#2 1 mi W
SCS-7	837	1/11/36	Bernalillo	San Ysidro	Puerco 52 mi NW
F-22	837	5/25/33	Bernalillo	Jemez Springs	
SCS-33	837	9/16/41	Melrose	Melrose	Fields 15 mi N
F-1	841	6/4/33	Silver City	Reserve	
SCS-2	843	10/07/34	Lordeburg	Red Rock	25 mi N
SCS-5	843	12/13/39	Santa Fe	Espenola	Trusco River 40 mi E
F-9	843	6/11/33	Magdalena	Magdalena	
F-21	844	5/10/33	Las Vegas	Las Vegas	
F-15	846	5/25/33	Silver City	Silver City	
BR-3	850	6/27/41	Carlsbad	Carlsbad	#1 3 mi NW
F-6	853	6/1/33	Las Vegas	Las Vegas	
F-11	855	5/24/33	Santa Rita	Mimbres	
BR-54	855	6/1/36	Engel	Elephant Butte	12 mi NW
F-31	857	11/03/35	Bernalillo	Jemez	
BS-1	859	10/08/38	Roswell	Roswell	Bitter Lake 12 mi NE
FWS-3	859	3/26/40	Roswell	Roswell	
SP-7	872	12/11/35	Tucumcari	Tucumcari	.5 mi S
SCS-32	879	9/16/41	Carrizozo	Hondo	42 mi SE
SP-3	881	12/07/33	Roswell	Roswell	Bottomless Lake 10 mi E
F-34	886	5/18/35	Silver City	Silver City	Beaverhead 92 mi N
F-7	1807	6/20/33	Grants	Grants	
F-13	1818	10/12/39	Santa Fe	La Madero	64 mi N
F-5	1818	4/30/34	Taos Junction	Vallecitos	
F-55	1818	5/22/40	Santa Fe	Vallecitos	74 mi NW
F-34	1818	6/16/35	Repumala	El Rito	
F-36	1818	6/3/36	Espanola	Espanola	El Rio 41 mi NW
F-2	1818	6/30/33	Silver City	Apache Creek	
BR-2	1821	6/17/35	Carlsbad	Carlsbad	3 mi NW
NP-3	1830 -V	8/17/35	Carlsbad	Carlsbad Camp	Carlsbad 3 mi NW
DF-2	1849	7/12/34	Silver City	Reserve	Tularosa 119 mi NE
F-32	1850	10/23/34	Cloudcroft	Mayhill	Penaseo 24 mi W
DF-17	1850	7/17/34	Capitan	Capitan	
SCS-1	1851	8/9/34	Silver City	Gila	Gila 32 mi W
DPE-1	1861	6/9/34	Silver City	Silver City	

PROJECT	CO. #	DATE	RAILROAD	POST OFFICE	LOCATION
NP-2	2354	8/22/39	Gallup	Crown Point	Chaco Canyon 79 mi NW
SCS-28	2356	6/20/40	Las Vegas	La Guava	26 mi NW
SCS-15	2356	7/12/38	Whitewater	Whitewater	1 mi NE
F-2	2358	11/01/39	Socorro	Apache Creek	Tularosa 108 mi SW
F-56	2358	6/15/40	Santa Fe	Coyote	69 mi NW
G-101	2806	5/2/41	Albuquerque	Bloomfield	167 mi NW
FWS-2	2810	10/28/39	San Antonio	San Antonio	Bosque Del Apache 13 mi S
F-31	2831	5/13/36	Bernalillo	Jemez	Polica 43 mi NW
SCS-4	2832	8/24/35	Espanola	Espanola	Chama 26 mi N
SCS-5	2834	8/20/35	Espanola	Espanola	Truches River 11 mi NE
SCS-25	2836	10/27/39	Socorro	Magdalena	Augustine 48 mi W
SCS-23	2836	6/27/41	Ft. Somner	Ft. Somner	2 mi NE
SCS-23	2836	6/27/41	Ft. Somner	Ft. Somner	27 mi NE
SCS-8	2836	7/26/35	Bernalillo	San Ysidro	Catron Ranch 44 mi NW
SCS-10	2837	8/14/35	Grants	Grants	San Mateo 25 mi N
DG-43	2838	8/15/35	Animas	Animas	1 mi E
SCS-26	2839	12/31/39	Silver City	Silver City	Mangas 19 mi NW
SCS-19	2839	7/22/35	Duncan, AZ	Duncan, AZ	Mesquitita 13 mi NE
SCS-24	2840	6/27/41	Hatch	Hatch	1 mi SE
F-11	2841	4/29/36	Silver City	Silver City	Camp Suly 42 mi NE
G-148	2842	10/01/39	Carlsbad	Carlsbad	Camp #3 3 mi NW
DG-41	2842	8/14/35	Lake Arthur	Lake Arthur	Hackberry Well 18 mi W
SCS-3	2843	8/20/35	Espanola	Espanola	Abiquiv 38 mi NW
SCS-22	2844	11/04/36	Hatch	Kingston	Kingston 50 mi NE
SCS-14	2844	7/26/35	Silver City	Silver City	Little Walnut 6 mi N
G-178	2845	10/05/40	Las Cruces	Las Cruces	Alameda 1 mi NE
SCS-18	2845	7/22/35	Silver City	Duckhorn	
DG-39	2845	7/28/35	Tularosa	Tularosa	Mescalero 5 mi E
SCS-15	2846	10/22/36	Whitewater	Whitewater	1 mi SE
BR-39	2848	4/22/41	Las Cruces	Las Cruces	1 mi SE
DG-38	2859	4/16/37	Las Cruces	Radit Springs	Jornado 24 mi W
SCS-21	2867	10/12/34	Mountain Air	Mountain Air	Manzano 15 mi W
SCS-27	2867	6/30/40	Albuquerque	Albuquerque	6 mi E
F-53	2868	5/28/38	Glorieta	Glorieta	2.5 mi E
BR-39	2868	6/22/41	Las Cruces	Las Cruces	1 mi NE

PROJECT	CO. #	DATE	RAILROAD	POST OFFICE	LOCATION
F-37	2868	7/22/35	Carlsbad	Carlsbad	Guadalupe 45 mi W
G-101	3341	7/26/38	Albuquerque	Bloomfield	167 mi NW
F-11	3343	10/14/39	Silver City	Mimbres	42 mi NW
F-34	3343	6/28/40	Silver City	Mimbres	Beaverhead 92 mi NW
SCS-24	3344	10/30/39	Hatch	Hatch	1 mi SE
F-37	3347	11/18/39	Carlsbad	Carlsbad	Guadalupe 46 mi SW
F-32	3347	4/16/40	Alamogordo	Mayhill	Penasco 46 mi E
SCS-23	3349	7/7/39	Ft. Sommer	Ft. Sommer	2 mi NE
G-69	3350	7/26/38	Alamogordo	Orugrande	Prathers East Well 64 mi SE
SP-8	3351	12/01/39	Newkirk	Conchas	Conchas Dam 26 mi N
BR-3	3352	7/25/38	Carlsbad	Carlsbad	3 mi NW
G-150	3353	10/01/39	Columbus	Columbus	.1 mi S
SCS-5	3354	7/25/38	Carrizozo	Ft. Stanton	Ft. Stanton 25 mi SE
BR-39	3355	8/2/38	Las Cruces	Las Cruces	.5 mi S
G-37	3356	7/19/38	Engel	Cochillo	Davis Well 33 mi NW
G-103	3357	4/8/39	Socorro	Quemado	108 mi NW
G-147	3808	10/11/39	Socorro	San Antonio	Tokay 23 mi SE
DG-40	3808	8/6/35	Carrizozo	Carrizozo	1 mi N
BR-82	3820	6/30/41	Carlsbad	Carlsbad	#2 3 mi NW
BR-39	3829	8/14/35	Las Cruces	Las Cruces	.5 mi SW
DG-37	3831	8/15/35	Engel	Cochillo	Davis Well 32 mi NW
BR-9	3832	10/15/36	Engel	Elephant Butte	12 mi NW
DG-38	3832	8/15/35	Las Cruces	Radium Springs	A.H. Ranch 22 mi N
SCS-29	3833	6/21/40	Alamogordo	High Rolls	14 mi NE
SCS-34	3833	8/12/41	Alamogordo	Mayhill	Penasco 46 mi E
SCS-16	3833	8/14/35	Las Cruces	Las Cruces	Almeda 2 mi NE
G-149	3834	10/25/39	Roswell	Roswell	#1 1 mi W
DG-42	3834	8/15/35	Magdalena	Magdalena	Augustine 21 mi W
F-24	3835	10/30/37	Alamogordo	High Rolls	
F-24	3835	10/11/39	Silver City	Glenwood	66 mi
F-54	3835	4/29/41	Carrizozo	Ruidoso	44 mi SE
F-54	3835	4/30/40	Alamogordo	Ruidoso	49 mi NE
F-41	3835	8/15/35	Corona	Corona	Oallinas 9 mi S
F-25	3836	10/11/41	Silver City	Glenwood	66 mi NW
F-25	3836	5/4/36	Silver City	Glenwood	67 mi NW

PROJECT	CO. #	DATE	RAILROAD	POST OFFICE	LOCATION
F-52	3836	6/1/38	Silver City	Glenwood	Willow Creek 96 mi NW
SCS-9	3837	8/15/35	Albuquerque	Albuquerque	Rio Puerco 27 mi W
G-174	3838	6/19/40	Deming	Cambrey	26 mi E
DG-36	3838	8/24/35	Deming	Deming	Mirage 9 mi NE
SCS-8	3845	12/15/39	Albuquerque	San Ysidro	Catron Ranch 60 mi NW
F-53	4816	10/18/41	Glorieta	Glorieta	2.5 mi E
G-69	4817	7/5/41	Alamogordo	Orogrande	Prather East Well 66 mi SE
G-150	4818	10/15/40	Columbus	Columbus	.1 mi S
NP-2	4819	10/15/40	Gallup	Chaco Canyon	79 mi NW

Appendix D

PROJECTS AND CAMPS IN UTAH

PROJECT	CO. #	DATE	RAILROAD	POST OFFICE	LOCATION
F-4	230	6/13/33	Carter, WY	Mt. View, WY	
F-7	231	6/13/33	Evanton, WY	Evanton, WY	
S-201	232	6/17/33	Bountiful	Bountiful	
DG-32	234	10/11/37	Thompson	Moab	Dalton Wells 26 mi S
G-26	288	4/6/39	Tintie Junction	Eureka	Jericho 15 mi S
G-114	293	10/17/38	Green River	Green River	Hanksville 57 mi SW
DG-35	469	10/12/37	Milford	Milford	.5 mi S
F-32	479	10/11/37	Salina	Salina	Salina Creek 1 mi SE
DG-29	482	10/16/37	Delta	Delta	Antelope Springs 45 mi NW
MA-1	482	8/21/41	Provo	Provo	.5 mi N
DG-27	529	10/25/35	Price	Castle Dale	Castle Dale 31 mi S
G-158	529	10/6/40	Price	Emery	Willow Springs 79 mi SW
SP-1	536	4/29/35	Kalton	Kalton	Locomotive Springs 12 mi E
SP-2	536	8/2/35	Woods Cross	Woods Cross	Farmington Bay 1 mi W at railhead
DG-32	561	10/25/35	Thompson	Moab	Dalton Wells 21 mi S
SCS-5	578	11/26/41	Mt. Pleasant	Mt. Pleasant	1 mi NE
SCS-2	585	10/25/35	Modana	Gunlock	Gunlock 54 mi SE
SCS-7	585	6/8/37	Cedar City	Leeds	Leeds 40 mi SW
SCS-3	593	10/25/35	Price	Price	1 mi SW
SCS-4	736	10/30/36	Brigham	Willard	Willard 7 mi S
SCS-9	736	10/31/39	Tremonton	Tremonton	At-railhead
G-36	794	10/5/39	Milford	Milford	.5 mi S
BR-2	794	6/18/40	Cox	Hooper	Ogden Bay Refuge 2 mi SE
F-5	940	6/17/33	Pleasant Grove	American Fork	
S-205	940 *	10/17/33	Woods Cross	Woods Cross	
F-48	940	10/18/35	Woods Cross	Bountiful	Bountiful 2 mi SW
F-49	940	6/2/38	Bountiful	Bountiful	Farmington Canyon 16 mi S
F-6	940	6/7/40	Park City	Kamas	Soapstone 30 mi

* integrated camp

PROJECT	CO. #	DATE	RAILROAD	POST OFFICE	LOCATION
F-1	957	5/26/33	Logan	Logan	Hyrum 12 mi NE
F-9	958	5/29/33	Nephi	Nephi	
F-30	958	5/7/34	Springville	Springville	Hobble Creek 9 mi SE
F-40	958	11/1/36	Provo	Provo	Rock Canyon 1 mi SW
F-51	958	7/6/41	Ogden	Huntsville	Ogden 14 mi E
F-10	959 *	5/29/33	Price	Orangeville	
F-28	959	6/1/34	Fairview	Fairview	
PF-223	959	11/2/34	Mt. Pleasant	Mt. Pleasant	2 mi NE
F-11	959	10/24/35	Price	Perron	Perron 45 mi SW
F-31	959	10/5/39	Cedar City	St. George	Veyo 77 mi SW
SF-16	959	6/20/40	Cedar City	Cedar City	Duck Creek 30 mi N
F-12	960	5/26/33	Park City	Kamas	
F-16	961	5/27/33	Cedar City	Cedar City	Duck Creek 35 mi NE
F-27	961	5/7/34	Cedar City	Panguitch	
NP-3	962	5/29/33	Cedar City	Bryce Canyon	Bryce 90 mi E
NP-4	962	9/1/39	Cedar City	Springdale	Bridge Mt. 62 mi S
S-204	1253	6/15/33	Brigham City	Brigham City	
S-204	1254	6/14/33	Provo	Springdale	
S-211	1255	6/15/33	Marysvale	Widtsoe	
S-212	1256	6/15/33	Cedar City	Alton	
SCS-6	1256	10/11/37	Thompson	Moab	Moab 37 mi SE
SCS-8	1256	6/24/40	Thompson	Monticello	Indian Creek 94 mi S
F-17	1335	5/25/33	Modena	Pine Valley	
F-26	1338	8/1/34	Fillmore	Fillmore	
F-18	1339 *	5/9/34	Marysvale	Escalante	
F-20	1345 *	5/25/33	Thompson	Moab	
F-29	1345 *	5/9/34	Salt Lake City	Roosevelt	
F-6	1346	5/25/33	Park City	Kamas	
F-16	1486	6/3/38	Cedar City	Cedar City	Duck Creek 30 mi E
DG-31	1507	10/26/35	Salt Lake City	Vernal	Vernal 185 mi E
NP-7	1507	11/23/41	Thompson	Moab	Arches 34 mi S
DG-30	1508	1/10/36	Cedar City	Cedar City	5 mi E
G-117	1508	10/9/38	Milford	Garrison	Burbank 72 mi NW
MA-1	1662	11/16/39	Provo	Provo	.5 mi W
G-155	1682	11/16/39	Modana	Modana	8 mi NE

* integrated camp

PROJECT	CO. #	DATE	RAILROAD	POST OFFICE	LOCATION
F-31	1923 -V	10/30/35	Modana	Veyo	Veyo 43 mi SE
DF-9	1928	7/23/34	Nephi	Nehpi	Nebo 10 mi E
BR-11	1958	10/19/35	Salt Lake City	Bridgeland	132 mi SE
DF-14	1964	7/23/34	Milford	Beaver	Beaver River 48 mi SE
DF-3	1965	7/23/34	Salt Lake City	Vernal	
F-35	1965	10/13/34	Green River	Vernal	Manila 63 mi NE
BR-12	1965	5/1/36	Odgen	Huntsville	Huntsville 14 mi E
NP-2	1966	7/23/34	Cedar City	Springdale	Zion 62 mi S
BR-12	1967	10/21/34	Ogden	Huntsville	Huntsville 9 mi E
DG-26	1967	11/30/35	Eureka	Eureka	Jericho 19 mi S
G-163	1967	10/31/39	Lucin	Lucin	5 mi W
G-103	1967	4/20/40	Kelton	Tremonton	Park Valley 12 mi NW
SCS-9	1967	6/17/41	Tremonton	Tremonton	At railhead
BR-11	1968	10/19/34	Salt Lake City	Bridgehead	Bridgehead 132 mi SE
BR-91	1968	9/27/39	Pleasant Grove	Pleasant Grove	1 mi SW
F-4	1979	5/29/35	Park City	Kamas	Soapstone 30 mi E
F-44	1980	6/10/35	Marysvale	Escalante	Aspen Grove 102 mi SE
BF-1	1985	4/25/34	Brigham	Brigham	Bear River Bird Refuge .5 mi W
F-43	2514	9/14/35	Pleasant Grove	Pleasant Grove	1 mi SW
F-6	2514	6/23/37	Park city	Kamas	Soapstone 30 mi NE
DG-28	2517	9/11/35	St. John	Clover	Clover Creek 10 mi SW
G-154	2517	11/11/39	St. John	Clover	Simpson Springs 49 mi SW
DG-33	2529	10/21/35	Marysvale	Henrieville	Henrieville 95 mi SE
G-155	2529	11/13/39	Black Rock	Black Rock	At railhead
G-115	2529	4/15/40	Delta	Delta	Callao 121 mi NW
DG-35	2530	10/21/35	Milford	Milford	.5 mi S
DG-29	2531	10/22/35	Delta	Delta	Antelope Springs 45 mi NW
BR-1	2539	10/22/35	Brigham	Brigham	Bear River Bird Refuge .5 mi W
G-160	2558	11/17/39	Cedar City	Hurricane	Hurricane 42 mi SW
Army-1	2574	6/24/35	Salt Lake City	Ft. Douglas	4 mi E
NP-4	2887	11/29/41	Cedar City	Springdale	Bridge Mt. 62 mi S
F-37	2910	10/5/34	Salt Lake City	Ducheane	Moon Lake 161 mi SE
F-27	2937	9/3/35	Manti	Mayfield	Mayfield 18 mi SW
NM-1	3233	6/17/36	Cedar City	Cedar Cily	Cedar Break 27 mi E
F-35	3239	4/14/36	Green River, WY	Vernal	Manila 57 mi SW

PROJECT	CO. #	DATE	RAILROAD	POST OFFICE	LOCATION
F-38	3240	4/14/36	Salt Lake City	Murrary	Big Cottonwood 15 mi S
DG-34	3241	4/14/36	Thompson	Blanding	Blanding 116 mi S
G-157	3241	11/27/39	Thompson	Moab	Dry Valley 68 mi SE
F-31	3255	11/1/39	Ogden	Huntsville	Huntsville 14 mi E
F-34	3265	10/12/37	Logan	Hyrum	Hyrum 12 mi SE
F-35	3544	10/31/35	Green River, WY	Manila	Manila 57 mi SW
F-6	3544	5/26/38	Park City	Kamas	Soapstone 30 mi NE
G-115	3556	10/14/38	Green River, WY	Green River, WY	1 mi W
G-32	3556	7/4/41	Thompson	Moab	Dalton Wells 26 mi S
G-157	3556	11/26/41	Thompson	Moab	Dry Valley 68 mi SE
SCS-5	3689	7/18/38	Mt. Pleasant	Mt. Pleasant	1 mi SE
F-36	3749	1/17/36	Fillmore	Xanosh	16 mi SW
F-32	3749	12/9/36	Salina	Salina	Salina Creek 1 mi SE
F-34	3796	5/18/36	Logan	Hyrum	Hyrum 12 mi SE
G-38	3803	12/4/41	Salt Lake City	Murray	Big Cottonwood 15 mi S
F-44	4429	6/20/36	Marysvale	Escalante	Aspen Grove 102 mi SE
F-42	4723	11/3/39	Marysvale	Escalante	Escalante 87 mi SE
F-41	4776	4/24/37	Thompson	Monticello	Indian Creek 94 mi S
F-16	4777	6/8/37	Cedar City	Cedar City	Duck Creek 30 mi E
F-44	4778	6/22/37	Marysvale	Escalante	Aspen Grove 102 mi SE
SCS-5	4780	10/29/36	Mt. Pleasant	Mt. Pleasant	1 mi NE
SCS-6	4791	4/25/37	Thompson	Moab	37 mi SE
BR-12	4792	10/20/36	Ogden	Huntsville	14 mi E
BR-54	4792	12/20/37	Heber	Heber	Deer Creek 1 mi W
F-35	4794	10/18/36	Green River, WY	Green River, WY	Manila 57 mi SW
G-114	6426	5/11/41	Green River, WY	Green River, WY	Hanksville 57 mi SW
NP-7	6428	7/19/40	Thompson	Moab	Arches 34 mi S
SCS-5	6430	7/8/40	Mt. Pleasant	Mt. Pleasant	1 mi NE

Selected Bibliography

Archives and Collections

Many collections and archives were consulted in the course of researching this book. The collections vary in depth and content; many contain resources such as oral histories, informal interviews, personal correspondence and diaries, photographs, and artifacts related to the Civilian Conservation Corps. Valuable information was found in the following collections: Arches National Park, Aztec Ruins National Monument, Bryce Canyon National Park, Capitol Reef National Park, Cedar Breaks National Monument, Center of Southwest Studies, Chaco Culture National Historical Park, Cline Library Special Collections and Archives at Northern Arizona University, Colorado National Monument, Denver Federal Records Center, Dinosaur National Monument, Dixie National Forest, Grand Canyon National Park, Mesa Verde National Park, the National Archives, Petrified Forest National Park, Pipe Spring National Monument, Sherratt Library at Southern Utah University, Utah State Archives, Utah State Historical Society, Walnut Canyon National Monument, Washington City Museum, Western Archaeological and Conservation Center, Wupatki National Monument, and Zion National Park.

Web Sites

Many Web sites contain information about the Civilian Conservation Corps. In addition to administrative histories, several national park and monument sites include details about local CCC contributions. For personal stories the James F. Justin Civilian Conservation Corps Museum is especially helpful (*http://members.aol.com/famjustin/ccchis.html*), while the CCC alumni Web site has detailed camp listings (*www.cccalumni.org/states.html*). Some state and local history Web sites also include history of the CCC, including *www.historytogo.utah.gov/* and *www.sanjuan.k12.ut.us/sjsample/CCC/CCCHOME/Index2.htm*.

Published Works

Alleger, C. N., and L. A. Glyre. *History of the Civilian Conservation Corps in Colorado.* Denver, CO: Western Newspaper Union, 1936.

Anderson, Michael F. *Polishing the Jewel: An Administrative History of Grand Canyon National Park*, Monograph No. 11. Grand Canyon National Park: Grand Canyon Association, 2000.

Baker, Robert D., et al. *Timeless Heritage: A History of the Forests of the Southwest*. Albuquerque, NM: U.S. Forest Service, Southwest Region, 1988. http://www.fs.fed.us/r3/about/history/timeless/th_index.html.

Braeman, John, Robert H. Bremner, and David Brody, eds. *The New Deal: The State and Local Levels*, Vol. II. Columbus, Ohio: Ohio State University Press, 1975.

Brown, Ronald C., and Duane A. Smith. *New Deal Days: The CCC at Mesa Verde*. Durango, CO: Durango Herald Small Press, 2006.

Brugge, David M., and Raymond Wilson. *Administrative History: Canyon de Chelly National Monument Arizona*. Washington DC: United States Department of Interior, National Park Service, 1976. http://www.nps.gov/cach/historyculture/upload/CACH_adhi.pdf.

Chavis, Tracey L., and William R. Morris. *Fire on the Mesa*. Durango, CO: Durango Herald Small Press, 2006.

Clemenson, A. Berle. *Casa Grande Ruins National Monument, Arizona: A Centennial History of the First Prehistoric Preserve 1892–1992*. Washington DC: National Park Service, 1992. http://www.nps.gov/archive/cagr/adhi/adhi.htm.

Cohen, Stan. *The Tree Army: A Pictorial History of the Civilian Conservation Corps, 1933–1942*. Missoula, MT: Pictorial Histories Publishing Company, 1980.

Degler, Carl N., ed. *The New Deal*. New York: Quadrangle Books, 1970.

Everhart, William C. *The National Park Service*. New York: Praeger Publishers, 1972.

Harper, Charles Price. *The Administration of the Civilian Conservation Corps*. Clarksburg, WV: Clarksburg Publishing Company, 1939.

Helms, Douglas. "The Civilian Conservation Corps: Demonstrating the Value of Soil Conservation." *Journal of Soil and Water Conservation*. 40 (1985): 184–88.

Hinton, Wayne K. *The Dixie National Forest: Managing an Alpine Forest in an Arid Setting*. Cedar City, UT: U.S. Forest Service, 1984.

Jackson, Jane E. "Monumental Tasks: The Civilian Conservation Corps at Mt. Elden." *Arizona Journal of History*. 48 (Autumn 2007): 289–304.

Leach, Nicky J. *The Guide to National Parks of the Southwest*. Tucson, AZ: Southwest Parks & Monuments Association, 1992.

Lister, Florence C. and Robert H. *Earl Morris and Southwestern Archaeology*. Albuquerque, NM: University of New Mexico Press, 1968. www.nps.gov/archive/azru/adhi/adhi.htm.

Lister, Robert H. and Florence C. *Aztec Ruins National Monument: Administrative History of an Archaeological Preserve*. Professional Papers No. 24. Santa Fe, NM: National Park Service, Division of History, 1990.

McKoy, Kathleen L. *Cultures at a Crossroads: An Administrative History of Pipe Spring National Monument*. Cultural Resources Selections No. 15. Denver, CO: National Park Service, Intermountain Region, 2000.

Melzer, Richard. *Coming of Age in the Great Depression: The Civilian Conservation Corps Experience in New Mexico, 1933–1942*. Las Cruces, NM: Yucca Tree Press, 2000.

Moore, Robert J. *The Civilian Conservation Corps in Arizona's Rim Country: Working in the Woods*. Reno, NV: University of Nevada Press, 2006.

Purvis, Louis. *The Ace In The Hole: A Brief History of Grand Canyon Company 818 of the Civilian Conservation Corps*. Columbus, GA: Brentwood Christian Press, 1987.

Rauch, Basil. *The History of the New Deal, 1933–1938*. New York: Creative Age Press Inc., 1944.

Roseman, Samuel I., ed. *The Public Papers and Addresses of Franklin D. Roosevelt*. Vol. 2. New York: Random House, 1952.

Rothman, Hal. *Bandelier National Monument: An Administrative History*. Santa Fe, NM: National Park Service Division of History, 1988. http://www.nps.gov/archive/band/adhi/adhi.htm.

Rowley, William D. *Reclamation Managing Water in the West, The Bureau of Reclamation: Origins and Growth to 1945*. Vol. 1. Denver, CO: Bureau of Reclamation, 2006. http://www.usbr.gov/history/OriginsandGrowths/Volume1.pdf.

Salmond, John A. *The Civilian Conservation Corps, 1933–1942: A New Deal Case Study*. Durham, NC: Duke University Press, 1967.

282

Schoch-Roberts, Lisa. *A Classic Western Quarrel: A History of the Road Controversy at Colorado National Monument*. Denver, CO: National Park Service Intermountain Region, 1997.

Scrattish, Nicholas. "Historic Resources Study Bryce Canyon National Park." Washington DC: U.S. Department of Interior, 1985.

Smith, Duane A. *Mesa Verde National Park: Shadows of the Centuries*. Boulder, CO: University of Colorado Press, 2002.

Storey, Brit. *Brief History of the Bureau of Reclamation*. Denver, CO: Bureau of Reclamation, 2000. http://www.usbr.gov/history/BRIEFHist.pdf.

Thompson, Erika. *Mesa Verde's Hidden Landscape: Designing a National Park*. Mesa Verde National Park, CO: Mesa Verde Museum Association, 2007.

Wirth, Conrad L. *Parks, Politics, and the People*. Norman, OK: University of Oklahoma Press, 1980.

Unpublished Theses and Dissertations

Baldridge, Kenneth Wayne. "Nine Years of Achievements: The Civilian Conservation Corps in Utah." PhD diss., Brigham Young University, 1971.

Hinton, Wayne K. "The New Deal Years in Utah: A Political History of Utah, 1932–1940." Master's thesis, Utah State University, 1963.

Johnson, William Charles. "The Civilian Conservation Corps: The Role of the Army." PhD diss., University of Michigan, 1968.

Pollock, Floyd Annen. "Navajo-Federal Relations as a Social-Cultural Problem." PhD diss., University of Southern California, 1942.

Purman, Donald Lee. "The Indian Civilian Conservation Corps." PhD diss., University of Oklahoma, 1967.

Index

About the Peaks, Plateaus & Canyons Association

The Peaks, Plateaus & Canyons Association (PPCA) is a group of nonprofit cooperating associations serving the federal and state land-management agencies of the Colorado Plateau. Linked by both terrain and mission, PPCA members exchange information and training and create joint projects to help associations of all sizes advance in their collective mission. To learn more about PPCA, visit us on the Web at www.ppcaweb.org.

ABOUT COOPERATING ASSOCIATIONS

The United States was the birthplace of national parks. The West was their cradle. The American public quickly discovered their national parks and developed a healthy appetite for more knowledge about them. Early on it became clear that the government, by itself, could not furnish visitors with sufficient educational materials to appease their hunger.

In 1920, just four years after establishment of the National Park Service as caretakers for national parks, Yosemite led the way in establishing cooperating associations to assist by supporting research and providing educational opportunities and materials for park visitors. By the early 1930s, parks across the West followed suit, and many of the oldest cooperating associations are located on the Colorado Plateau.

Cooperating associations are nonprofit, tax-exempt entities recognized by the United States Congress to aid the National Park Service and other public land agencies in their missions of education and service. These associations are dedicated to enhancing public understanding, appreciation, and stewardship of America's cultural and natural heritage.

About the Authors

Dr. Wayne K. Hinton holds degrees from Dixie State College, Utah State University, Brigham Young University, and University of California, Davis. After teaching for thirty-eight years at Southern Utah University, eighteen of them as history department chair, he retired in 2006. Dr. Hinton is a member of Utah State Historical Society, Old Spanish Trails Association, Organization of American Historians, Western History Association, and the Mormon History Association. He has authored four books, numerous journal articles and conference papers, and many other works. He and his wife, Carolyn, live in Cedar City, Utah. They have two daughters, two sons, and nineteen grandchildren.

Elizabeth A. Green is a freelance book editor and writer with particular interest in regional history. She has worked as a journalist, a nonprofit administrator, and a social worker. An avid community volunteer in Durango, Colorado, she currently serves on the local historical society board of directors and as a docent for public lands on a steam-powered narrow-gauge train. She lives near Durango with her husband, Allan, a retired forester whose father was a CCC camp superintendent in northern Wisconsin. She visits her children and grandchildren in Denver and Alabama as often as possible.